Y0-EIB-719

Discrimination and
Reverse Discrimination

BORZOI BOOKS IN LAW AND AMERICAN SOCIETY

Discrimination and Reverse Discrimination

Kent Greenawalt
Columbia Law School

ALFRED A. KNOPF NEW YORK

This book was originally developed as part of an American Bar Association program on law and humanities with major funding from the National Endowment for the Humanities and additional support from the Exxon Education Foundation and Pew Memorial Trust. The ABA established this program to help foster improved understanding among undergraduates of the role of law in society through the creation of a series of volumes in law and humanities. The ABA selected a special advisory committee of scholars, lawyers, and jurists (Commission on Undergraduate Education in Law and the Humanities) to identify appropriate topics and select writers. This book is a revised version of the volume first published by the ABA. However, the writer, and not the American Bar Association, individual members and committees of the Commission, the National Endowment for the Humanities, Exxon Education Foundation, or Pew Memorial Trust, bears sole responsibility for the content, analysis, and conclusion contained herein.

THIS IS A BORZOI BOOK
PUBLISHED BY ALFRED A. KNOPF, INC.

First Edition
9 8 7 6 5 4 3 2
Copyright © 1983 by Alfred A. Knopf, Inc.

All rights reserved under International and Pan-American Copyright Conventions. No part of this book may be reproduced in any form or by any means, electronic or mechanical, including photocopying, without permission in writing from the publisher. All inquiries should be addressed to Alfred A. Knopf, Inc., 201 East 50th Street, New York, N.Y. 10022. Published in the United States by Alfred A. Knopf, Inc., New York, and simultaneously in Canada by Random House of Canada Limited, Toronto. Distributed by Random House, Inc., New York.

LIBRARY OF CONGRESS CATALOGING IN PUBLICATION DATA

Greenawalt, R. Kent, 1936–
    Discrimination and reverse discrimination.

    (Borzoi books in law and American society)
    Includes related documents.
    Bibliography: p.
    Includes index.
    1. Race discrimination—Law and legislation—
United States. 2. Sex discrimination—Law and legisla-
tion—United States. 3. Reverse discrimination—Law
and legislation—United States. I. Title. II. Series.
KF4755.G73 1982   342.73'087   82-18747
                        347.30287
ISBN 0-394-33193-1 (Paperbound)   394-33577-5 (Casebound)

Manufactured in the United States of America

TO MY PARENTS,
WHO INTRODUCED ME TO
IDEAS OF JUSTICE

Preface

This book develops in an integrated manner the legal and ethical problems of discrimination and "reverse discrimination." It consists of an essay that interweaves the two perspectives, and a set of legal materials, mainly Supreme Court opinions and federal statutes, that reflect the influence of moral opinion on legal decisions but also show how resolutions of legal issues differ from moral judgments. The book is intended for use mainly in courses in philosophy and government or in courses in which a historical or interdisciplinary approach is taken to civil rights. How exactly the book can best be used will depend on the nature of the course and the particular aims of the instructor; but I herewith offer a few words suggesting my primary aims, the ways in which the essay can be related to the legal materials, and some desirable supplements to what is contained in the book.

The book has a number of distinct, though related, aims. It is meant to provide an adequate basis for the student to work out a rational and coherent approach to problems of discrimination and reverse discrimination, and to develop a technique for approaching other social issues that have an important moral dimension. It is meant to illustrate similarities and differences of moral and legal reasoning. It is meant to serve as a basis for reflection about the proper role of the courts when they interpret authoritative constitutional and statutory standards of varying specificity. By affording a reasonably comprehensive picture of the present law of discrimination and reverse discrimination, it is also meant to encourage the student to consider how far the law should reflect ethical evaluations and to scrutinize the existing law in the light of his or her own moral judgments.

One value of the legal materials, especially the cases, is to put the relevant social issues in a highly concrete setting. No doubt, many questions about discrimination can be considered without reference to the law; but the cases sharpen one's focus and introduce a powerful note of reality. The legal materials help to remind the student that resolving social issues is more complex than deciding what would be moral acts and practices for ideal persons with perfect information. Legal standards and the standards used by such entities as universities and employers to confer benefits must take account of the imperfect dispositions of most people and of the need for criteria that are administrable in the face of limited information. A comparison of older and more modern cases dealing with discrimination illustrates strikingly the extent to which popular notions of what is just treatment have altered in the last century, giving the reader a sense of how moral judgments change over time and an insight into the dimensions of current social problems. The constitutional and statutory provisions and the judicial opinions are a crucial starting point for thought about how far the law should intervene in social relations and about the respective responsibilities of various lawmaking authorities. The law can also aid one to understand the way in which particular distinctions based on race or gender are part of a larger whole. Like any rational approach to moral judgment, those who make and interpret law try to achieve consistency of treatment of essentially similar phenomena; and looking at the broader scope of the law dealing with discrimination allows one to make appropriate comparisons and, in particular, to address problems of reverse discrimination in a relevant context.

Although the essay that begins the book can be read and understood by someone who has not yet looked at the legal materials, it is not meant to stand alone. Rather, it seeks to introduce those materials by commenting on some significant relations between law and morals, by briefly describing the development of the law, by summarizing the arguments for and against legal restraint of discrimination, and by analyzing in greater depth the moral arguments relevant to reverse discrimination. The essay can be read as a single piece, or relevant parts can be considered with the corresponding legal materials. Perhaps best use can be made of the essay if one reads through it once as an introduction to the materials and the issues they raise, and then comes back to its sections with more care as the cases and statutes are examined.

The essay is more thorough in respect to some of the aims of the book than to others. It provides a relatively full survey of the ethical arguments about discrimination and reverse discrimination and, with the materials, should afford an adequate basis for discussion in depth of those arguments. Nonetheless, instructors, particularly those in ethics courses, can profitably supplement the book with some of the recent and rich philosophical literature on reverse discrimination— there being of course no complete substitute for addressing positions in the words of the authors who advance them. What the essay has to say about judicial role and legal interpretation is much more sketchy. The essay and materials alone are sufficient to engender fruitful consideration of the interpretation of authoritative standards, the proper place of ethical evaluation in such interpretation, the special character of constitutional norms, and the appropriate limits on the exercise of power by judicial officials who are not politically responsible. But I do not attempt in this book to address these subjects in a systematic manner. Instructors for whom one or more of these is a primary concern will probably want to assign readings in which such a systematic view is undertaken. The essay, the legal materials themselves, and the notes that accompany the materials reveal a good bit about the history of discrimination and civil rights; but again, no attempt is made at a comprehensive historical description, and instructors will not wish to depend on this book alone for that purpose.

To assist the student in addressing important issues, questions are posed after cases and other legal materials. Instructors will want to review these in advance in order to see which inquiries they regard as being of central concern, and to decide whether to eschew use of some of the questions and to add others. Students, and instructors, may feel that some of the questions, particularly those that address the correctness of legal conclusions, demand more knowledge of the law and its workings than they can reasonably be expected to have. The point of these inquiries is not to call for the understanding a sophisticated student of the law might bring to bear; nor is it to elicit a response identical to the reader's moral evaluation. Their aim is to get the reader to think seriously about the special role of courts and about the relevance of authoritative constitutional or legislative language the court is interpreting. Laymen are perfectly able to comprehend most of the crucial issues that divide legal scholars. How much weight should courts give to the verbal formulation of guiding standards? How much should they try to implement the judgments of those who adopted the language? How far should they interpret vague language to conform with their own judgments of what is morally right or socially desirable? These are questions that nonlawyers can discuss intelligently even if they are aware that further study of legal institutions might deepen their insights and change their minds. These questions will have served their purpose if they provoke the undergraduate's interest in these problems, even if it is still too early for him or her to give confident responses to them.

Acknowledgments

I am grateful to the American Bar Association and its Commission on Undergraduate Education in Law and the Humanities for their support of the development of these teaching materials. Both in working out my original conception and in proceeding through stages of revision, I benefited greatly from comments of the members of the Philosophy Advisory Panel: Edward Levi, chairman of the commission; Gerald Fetner, its director; and Joel Feinberg, Martin Golding, Thomas Grey, and Richard Wasserstrom. The criticisms of persons who used or reviewed the materials in an earlier version were especially helpful when I undertook substantial revision of the essay prior to publication. These included valuable suggestions from Lief Carter, William McBride, Peter McCormick, Rosemarie Tong, Carl Wellman, Harry Witte, and A. D. Woozley, and a comprehensive critique by James Nickel. I also wish to thank Daniel Cobrinik and John Orenstein, who helped prepare the bibliography, and members of the Faculty Secretariat of Columbia Law School, who typed successive installments of the work.

Acknowledgments

Contents

Essay

I.

Preliminary Reflections

Any list of the gravest injustices in American history would have mistreatment of blacks and American Indians close to the top. Broader discrimination against persons because of their race, ethnic background, religion, and gender has also been striking and pervasive. Prejudice and its baleful effects continue, but even if prejudice and decisions based on it could quickly be eliminated, a most unrealistic hypothesis, the consequences of earlier practices would affect the lives of this and many future generations. Unjustified discrimination has been, and remains, a major problem of American life. Dilemmas over how to respond to the problem raise some of the most profound and delicate questions of morality, politics, and law.

These dilemmas have an important personal dimension. If a young woman recognizes that she harbors irrational negative feelings toward members of other races, should she try in some manner to purge herself of the feelings or attempt to behave toward others as if the feelings did not exist, or should she accept the feelings and avoid contacts with those who gave rise to them? How far should a man be willing to change the understood conditions of his family life if he recognizes that his wife is frustrated by expectations about her role that both had unthinkingly accepted at the time of their marriage? When should one appropriately criticize or reject others who engage in acts of discrimination one believes are morally wrong?

What dominates public discussion is not this personal dimension but the possible social responses to discrimination: how organizations, and particularly the government, should react to discrimination that causes harm to large classes of people. At a moral level, the concern is about principles of social justice, liberty, and welfare. Judgments must be made about what society owes to those who have suffered from discrimination and about the restraints on the liberty and opportunity of others that may be undertaken to satisfy these debts and to reduce future discrimination and its harmful consequences. Those in positions of responsibility must also gauge the political feasibility of various alternatives. Legislators at all levels of government have to determine how far the law should be used to accomplish the purposes they believe are socially justifiable. Judges must decide whether existing legal norms should be interpreted to forbid or require actions by private and public agencies.

One controversial and painful question at each level is whether giving preferences to members of groups who have suffered discrimination is among the appropriate government responses. Are such preferences—in jobs, financial assistance, education—morally acceptable, or even morally required? Are they politically wise? Are they forbidden, allowed, or demanded by federal and state constitutions and statutes?

This essay and the materials it introduces deal with the social aspect of discrimination, paying special attention to what has been called "reverse discrimination" or preferential treatment. Before proceeding to develop the substantive ethical and legal issues, I make some general observations about the relations between ethics and law, and provide an elementary exposition of important features of our legal system for readers not familiar with that subject.

II.

Law and Philosophy

A. LEGAL SOURCES AS RAW MATERIAL FOR ETHICAL REFLECTION

Legal cases provide a rich storehouse of examples of social dilemmas to which ethical considerations can be applied. A conflict reflected in a legal case has mattered a great deal to at least two people, who have probably expended a good deal of energy, time, and money to get it settled. Most cases remind us of a truth we know from personal experience: that the stuff of real ethical questions can be immensely complex, bearing little relation to the straightforward issues of right and wrong on which we cut our teeth.

Consideration of actual and important social questions provides a useful way for us to test the application or persuasiveness of an ethical theory. For example, suppose one believes that an ethical decision is correct if it produces a balance of favorable over unfavorable consequences. These materials suggest how various are the consequences and likely consequences of reverse discrimination; and we can begin to perceive how difficult the resolution of many ethical problems can be, even if we think we know what theory to use. Performing that exercise also compels us to ask whether consequences are all that matters, or whether separate considerations of justice are also important, perhaps more important. By working through genuinely significant ethical questions, we can see how far broader ethical theories conform with the way we try to resolve particular ethical problems; and if we care about relating our thoughts to our lives, we try to bring these into some sort of congruence.

B. REASONING BY ANALOGY, BY GENERAL PRINCIPLES, AND BY *REDUCTIO AD ABSURDUM*

Some important forms of ethical reasoning also characterize legal reasoning, as a look at almost any judge's opinion or lawyer's brief will show. Reasoning by analogy is a staple of the law. A determination has been made about the resolution of a certain issue. A somewhat different issue arises, and one side urges that this issue is so essentially similar to the first that the outcome must be the same. The other side resists the analogy by arguing that important features distinguish the second situation. In ethical reasoning, the process is similar; however, in lieu of previous authoritative determination may be agreement on how the first issue should be resolved. For example, two disputants about abortion may begin by agreeing that a couple may ethically take steps to prevent bringing a fetus into being but may not intentionally destroy a newborn baby. The argument then may proceed on whether destruction of the fetus is most analogous to birth control or to infanticide.

A second feature of legal reasoning is the attempt to state general principles that may be applied to cases other than the particular one a court is deciding. Part of the aim is for courts to give guidance for future cases—an especially important function for an appellate court such as the Supreme Court of the United States, whose decisions largely control the legal principles that other courts apply. In this respect, stating legal principles may resemble moral *instruction*; but we are more interested in a different aspect. If a court can formulate a generalization that has applications wider than the case before it, then it has some greater assurance that it is making the decision properly. The statement of principle is some safeguard, although by no means a complete one, against bias and passion. Principle plays a similar role in ethical decision. Suppose two friends of yours, Carol and Mark, are dating one another and Carol has told you that she is not seriously interested in Mark but finds him sexually attractive. Mark asks you whether you think Carol really cares about him. You must decide how far you should tell Mark the truth, aware that the full truth may hurt him and may possibly breach a confidence between you and Carol. You also know that telling the truth may make Mark angry with you, as the messenger of unpleasant news, and may also make Carol angry with you, if she ever comes to suspect that you helped dampen Mark's enthusiasm. It may help you to make a decision to reflect on what you would want, or expect, someone to do if you were in Carol's or Mark's situation, and also what you think would be generally desirable behavior of friends in such circumstances. This sort of reflective effort to arrive at some generalized principle helps one to obtain distance from one's personal feelings about the particular situation and to test original intuitions against a larger screen.

One part of reasoning by principles is argument by *reductio ad absurdum*. A particular possible decision falls within a principle, and it is shown that the principle has implications that are obviously unacceptable. For example, suppose that when you must decide whether to reveal Carol's lack of serious interest in Mark, you are offered the principle that in no event should you actually lie to Mark because lying is always wrong. You are then able to think of a situation in which you are confident it would be a proper to lie (a crazed man bent on murder asks if a loaded gun is handy and you know that one is). Therefore you reject that principle as formulated because it would imply an absurd conclusion. Either the principle must be altered, or another more adequate principle must be found to substitute. Much legal argument and opinion writing takes this form. Principles offered in resolution of problems are criticized on the ground that they would yield obviously unacceptable results if applied to other cases that they cover. Of course, judges do not always agree on what results are obviously unacceptable or on whether a particular principle does imply a particular result. But in law, as in ethics, this interaction between concrete problem, proposed resolving principle, and hypothetical example to test the principle is an essential part of the fabric of reasoning toward decision.

C. SOME SIGNIFICANT DIFFERENCES
BETWEEN LAW AND ETHICS

Although law and ethics deal with many of the same problems and share forms of reasoning, a proper ethical resolution of an issue is not necessarily a proper legal resolution.

When courts make decisions, they are largely guided by authoritative texts. These constitutional provisions, statutes, administrative regulations, and earlier judicial decisions do not always conform with a judge's personal views of what is ethically right; yet in the role of judge, he or she may be bound to follow them. To take an extreme instance: It is clear that before the Civil War, slavery was legal in America, its legitimacy being recognized in the Constitution itself. A judge in that period was required by law to render some decisions enforcing the rights of slaveowners, even if he realized the great immorality of that institution. Of course, a law may be so wicked that the ethical duty of a citizen, or even a judge, is to refuse to obey or enforce it; and slavery may have fallen into that category. But even if that were so, it would not indicate that the law forbade slavery; only that slavery raised a conflict for the judge between legal duty and ethical duty.

Ethical reasoning, as ordinarily developed in philosophical writings, is different from legal reasoning in not starting with some authoritative text. In this respect, the law more nearly resembles the process of moral decision within religious traditions that do recognize texts, such as the Bible or the ex cathedra statements of popes, as authoritative because divinely inspired. Within such traditions, the search for correct ethical decision often consists of, or includes, the attempt to fathom the guidance of such texts.

Unlike courts, legislatures are free, within a wide range of constitutional limits, to resolve problems as they think best. But even the role of the legislator is not quite the same as that of an individual making an ethical choice. Legislators represent other people, and they should be guided to some extent by what they perceive to be the ethical opinions of their constituents. To take an extreme example, a legislator who became a vegetarian because he believed that killing animals to eat them is morally wrong would probably not be justified in the present meat-eating climate of opinion in trying to enact a law that would forbid people to eat meat.

Features of the law other than the special roles of judges and legislators distinguish it from ethics. Law operates in a social context and involves the intervention of the government. The intervention can be direct, as in the criminal process, where the state prosecutes and punishes transgressors; or the intervention can consist in requiring one private individual or company to pay for damage done to another. In either event, it is desirable for the law often to demand less, and occasionally more, than ethical principles require. Think of the many ways in which family members and friends can act immorally toward one another: A husband can intentionally manipulate his wife's weaknesses for his own satisfaction; a person can undermine the friendship of two acquaintances in order to have a close relationship with one of them. Given the law's limited engines of monetary damages and imprisonment, the expensiveness of its processes, and the manifold subtleties of human interaction, it would plainly be undesirable to make every unethical act toward a family member or friend a crime or the basis for a claim of damages. Moreover, the law's intervention in a particular way, even on the side of the ethically virtuous, may be destructive of vulnerable but valuable relationships. A related point can be true about some less personal interactions. If institutions providing mortgages were never allowed to foreclose those mortgages against poor people caught up in trying circumstances, the institutions might stop offering mortgages to persons who might become poor, making such people worse off instead of better off.

Even when what is ethically right seems clear and the matter is not one whose very nature renders it inappropriate for legal regulation, there may be serious questions about how far and how fast the law should go. Ethics may posit an ideal of behavior, but the law must deal with people in a given society. It should not demand of them more than they are capable of performing; nor should it often make demands that create severe social tensions, threatening the fabric of community life. Unquestionably, legislators must trim their vision of the ideal to the realities of social life, taking into account what kinds of laws will be acceptable at a given place and time. Such considerations undoubtedly also influence judicial decision on occasion, although whether they appropriately do so is more controversial.

When laws are adopted or judicial determinations made, they ordinarily speak to a generality of situations. Although we have already seen that the search for general principles plays an important role in ethical choice, nevertheless personal ethical choices are often tailored to the unique circumstances of individual cases. The legislature does not have time to evaluate each particular case; and a court, although it has a particular case in front of it, typically wishes to base its decision on some generally applicable ground. Both legislatures and courts are interested in giving guidance to government officials on how to treat classes of similar cases, and they are also interested in avoiding charges of partiality against particular persons or interests. Thus a legal rule can usually be reduced to some general formulation that isolates certain relevant factors of human situations and dictates a result if those factors are present. These formulations guide officials as to how they should treat citizens and help to ensure that the operation of the law is even-handed, not dependent on the particular evaluation or prejudice of the individual official who happens to deal with a case. One consequence is that some possibly relevant ethical factors may not be legally relevant. For example, the law of murder in most states does not itself take into account whether one kills selfishly for money or unselfishly to relieve the victim of pain, although such considerations will play a part in the sentence that is assessed after one has been found guilty.

The law is also different from academic discussions of ethics in its treatment of facts, although here the dilemma that the law faces is one that is also present for ethical decision in actual life. The problem is uncertainty about relevant facts: uncertainty about what has taken place in the past, and uncertainty about the consequences of alternative courses of action. In theoretical discussions of ethical issues, the facts can usually be stipulated; but when we make actual decisions, stipulations unfortunately are no longer available. We must often act on the facts as we understand them, no formal process of discovery being available. When people formulate legal rules, they must also accept the uncertainty of relevant facts. Despite decades of study and discussion, for example, it is still not conclusively established whether capital punishment deters a significant number of murders, and yet for many people the possibility of deterrence would be the only legitimate reason for permitting capital punishment. But there are other more specific facts on which the operation of rules of law turns. Did A actually kill B, and if so, did he kill B intentionally? For such facts, the law provides complex and formal procedures, and the main issue in many legal cases is not over a rule of law but over the facts. If the law has any lessons to teach here, they are the difficulty of determining what actually happened in many instances and the importance of determining the facts in as fair and impartial a way as possible.

The crucial point for our purposes concerns the relationship between rules of law and the realistic possibility of determining certain facts. The application of a legal rule cannot sensibly turn on the existence or nonexistence of facts that are impossible or very difficult to ascertain by processes that are socially acceptable for this purpose. A rule of criminal liability should not employ subtle distinctions in motivation that are undiscoverable in the courtroom. The obstinacy of facts, then, constitutes another reason why most legal rules cannot be so finely tuned that they are responsive to all the elements of ethical relevance in a human situation.

Precisely what the proper roles of government and law are in the regulation of human life raises the deepest questions of political philosophy; and whenever one discusses whether there should be a law on a particular subject, one must deal with those questions, at least by implication. As the problem of reverse discrimination richly illustrates, discussion of the proper role of law cannot be limited to the realm of grand theory concerning individual liberty and social restraint but must also address the gritty subjects of what the law can effectively discover and what it can effectively accomplish.

Especially in a constitutional scheme such as that of the United States, a related and also important question of political philosophy is what role should be played by the courts with respect to the other branches of government. The issue of reverse discrimination also raises that question in stark form and in more than one dimension.

D. ETHICAL CONCLUSIONS
AND LEGAL DECISIONS

Most of the preceding discussion has been a caution against the fallacy that whatever is the ethically right outcome for a human situation is the outcome that a legislature or a court should dictate. But ethical evaluation may still be vitally important for legislative and judicial action. The point is most obvious for legislation. Representatives often vote on the basis of their own moral convictions, or what they perceive to be the convictions of their constituents, or some combination of the two. The entire problem of reverse discrimination would never have arisen if it still seemed ethically acceptable to consign blacks and members of other minority groups to a permanent underclass. That judges interpreting the law may be influenced by ethical opinions is less apparent, but the authoritative law is often not clear. Sometimes the crucial terms of a legal standard, such as "equal protection of the laws" or "cruel and unusual punishment," may themselves be open-ended, affording scope for ethical judgment in the interpretation of their application to various circumstances. Whether judges applying such terms should be guided by assessment of the ethical values of those who adopted the standard, by the ethical values of present members of the political community, by their own ethical values, or by some combination of these is a matter of debate. So also is the degree of deference that should be given to legislative judgment and the implications of prior decisions. What is not debatable is that in many cases some form of ethical evaluation is unavoidable. Other legal terms do not themselves introduce moral evaluation; but the legal arguments for differing interpretations may be fairly evenly balanced, and the judge's view of what solution is socially desirable or ethically right may determine the outcome. (In the questions following a number of cases in the materials, I ask whether the Supreme Court should have departed from the historical understanding about the equal protection clause. These questions raise some of the profound issues about judicial role and the scope of ethical analysis in constitutional interpretation.)

Because of their public and political nature, legal justifications offered by judges have a special character. If one were attempting to offer a genuine ethical justification for a decision, one would honestly report the moral considerations that carried the greatest weight. Legal opinions are in part an explanation of the reasons that moved judges to a decision, but they are something more. They are attempts to guide the lower courts, they are symbols of legal continuity, and they are efforts to defend the exercise of judicial power. On occasion, and especially in a controversial case, judges will wish to emphasize the extent to which their decision was required by existing law and they will downplay the influence of ethical judgment. Though it is surely a mistake to dismiss all discussion of legal sources as legalistic rhetoric that is meant to conceal the true bases of decision, nevertheless such discussion cannot always be taken at face value. The steady influence of ethical opinion on the development of the law may not always rise to the level of self-consciousness for the judge; and even when it does, his or her opinion is not likely to reflect its true weight.

Of course the relationship between law and social morality is not a one-way street. Such Supreme Court decisions as *Brown v. Board of Education*, 347 U.S. 483 (1954), and *Roe v. Wade*, 410 U.S. 113 (1973) (declaring a woman's constitutional right to have an abortion), and also such important congressional enactments as the Civil Rights Act of 1964, affect opinions about what is ethically right, as well as being affected by them. Over time, the nexus between the ethical judgments of members of society and the law of that society is inevitably fairly close. And so ethical perceptions of discrimination and reverse discrimination will be influenced by, as well as influence, legal treatment of those subjects.

III.

A Brief Summary of Some Features of Law and Legal Institutions Relevant to Discrimination and Reverse Discrimination

The content of this section is elementary for lawyers and students of American government. Nevertheless, an examination of legal materials on discrimination and reverse discrimination can generate considerable confusion about what is at stake in a particular case unless one has in mind some cardinal features of the American polity and judicial system. The aim here is to provide sufficient background to make clear the particular context in which various questions of discrimination arise.

A. THE FEDERAL CONSTITUTION, CONGRESS, THE STATE LEGISLATURES, AND ADMINISTRATIVE BODIES

As the framework for the American system of government, the Constitution controls the powers exercised by both the federal government and the state governments. The national government has limited powers, Congress in theory being permitted to legislate only for designated subjects, such as raising armies and regulating interstate commerce. The federal government is free to spend money in any way that promotes the general welfare of citizens, but attempts to further the general welfare by other means are left to the states, which are not restricted in the scope of their powers. This is the original theory of the Constitution, but it has evolved somewhat differently. The commerce power has been so broadly interpreted that a great many things Congress wishes to do in regulating the lives of citizens can be justified as an exercise of that power. And federal financing of state and private institutions has become so pervasive that the federal government can exercise a high degree of control by demanding that requirements be met as a condition for the receipt of federal money. Much antidiscrimination legislation has been grounded either in the commerce power or in the spending power. The federal bar on discrimination by private employers, for instance, is a regulation of commerce, and the restraint on discrimination in university hiring derives from the spending power. The third significant source of federal power to combat discrimination is found in the Thirteenth and Fourteenth amendments, which give Congress the power to enforce their provisions, including the guarantee of equal protection of the laws.

Federal administrative agencies, such as the Labor Department, are responsible for administering the laws that Congress enacts. Typically, they will prescribe much more detailed regulations and procedures than Congress has provided. These administrative regulations may help guide courts as to what Congress intended, when that is in doubt. And so long as the regulations are consistent with the statute they enforce, they become a subsidiary source of federal law, to be enforced by the courts if that becomes necessary.

Although some subjects, such as the waging of war, are of exclusive federal concern and some other subjects have been barred to the states by congressional action, congressional involvement in an area does not ordinarily preclude state legislative activity. In respect to antidiscrimination laws, state and local efforts in many northern states preceded federal legislation, and federal law in many places actually defers to enforcement by state and local authorities. For matters left open by federal statutes and regulations, state legislatures, local governments, or such specialized bodies as state universities may make decisions about desirable rules and policies. What a state may not do, however, is adopt or enforce any legislation or policy that conflicts with federal law. The federal government is supreme, and if it has acted validly, any inconsistent state practices must yield.

Both federal and state government bodies are restricted in another way. They may not act in a manner that violates individual rights guaranteed by the federal Constitution. A few of these guarantees, such as a rule against retroactive criminal legislation, are found in the original Constitution; but the most significant individual rights are contained in the Bill of Rights, adopted two years later, and in the Thirteenth, Fourteenth, and Fifteenth amendments, passed after the Civil War. Although the Bill of Rights was additionally addressed only against the federal government, and the Civil War amendments were directed mainly against the states, the course of interpretation has almost entirely merged the restrictions on federal and state governments. For our purposes, we can assume that the relevant limits are identical. Because constitutional limits generally apply only against governments, private persons and institutions cannot, with few exceptions, violate the Constitution, although they may violate statutes that place similar restrictions on the private sector.

We are now in a position to understand, for example, the various challenges that can be made to a state university decision to prefer applicants for admission who are members of minority groups. It may be argued that such a policy violates a state statute or the state constitution, since a university that is an organ of the state is bound to comply with valid state constitutional and statutory law. It may be argued that the policy violates a federal statute or the equal protection clause of the Fourteenth Amendment. In *University of California Regents v. Bakke*, both of these challenges were made under federal law, and a state constitutional claim was also made.

B. THE UNITED STATES SUPREME COURT AND FEDERAL AND STATE COURTS

The United States has parallel federal and state courts; at the apex of each of these two pyramidal structures is the United States Supreme Court. Cases that involve a federal issue, such as the legitimacy under a federal statute or under the federal Constitution of admissions preferences for blacks, can begin in either a federal or a state trial court. Once the facts are determined and the trial court has reached a decision, the losing litigant may appeal the decision to an appellate court. If the case has started in a federal district court the appeal goes to the federal court of appeals; if the case has started in a state trial court, the appeal proceeds through the state appellate system that is provided. The appellate courts must accept the facts as found by the trial court; their job is to review the legal determinations made by the trial judge. After the case has been decided by the federal court of appeals or the state supreme court, the only recourse left is to the United States Supreme Court. With some exceptions, the Supreme Court has discretion to choose the cases it wishes to hear, which it does formally by granting certiorari. It will take a case from a state court only if an issue of federal law is crucial to the decision; as far as purely state law questions are concerned, the state supreme court is the ultimate interpreter. When the Supreme Court takes a case, it then receives full written arguments, called briefs, from the lawyers in the case, as well as amicus curiae briefs (friends of the court) from other interested organizations. It also hears oral argument. Sometime later it renders its decision, typically with opinions that explain the outcome.

What the Supreme Court says about federal law is authoritative in future cases for all the lower courts, state as well as federal; and in practical terms, the Constitution means what the Supreme Court says it means. The Supreme Court treats its own prior decisions with great respect and will usually attempt to decide a new case consistently with the decisions in cases that have preceded it. But it can change its mind and overrule an earlier case, indicating that a decision is no longer authoritative. More often, it will narrow the scope of an earlier decision without rejecting it outright. Thus major constitutional issues are open to continuing reexamination, and one can never be quite sure what weight an earlier decision will carry.

IV.

"Discrimination," "Reverse Discrimination," and Related Concepts

When one deals with a sensitive topic, one must be as careful as one can about the use of related terms, since variant connotations can themselves be the source of serious misunderstanding. In one sense, "to discriminate" is merely to perceive a difference ("she can discriminate between persons of Chinese origin and those of Korean origin") or to treat differently ("in setting a regimen for practice, the coach discriminates among his players, giving each the work he needs to develop his special skills"). In these usages, no implication need be present that one person or group is treated worse than another. But in most discussions of social issues, to say that discrimination exists is to suggest that one group of people is treated worse than another. Moreover, the term usually implies that the grounds for unfavorable treatment bear no close relation to the benefit or burden involved; we are more likely to speak of an employer's discrimination against blacks or in favor of veterans than of its discrimination against stupid or clumsy people. Ordinarily, if the basis for differentiation is not closely related to the benefit, the differentiation is not justified, and the term "discrimination" often signals that negative evaluation; but to describe veterans' preferences in public employment as discrimination in favor of veterans is not necessarily to condemn the preferences.

When I use the term "discrimination" standing alone in this essay, I mean only that a difference of treatment is to the disadvantage of members of some group. I shall analyze the crucial questions—whether the disadvantage bears significant relation to the benefit or burden and whether it is unjustified—without making application of the word "discrimination" turn on my conclusion.

"Reverse discrimination" means a difference in treatment that reverses the pattern of earlier discrimination. Typically, more favorable treatment, say in admission to an academic institution or in employment, is given to members of groups that have been discriminated against in the past. Some people who support such programs object to the term "reverse discrimination" because they fear that the label will tar such programs with the assumption of unjustifiability that accompanies other practices called discrimination. In many sorts of discussions, use of a different, less freighted, vocabulary may be wise; but I hope that here, where terms are set out with some care, the reader will understand that I do not mean to smuggle in normative conclusions by referring to "reverse discrimination."

Like "discrimination," the term "preferential treatment" is usually applied when the reasons for giving persons an advantage do not relate directly to the relevant benefit or burden; one does not think of professional teams giving preferential treatment to the most skilled athletes. Because it does not carry some of the more negative connotations of "discrimination," a phrase such as "preferential treatment for minorities" may convey the nature of a program in a more neutral way than does "reverse discrimination." True reverse discrimination or preferential treatment goes beyond merely measuring qualifications by a more accurate yardstick than has traditionally been used. If, for example, it could be shown that aptitude tests consistently underpredicted the performance of blacks in universities, then it would not be reverse discrimination to discount their relevance for black applicants.

"Affirmative action" is a phrase that refers to attempts to bring members of underrepresented groups, usually groups that have suffered discrimination, into a higher degree of participation in some beneficial program. Some affirmative action efforts include preferential treatment; others do not. Publicizing the availability of jobs more broadly than had been done previously and changing hiring practices to minimize the risks of discrimination against blacks may be done without affording blacks any employment advantage.

Two other terms that often appear in discussions of reverse discrimination and affirmative action are "quotas" and "goals." They will be treated in context as the discussion proceeds.

V.

Discrimination and Reverse Discrimination: Justice and Utility

The pattern of the rest of this essay is to weave ethical analysis with legal development. The description of legal developments corresponds for the most part with the order of the legal materials that appear in the latter part of the book. Within the past two and a half decades, the movement of the law has been from resolution of the easier ethical issues concerning discrimination to the more difficult ones, so that the progressive explication of the law fits naturally with the development of ethical issues from relatively simple to more complex. Arguments about the law's intervention in matters of discrimination fall into two broad categories, arguments about consequences and deontological arguments; or, more roughly, arguments of utility and arguments of justice.

The proper place of various sorts of moral arguments is, of course, one of the central inquiries in moral philosophy. The following summarized and oversimplified account is not intended as a satisfactory treatment of that inquiry, which many students will already have undertaken in some depth. For them, these passages can serve as a reminder of the way in which the broader theoretical issues bear on social problems of responding to unjustified discrimination. For the readers for whom these theoretical issues are new, this discussion can highlight the way in which perplexities over a practical social question can lead one to examine much more general doubts about the appropriate standards of human action.

A. CONSEQUENCES AND UTILITY

The moral significance of likely consequences is a long-debated issue. Some thinkers have asserted that when people say X is right, what they *mean* is simply that X will be more conducive to desirable consequences than any alternative. These thinkers also claim that the desirability of consequences is the final test of whether an act is immoral or moral. Other thinkers join them in this second claim, without believing that the standard of consequences is necessarily what is meant when people speak of right or wrong. Thinkers who accept this second proposition, whether or not they accept the first, may be called consequentialists, or utilitarians.

In the utilitarian philosophy developed by Beccaria and Bentham, a cardinal tenet was that the ultimate standard of good consequences is the greatest happiness of the greatest number. But utilitarianism is now often understood in a broader sense. Thus one who believes that the spread of knowledge and the maximum development of human faculties are desirable consequences, quite apart from whether or not they contribute to happiness, could be a "utilitarian" in this sense, although his theory would depart from Bentham's in a fundamental respect. I follow that usage rather than employing the less familiar word "consequentialist."

The modern disagreement between act-utilitarians and rule-utilitarians is important for our purposes and requires brief explication. An act-utilitarian believes that the criterion for evaluating any particular act is whether the consequences of that act will be beneficial or harmful. A rule-utilitarian says that the criterion is whether the act conforms to a standard or rule that, if followed generally, would lead to desirable consequences. Thus the act-utilitarian would ask if a particular lie will have desirable consequences; the rule-utilitarian would inquire whether lies, or this sort of lie, would generally have good consequences. This way of putting the distinction makes it more stark than it is likely to be in practice. A sophisticated act-utilitarian will take into account for any given act the desirable consequences of stability from following a settled rule and the consequences of example for future actors. Thus an act-utilitarian might oppose euthanasia in even the most appealing cases on the ground that the example of killing innocent persons in such circumstances poses too great a danger of diminishing respect for life generally. A sophisticated rule-utilitarian, on the other hand, must sensibly admit some qualifications to simple rules. He may say lying is wrong, *unless* the lie prevents physical harm to innocent people (as in the example of the prospective killer looking for a gun) or saves someone from unproductive emotional trauma (a terminally ill person clearly unequipped to deal with the prospect of imminent death asks if he will get better), etc. As the rules of the rule-utilitarian become more and more refined, there is less and less to distinguish him or her from the act-utilitarian.

Whichever approach is more sound from the standpoint of moral philosophy, when legislators and judges take a utilitarian perspective regarding the establishment and interpretation of legal rules, they usually function like rule-utilitarians, asking whether the rule they make or employ will have generally desirable consequences.

B. DEONTOLOGY AND JUSTICE

A deontological theory of ethics asserts that some practices are to be done or avoided for their own sakes, independent of the consequences they produce. Thus a lie, or some subclass of lies, may be regarded as wrong even if likely to promote happiness or other desirable results. A person who concludes that some acts are intrinsically wrong may still have to choose between an approach that is consequentialist in a sense and one that is not. He or she may face an occasion in which the commission of one intrinsically wrong act will reduce the total number of intrinsically wrong acts—as, for example, when the telling of one lie will prevent the telling of more lies. Then the person will have to decide whether his or her moral responsibility is to tell the truth in this instance or to promote truth-telling. Those who approach ethics from a deontological perspective have typically focused on the individual's duty not to commit inherently wrongful acts; but one might count as morally relevant the contribution of one's action toward the moral quality of subsequent acts by oneself or others.

Whether or not one believes that acts can be intrinsically wrongful independent of their potential to produce beneficial results, one may think that the pursuit of desirable consequences must be constrained by distributive principles; that, for example, a distribution that is more equal or in which benefits are more closely correlated to moral desert is to be preferred to a distribution that includes a higher total of beneficial consequences but is less equal or correlates benefits less closely to moral desert.

Nonutilitarian arguments about government intervention to stop discrimination, and about reverse discrimination, can, with a little stretching, all be classed as arguments of justice. Either they are arguments about the distribution of benefits and burdens, in which event, as explained below, they obviously concern justice; or they are arguments about rights the government should accept or support. Although usage here may be a little less clear, government violations of moral rights, and government failures to support moral rights that it should support, constitute forms of injustice.

The two notions of justice that have most obvious application to problems of reverse discrimination are distributive justice and compensatory justice. Since the time of Aristotle, the idea of distributive justice has been held to require that equals be treated equally and unequals unequally. This principle precludes arbitrary distinctions based on irrelevant characteristics. More broadly, we might say that members of society should have a fair share of the benefits and burdens of a social order. Neither the notion that equals should be treated equally nor the notion of a fair share gets us very far by itself. We must know by what criteria people are to be judged equal or unequal and also decide what will count as equality of benefit or burden. Suppose two berry pickers work equally hard but one is able to pick twice as many berries as the other. Should he be paid twice as much or the same amount? If one person requires $100 a week for medical care to keep in excellent health and another requires an expensive machine costing $200 per week even to stay alive, are they being treated equally or unequally if each gets a check for $100 each week? To fill in the formula about equals being treated equally or about a fair share, we require a rather complete account of the qualities that should matter, and how much each should matter, in respect to a wide range of benefits and burdens. And if we are talking about treatment by the government, we also require a philosophy about the proper extent of government involvement in the private order. For one alternative almost always is for the government to leave as is whatever private ordering occurs. For example, as far as the berry pickers are concerned, the government may simply leave wages to be determined by the private employer.

Reaching agreement on all the qualities that should count is typically much more difficult than reaching agreement on some qualities that should not count, and here the formulas of distributive justice can be helpful. Suppose it is agreed that for the distribution of civic benefits and burdens, such as government jobs and taxes, one's religion should not be relevant. We are then in a position to say that no one should suffer in competition for a job or have to pay higher taxes because of his or her religion. This is the sort of position that is commonly asserted not only about religion, but also about race, national or ethnic origin, and increasingly, gender.

Someone is being denied distributive justice when he or she loses a benefit because of an irrelevant characteristic. In the clearest instance, this occurs at the moment an arbitrary choice is made. But the claim can be somewhat more complex. It may be that because of decisions on the basis of irrelevant characteristics at an earlier stage, a person has been deprived of the opportunity to acquire traits that are relevant to receipt of the benefit. Highly developed writing and analytical skills are, for example, valuable for lawyers. Organizations hiring lawyers and law schools choosing students understandably care whether applicants possess these skills. Let us suppose that a group in society has been systematically and unjustifiably denied the chance to develop these skills and that, therefore, opportunities in law, which carry substantial income, prestige, and power, are not available to members of that group. Even if it were true that no law school and no employers of lawyers discriminated on arbitrary grounds, nevertheless members of the group in question might say their inability to become lawyers represents a denial of distributive justice. The assertion would seem especially powerful if they were blocked from other positions of power and wealth for the same reasons. If persons have thus far suffered disabilities because of distributive injustice, they have a claim of distributive justice to be given the share that they would have had but for the original wrong.

The second concept of justice that is important to us is compensatory justice. The notion here is that if one is unjustly deprived of something one rightfully possesses, one should be paid back. In the simple case, A steals B's bicycle. Principles of compensatory justice require A to return the bicycle to B, or if the bike is no longer around, to give B enough money to buy a replacement. Persons who have suffered because they have been wrongly treated on the basis of some arbitrary characteristic may claim that those who wronged them should pay them back for the harm done. To a substantial extent, the demands of compensatory justice will coincide with demands of distributive justice: that people be placed in positions they would have obtained in the absence of original wrongs. But the principle of compensatory justice may go further. Suppose Adam is a shiftless man of thirty years who has never worked and does not plan to. He barely survives on welfare. The local sheriff knowingly "frames" him for a theft, and as a consequence, Adam goes for five years to prison, where he is miserable. As soon as he is out, he returns to his previous existence. As far as distributive justice is concerned, he *now* has no complaint concerning the sheriff's behavior. Although Adam undoubtedly had a complaint of distributive injustice while in prison (i.e., he was being made to suffer harm he did not deserve), he would now be, we are assuming, penniless and living on welfare whether or not he had been framed. But Adam does still have a claim of compensatory justice against the sheriff; he wants to be paid back for the hellish existence and loss of liberty that he has had to endure for five years.

I have suggested that a third concept of justice is that moral rights be adequately recognized by the government. Restrictions on private discrimination may be said, for example, to violate the basic rights of liberty and property of persons who choose to discriminate. On the other hand, discrimination of many kinds may be thought to offend a moral right to compete for benefits on the basis of one's relevant skills. Such a right would be directly violated by governmental discrimination; governmental inaction against private discrimination might be considered an unjust failure to support the moral right to compete that private individuals have against other private individuals and enterprises. This particular claimed right could also be interposed against remedies for past discrimination that include preferential treatment for members of groups previously victimized. A frequent part of discussions of discrimination is a claimed right to adequate or equal opportunity. What is often meant is something more than a fair chance to compete on the basis of one's present skills; namely, a claim that the government should afford minimally satisfactory, or equal, opportunities to develop talents and skills. Such claims may be understood as one point of view about what distributive justice requires in respect to opportunity—opportunity being a special kind of benefit that a society may distribute in various ways. In instances of reverse discrimination, both sides can present arguments based on equal opportunity. Members of previously harmed groups may say that present preferences help make up for earlier deprivations; those who lose a benefit because of a preferential program may say they are being presently denied equal opportunity.

Yet another notion of justice, procedural justice, is very important in the law and bears on problems of discrimination and reverse discrimination. Most straightforwardly, once it is determined what characteristics are to count as relevant for distributions of burdens and benefits and what sorts of injuries warrant compensation, then a fair way of determining who qualifies is required if these accepted principles of justice are to be realized in practice. The relationship between procedure and substantive principle is more complicated, however. "Ideal" substantive principles may have to be tempered to some degree in the interest of having standards that can be applied fairly and at acceptable expense.

It may also be thought that justice requires a fair input into social decisions about how benefits will be allocated. Since we know that political decision makers are often not disinterested and are responsive to pressures, and since we know also that various decisions about distribution will affect people differently, we can conclude that if members of a group are unfairly represented in the political process, the chances that their claims of justice will be disregarded are increased. In practical terms, the realization of other aspects of justice depends heavily on a degree of political justice.

C. UTILITY AND JUSTICE

How do considerations of justice relate to utility? At least three possibilities suggest themselves. The first is that all proper considerations of justice are reducible to utilitarian benefits. The second is that principles of justice set "side constraints" on the pursuit of utilitarian objectives. The third is that when principles of justice conflict with utilitarian considerations, the decision maker must resolve on some ad hoc basis which principles are to be satisfied. A utilitarian might say that the way to fill out the formulas of justice is to ask what criteria of initial distribution will promote the most desirable consequences for members of society, and what standards of compensation will reduce insecurity and unhappiness for those who suffer loss and will deter those tempted to take things from others. For the utilitarian, principles of justice would be merely useful subcategories of more general principles of utility.

We can, however, conjure up some instances in which utility would not seem to be served by adhering to principles of justice. Suppose it could be shown that in families, all members are happier and psychologically healthier if there is a clear hierarchy that eliminates any competitive wrangling among supposed equals. Imagine twins identical in every respect except a small birthmark on one that allows the parents to tell them apart. Should the parents arbitrarily choose one and raise him to a higher status over the other? Calculations of utility would suggest doing so, but distributive justice would appear to be violated. Perhaps a similar, and certainly more realistic, example concerns doing experimentation in which otherwise similar patients are intentionally treated differently. Is any principle of justice violated when some patients receive probably valuable medicine and others get a placebo—a practice that in the long run helps develop the best possible medicines and saves lives? Compensatory justice may not serve utility when we know that the only compensation available will be misused. Suppose Adam, the jobless man framed and put in jail, will, if he receives monetary compensation from the sheriff, waste it on drink, which makes him miserable; further suppose that the sheriff has undergone a reformation and now donates all his money except modest living expenses to worthwhile charities. Adam deserves compensation under principles of justice but his getting it will disserve utility. The rigorous act-utilitarian must say that if principles of justice, or other claimed principles of moral right, actually conflict with the aim of achieving the most desirable consequences (and this conflict is obvious to those making the choice), the principles must yield.

A rule-utilitarian may urge that the *rules* of compensatory and distributive justice do serve utility, and that isolated exceptions are beside the point. Perhaps he or she would recognize some rulelike exception that covers experimentation, in which the practice of treating equals unequally is at the heart of the method.

A position that straddles between the typical utilitarian and deontological views is one in which what philosophers should judge to be the most adequate set of moral standards is the set whose acceptance will produce the most desirable consequences, that set turning out to be largely nonutilitarian because societies will actually achieve the best consequences if their members adopt some other set of standards. The person who adopts such a stance shares with the utilitarian the ultimate criterion for judging moral practices, but he or she rejects the utilitarian's view about how actual people should approach moral problems and evaluate social institutions.

If one concludes that valid claims of justice have a weight that is not reducible to utilitarian considerations, one must decide how conflicts between justice and utility are to be resolved. Some people believe that a true claim of justice must take priority; that desirable consequences may be pursued only if no injustice is done. Others believe that utility can override valid claims of justice if the consequential considerations are powerful enough. As the earlier discussion of deontological standards indicates, the issue about consequences can arise even if one focuses on justice alone. One might believe that doing justice for some present victims of injustice will actually reduce the possibilities for justice in the future, by, for example, creating such resentment among those who have to pay the price that they will be disposed to inflict new wrongs on the original victims or on others. Should one perceive such a conflict, one would have to choose between doing justice and promoting justice.

As you address the problems of discrimination and reverse discrimination, you will want to consider carefully whether you think claims of justice carry weight independent of the likely consequences of recognizing them, and if so, how conflicts between doing justice in the present and promoting desirable consequences (possibly including encouraging justice in the future) should be resolved. Your decisions on these points may or may not affect your view of the circumstances, if any, in which discrimination and reverse discrimination are warranted.

Whatever their ultimate moral significance, certain principles of justice are commonly dealt with by legislators and judges, who usually will not try to work out systematically the social consequences of following them. For the legislator, the explanation may be that the principles are widely accepted or simply that they appear to be of obvious moral weight. For the judge, the principles may be deeply reflected in the legal materials with which he or she works, and the judge may accept them as authoritative without reflecting on whether their pursuit will in particular instances promote a better society. There is even some question whether such reflections are the judge's business. Some scholars believe that in every case, the judge's duty is simply to decide in which direction the existing legal materials point; that the side that would win on this basis has an institutionalized *right* to a decision in its favor. In this view, general weighings of considerations of social advantage are to be left to the legislature. The competing view is that at least in very close cases, for which the legal materials produce no clear answer, a judge does appropriately take into account the same sorts of considerations of social policy that influence legislators. Since proponents of the "rights thesis" acknowledge that some legal standards do direct judges to make decisions about social desirability and moral acceptability, and since proponents of the view that judges appropriately weigh considerations of policy and morality agree that the legal standards often preclude such inquiry in particular cases, the theoretical disagreement, in practical terms, seems to come down to how often such matters may be taken into account. Such questions about the appropriate role of judges lurk in the background of many lawsuits over discrimination and reverse discrimination. In any event, the main point here is that even if concepts of justice are largely reducible to utilitarian considerations, it may be that for judges, these concepts should often be taken as givens of the legal system not demanding further justification.

VI.

Development of the Law Against Discrimination: The Easier Ethical Problems

A. THE LAW THROUGH *BROWN V. BOARD OF EDUCATION*

Despite the stirring assertion in the Declaration of Independence that "All men are created equal" (see Materials, p. 89), neither blacks nor American Indians were treated as full human beings at the time this country was founded. Indians were hounded brutally from their lands when whites wished to move westward, and blacks were torn away from their homes and culture, transported across the ocean in intolerable conditions, enslaved without even the rights that slaves had in the ancient world, prohibited from learning to read and write, and in many instances at least, denied the chance to develop a stable and secure family life. This wicked system was even enshrined in the American Constitution, which forbade federal abolition of the slave trade before 1808, required states to return fugitive slaves from other states, and established the formula that each slave would count as three-fifths of a free person in calculations of population for the purpose of determining the allocation of seats in the House of Representatives (see Materials, pp. 89–91).

This legal regime was overthrown only by the Civil War. In its aftermath were adopted the Thirteenth Amendment, which forbids slavery and involuntary servitude, the Fourteenth Amendment, which guarantees all persons the right not to be deprived by a state of due process of law and equal protection of the laws, and the Fifteenth Amendment, which prohibits racial discrimination in voting (see Materials, pp. 91–92). It was apparent, as the earliest important Supreme Court opinion interpreting the Fourteenth Amendment indicated, that the main purpose of these amendments was to improve the status of the recently freed blacks (see *Slaughter-House Cases*, Materials, pp. 95–99). But their language was general, and the words of the Fourteenth Amendment were potentially very broad, carrying within themselves the seeds of the dilemma of reverse discrimination.

For our purposes, the crucial phrase in the Fourteenth Amendment is that "No State shall . . . deny to any person . . . the equal protection of the laws." The nature of laws is to classify, to treat some people differently from others in some respects; so the amendment obviously cannot mean that all people must be treated equally in every respect. The clause might be read only to embody a formal principle of justice; that once the legislature has decided which persons are to receive protection under various laws, those persons should equally be accorded that protection. So interpreted, the clause would be only a guarantee of fair administration. But as the Supreme Court has consistently recognized, such an interpretation would be insufficient, for it would permit legislative classifications denying basic rights to blacks, and it was that which the amendment most obviously was meant to forbid.

From the outset it was understood that some rights could not be denied to blacks. What the framers of the amendment most clearly had in mind were rights protected by the 1866 Civil Rights Act, such as the rights to own property and to make contracts; and the amendment was passed largely to ensure constitutional support for those rights (see Materials, pp. 92–95). The Fourteenth Amendment alone was not, however, believed to guarantee blacks equality in all rights. Many northern states then had racially segregated schools and excluded blacks from voting and jury service, and they plainly did not assume that the vague wording of the amendment rendered all those practices unconstitutional. The Fifteenth Amendment was later thought necessary to ensure equality of voting rights; but in 1880, the Supreme Court held that exclusion of blacks from jury service did violate the equal protection clause, implicitly rejecting the claim that it was not meant to reach political rights (see Materials, pp. 99–101). In subsequent nineteenth-century cases, the Court declined to expand the coverage of the language much further. It did in 1886 confirm that the equal protection clause protected some groups other than blacks (Materials, pp. 101–102); but in 1883 it held invalid the Civil Rights Act of 1875, saying that the post–Civil War amendments did not authorize congressional restraint of private racial discrimination (see Materials, pp. 102–105). And in 1896, in *Plessy v. Ferguson*, it upheld segregation of public facilities, a practice that was only then becoming a dominant part of the southern approach to race relations (Materials, pp. 105–111). Partly on the theory that the Fourteenth Amendment did not deal with "social rights," and partly on the theory that racial segregation did not necessarily mean inequality, the Supreme Court rejected the argument that it was unconstitutional, overriding the eloquent plea in the dissent of the first Justice Harlan that the Constitution required government to be "color blind." Through the first half of the twentieth century, the doctrine of *Plessy* survived. It was unconstitutional for states to deny rights to blacks, but so long as facilities were equal, separation on a racial basis was permissible. Of course in practice, facilities were not equal, and often schools for blacks were pitifully inadequate. Moreover, systematic denial of voting and other rights also was beyond effective correction by the federal courts, although when important cases rose to higher courts the claims of blacks were usually sustained.

One class of persons that enjoyed no success at all in claims under the equal protection clause was women. Women were not constitutionally assured of the right to vote until the Nineteenth Amendment was adopted in 1920 (Materials, p. 92), and although the sweeping legal inequalities that characterized their status were moderated by legislation through the first half of the twentieth century, it remained accepted until quite recently that gender was a permissible basis of classification for many matters.

Brown v. Board of Education, decided in 1954 (Materials, pp. 121–126), marked a revolution in interpretation of the equal protection clause. It sparked invigoration of the clause in its application to racial classifications, and it presaged a more general expansion of coverage that has imposed stringent limits on classifications based on gender, alienage, and recent movement into the state. It has also significantly curtailed state choices about how to apportion population for legislative districts and whether to impose fees as a condition for exercising rights in the political and criminal processes.

In this section of the essay, as well as in the materials, our main concentration is on racial discrimination. But a brief comparison of the problem of discrimination on the basis of sex follows the discussion of racial discrimination.

B. RACIAL DISCRIMINATION BY THE GOVERNMENT: THE ETHICAL ISSUE

Whatever the proper constitutional analysis, the problem of social ethics the Supreme Court dealt with in *Brown* seems rather easy to most of us today. Racial segregation in schools reflected white belief in the inferiority of blacks, it helped perpetuate that belief among succeeding generations of school students, and it largely deprived blacks of sufficient educational opportunity to achieve upper-middle-class positions in society. Few tenets of social philosophy would now be more strongly held than the belief that the state should not exclude persons from social benefits because of their race and should not encourage racial stereotypes. Exclusion on the basis of race violates distributive justice because it arbitrarily classifies on the basis of irrelevant characteristics. It also creates unhappiness, hostility, and frustration of potential in members of the group subjected to discrimination, and sows seeds of bitter divisiveness within society; thus such action is hard to defend on utilitarian grounds.

Of course it might be said, and was for many years, that because of public attitudes, the consequences of nondiscrimination by government would be so catastrophic that segregation and other forms of unequal treatment were a preferable alternative; that whatever might be the ideal in government treatment of members of different races, the reality of intense racial hostility rendered it undesirable that the law try to reflect this ideal at the present time. Perhaps this argument always overestimated the intransigency of attitudes of racial hostility. In any event, because of education, legal change, media portrayals of minorities, and growing awareness by whites of nonwhite societies, the last two decades have marked a tremendous shift toward acceptance of a genuinely multiracial society; and the time has passed when it could plausibly have been asserted that broad government discrimination by race was necessary to avert racial strife. Whether segregation to avert strife is ever warranted in narrow emergency circumstances, say in response to a race riot among prisoners, is a much more troublesome question.

We shall proceed in a moment to the more perplexing problem of the remedies for school segregation, but we may note that a fixed principle for discussions of reverse discrimination is the immorality and unconstitutionality of racial separation that occurs at the behest of the majority and dominant group of whites and systematically suppresses the opportunities in life of members of a minority.

State denial of benefits, such as jobs, to members of a racial minority is even more obviously improper, morally and constitutionally, because in that situation there is not even the veneer of equal treatment which the "separate but equal" formula for segregated facilities suggests. Yet such denials are not wholly without conceivable justification. Apart from the argument that racial harmony will be promoted by excluding blacks from certain jobs, a claim just considered in regard to school segregation, it might be said that a significant correlation exists between racial identity and performance in the relevant position, and that since most blacks will perform less well than most whites, it makes sense to choose whites. Such a justification strikes us now as hollow and hypocritical; but if we take the claim more seriously than it may deserve, we can learn something about our moral judgments concerning discrimination. Initially, we would be skeptical that the claimed correlation exists; but even if it were proven, the conclusion that whites should be chosen would not follow. The state can engage in a more careful evaluation of individual qualifications. If it were urged that picking whites is more convenient, we might respond that disqualifying people because of immutable characteristics such as race cannot be justified on the basis of administrative ease. Suppose the proponent of such a policy challenged us to explain whether we would accept choosing people on the basis of intelligence if the correlation to performance were no greater than in respect to race and the difficulty of making more individualized assessments of capacity the same. We might of course say no, that intelligence alone should never be used as a basis for choosing people unless the correlation between measured general intelligence and actual performance is very high. But we might also distinguish intelligence from race. Testable intelligence is not a wholly immutable characteristic; people can make themselves more intelligent. More important, if blacks generally perform less well than whites, we strongly suspect that the historical reason is the cruel suppression of blacks by government and society. To exclude all blacks, some of whom may be perfectly able to perform, because the level of performance of most blacks has been lowered by past unjust discrimination seems obviously unfair. Finally, when blacks have been denied job opportunities, these denials have not been isolated incidents in respect to particular jobs, they have been part of a pattern of system-wide discrimination against a clearly identifiable segment of society that has a powerful sense of group consciousness. Such discrimination perpetuates notions of class inferiority and racism, and forecloses opportunities for advancement for future generations. Whatever marginal gains in administrative ease might be achieved by excluding blacks could not possibly justify that practice.

Does this analysis lead to the conclusion that whenever a state imposes substantial disadvantages only on a minority group, its actions are unjustified? Not necessarily. If a grave threat is posed by some members of a minority and authorities are genuinely unable to determine which persons these are, perhaps they may take preventive steps against all members of the group. So at least thought the Supreme Court when, during World War II, it sustained a curfew on the West Coast for all people of Japanese ancestry and then approved the much more drastic step of their exclusion from the area (see Materials, pp. 113–117). Many, including myself, believe that the showing of danger of espionage and sabotage was much too weak to warrant such treatment of American citizens of Japanese descent; but the situation illustrates the possible conflict of considerations of general welfare on the one hand and the claims to equal treatment and recognition of rights of one part of the community on the other. If someone believes that such treatment of minorities can ever be justified, he or she must acknowledge that very pressing utilitarian needs can override what would otherwise be the unchallengeable demands of justice.

C. PRIVATE DISCRIMINATION AND GOVERNMENT PROHIBITION

In 1964, partly in response to Lyndon Johnson's stirring plea that such action would be a fitting memorial to the slain President Kennedy, Congress passed substantial civil rights legislation, forbidding racial discrimination in jobs (Materials, pp. 153–154) and in the use of places of public accommodation (Materials, pp. 150–152), as well as bolstering existing constitutional prohibitions against segregation of state facilities. These efforts were complemented by major voting rights legislation in 1965. The federal fair employment and public accommodations laws, as well as the later prohibition of housing discrimination (Materials, pp. 155–156), followed initiatives taken earlier in many northern states.

Governmental prohibitions of private racial discrimination present a question that is somewhat more complex than the moral legitimacy of discrimination by the government itself, because of a competing claim to liberty—a claim that is absent, or much weaker, when government officials wish to discriminate. (I here pass over the troublesome legal question of what involvement by the state is sufficient to make it responsible for what is initially private discrimination [see Materials, pp. 117–121].)

We may ask, first, whether private racial discrimination is morally justified and, second, whether government interference with a private choice to discriminate is justified. We may be tempted at the outset to say that differentiation of treatment on racial grounds alone can never be morally justified. Perhaps in some ideal society in the future that could be true, but it is too extreme a position in our society. We are all conditioned to have preferences and aversions that we acknowledge to be arbitrary from the standpoint of distributive justice. In deciding whom one is to date or to marry, there is nothing unethical about choosing someone with whom one feels compatible, even if the qualities that help create compatibility are racial, religious, or ethnic similarity. What if, instead, one is an individual employer, hiring a cashier with whom one will have very little personal contact? Since a job is a valuable position and since the employer's own personal feelings are not involved intensely on a day-to-day basis, perhaps one would act immorally to indulge one's arbitrary personal preferences. Here, at least, the conscientious employer faces a serious ethical question. How far the employer's own preferences match those of the rest of society may matter. If one is partial to left-handed or green-eyed applicants, one may take the attitude that acquisition of this particular job is not crucial for anyone and that indulging one's preferences will not harm anyone seriously. But if one's preference is for whites, or men, or Protestants, one must recognize that if this preference is shared by a great many other employers and one indulges the preference, one will be contributing to a pattern of hiring that seriously disadvantages substantial segments of the society on an arbitrary basis. In such a situation, the claims of equal opportunity seem powerful enough to require the employer to put aside pesonal arbitrary preference. Even if what has been said so far is correct, there will be room for disagreement over when a relationship becomes close enough so that no wrong is done in indulging an arbitrary preference shared by many members of society. Do a couple renting a room in their own apartment to a boarder, or hiring a governess for their children, do anything ethically wrong in refusing to rent to or hire black applicants because they feel uncomfortable with blacks?

The primary employers in society are, of course, no longer individuals but major corporations. The "owners" will have absolutely no contact with most employees, so their arbitrary preferences can hardly count for very much. But the managers of such firms, along with individual employers, might raise a different argument, namely, that the shared preferences of other employees and customers are such that honoring these preferences will promote harmony within the firm and patronage by potential clients or purchasers. Since the present employees and customers have no moral right to have the employer hire whites instead of blacks, an employer who offers this defense of its discrimination is relying on utilitarian grounds. Often such an argument has been a rationalization for less considered reasons for discrimination, but sometimes it has had substance. We may believe that individual firms, especially larger ones, should be willing to accept some business sacrifice in the interest of distributive justice; but that they have an ethical responsibility to commit economic suicide is doubtful.

The question whether the government should forbid discrimination of a particular sort is a somewhat different issue from whether the original discrimination is morally wrong. If discrimination is in an area of intimate personal choice, such as whom to date, then, for many reasons, the government obviously has no place. The original exercise of an arbitrary preference is not wrong, attempted government compulsion could not possibly work, and if it would, the infringement of liberty would be much too severe. A moral claim of liberty can be made against government control even when the conduct engaged in may be unethical; and this is a claim that has some relevance in regard to the individual employer, whether or not the discrimination can be defended on ethical grounds. Nevertheless, the general consensus now is that, putting aside cases in which the relationship is highly personal, the moral claims of liberty of individual employers, and of owners of public accommodations, are too weak to outweigh the interest in fair equality of opportunity for groups that have suffered systematic discrimination.

The claim to be free of government intervention is much weaker for the large firm than for the enterprise individually owned and run. Since the personal feelings of the owners of large corporations are not engaged so closely, a moral claim to liberty on their behalf would have to rest on a very expansive view of the moral right of persons to handle their property as they choose. Since property is a social institution, possible in complex forms only because of the operation of law, modest regulation in support of the general welfare seems obviously appropriate, and very expansive views of the moral rights that attach to property must be rejected. The argument about customer preference largely vanishes if all firms must hire on a nondiscriminatory basis, since customers will have to deal with one of them and none will suffer a competitive disadvantage from hiring blacks, or women, for positions in which most customers prefer white men. This leaves the argument about employee harmony. Here the response is that almost all members of society can, if they need to, learn to deal with members of other races and religions, at least in nonintimate relationships, and it is appropriate for government not to be stymied by existing and obstinate preferences but to encourage a broader tolerance.

A more general utilitarian argument can, of course, be made that regulation interferes with productivity and affords government officers opportunities for arbitrariness. Such an argument has more relevance when complicated mechanisms of enforcement are involved than when all the government does is to mandate nondiscrimination, leaving enforcement to private victims. On some occasions, no doubt, these general reasons for avoiding regulation should tip the scale against government intervention that would otherwise be acceptable. However, when protective legislation safeguards the basic moral rights of citizens, only very strong arguments about lost productivity should persuade us that the protections may be repealed.

D. GENDER DISCRIMINATION

In many respects the analysis of sexual discrimination is similar to that of racial discrimination, but there are some important differences. For most of Western history, unequal treatment of men and women has been perceived by most men, and many women, as being for the benefit of members of both sexes, and as an essential foundation of stable family life. It was widely supposed that God or the natural order, or both, assigned men and women to variant roles in life and that human institutions should recognize those assignments. The appropriate roles of women were home-centered; but these were not always portrayed as intrinsically inferior, as the place of Mary, the mother of Jesus, in the Christian tradition and the legends of chivalry in their own way reflected. Women were systematically denied legal rights, the stated justification being that men were their natural protectors in affairs of the world. The view of reality that conceived male control as for the good of all may have been the ideological delusion of an oppressor class casting a veneer of legitimacy over a starkly unjust social order. Supposedly benign motives are often a cover for exploitation, and although male domination of women was softer and less blatantly self-interested than white domination of blacks, nevertheless that domination foreclosed broad avenues of personal development for women (and indeed in its implicit demands on men, largely foreclosed other avenues for them, too).

Because women fulfilled an essential and respected place within the family, legal disabilities often did not carry with them the extreme social inequality that accompanied racial oppression. And at least in this century, education through college and general cultural levels has been roughly equal between the two sexes. One consequence of this situation has been that when positions in professional schools and ordinary jobs have become open to women on an equal basis, many women have been qualified to fill them.

Another special characteristic of gender discrimination has been that in direct practical effect, some differences in treatment have unambiguously favored women and others have had mixed effects. It is favorable rather than unfavorable treatment to be eligible for alimony, to be given a preference in child custody disputes, not to be subject to a wartime draft. If women do not want custody or alimony, they are not compelled to take them. Women who wish a military career and are denied the opportunity have undoubtedly suffered a disadvantage; but a draft takes persons who have not chosen that course, and freedom from compulsion imposed on other persons is, viewed by itself, advantageous. Even these preferences, however, may reinforce negative stereotypes about women, and their being favored in child custody disputes may help keep them at home. Thus individual classifications that have undeniably favored women may well have contributed to an entire pattern of relations that has thwarted their opportunities. Examples of gender discrimination that has mixed effects would be legislation setting maximum hours, or load limits, applicable only to women. Women who work may have less onerous jobs than similarly situated men; but a parallel consequence is that significant job opportunities are denied to women. Or legislation may on its face favor one class of women and disfavor another. Suppose, for example, wives of deceased male workers automatically get benefits that do not go automatically to the husbands of deceased female workers. This classification can be viewed as disadvantageous to female workers or advantageous to spouses of male workers. Like many of the individual classifications that have undeniably favored women, these "mixed-effect" classifications may also promote an overall pattern of frustrated opportunities for them.

The progressive elimination of gender discrimination unquestionably has had the main effect of affording new and desired opportunities for women; but in contrast to the elimination of historical patterns of racial discrimination, not every change toward equality works in their favor. Perhaps partly for this reason, as well as because the conception of a special role for women still enjoys acceptance among many people, the inappropriateness of gender discrimination is not yet as firmly settled in our society as the inappropriateness of racial discrimination. The increasing distaste for gender classification is reflected both in Supreme Court decisions (see Materials, pp. 138–149), and in Congress's proposal of the Equal Rights Amendment (Materials, p. 149). Both the Court's unwillingness to subject gender classifications to quite as strict a test as it has used for racial classifications, and the ultimate failure to achieve adoption of the Equal Rights Amendment, reflect the continuing uncertainty about some distinctions made on sexual lines. Still, whatever disagreements remain, almost everyone acknowledges that women who choose to work outside the home should have the chance to do so and should have the same salary and access to desirable positions as similarly qualified men. Once that is granted, government discrimination in most jobs and in educational possibilities is clearly unwarranted, and government mandates of nondiscrimination in the private sector are justified, for much the same reasons that apply to the bars on racial discrimination. Whether sexual segregation in education is acceptable even if racial segregation is not, and whether some jobs at least (e.g., combat positions in the military) can fairly be given only to men, are troublesome questions left for your own thought and discussion.

If the preceding discussion has suggested that the problem of gender discrimination may be somewhat more tractable than the problem of racial discrimination because of the educational and cultural opportunities many women have enjoyed, this is only part of the truth. Attitudes about gender differences affect most people much more intimately than racial attitudes and may be more resistant to change. As long as many marriages are grounded on the assumption that the primary responsibility for housework and child care should fall on the wife, many women will be at a serious disadvantage in the competition for other positions, even if there is no gender discrimination in the allocation of those positions. Whether one views such a prospect as unfortunate or unfair will depend on whether one thinks that, in general, women naturally have greater capacities for rearing young children than do men and on whether one believes that many women will *freely* choose to accept that role, even at the cost of reducing their chances for advancement in the "outside" world.

Most of the positions taken in the previous pages about discrimination and the government's role in forbidding it are not self-evident, and you may dispute some of the conclusions. But I believe they represent a fairly broad consensus of opinion in this country and beyond and would be accepted by most of those on both sides of the question of reverse discrimination. If these conclusions are correct, the government may not generally discriminate on the basis of race, religion, national origin, or gender; and it acts appropriately when it forbids discrimination on those grounds in such nonintimate social interactions as the use of restaurants and hotels, the sale and rental of housing, and the hiring and promotion of employees. This is enough to justify the major outlines of the federal and state civil rights legislation that affects the private sector.

====================   **VII.**   ====================

Remedies for Specific and Illegal Past Discrimination and the Problem of de Facto Segregation

I come now to the question of remedies for discrimination that violates the Constitution or statutes, discussing also the thorny problems of whether discrimination can occur that is not intentional, and voluntary efforts to integrate schools. I spend as much time as I do on these subjects because of their close relationship to what are thought of as typical instances of reverse discrimination, which is, after all, usually conceived of as a broadly directed attempt to remedy discrimination. More particularly, classification by race or sex is often used to remedy specific violations of law, and racial criteria may be used to counteract de facto segregation. Further, a point that is often overlooked, claims of justification that are central to reverse discrimination may be required to support certain remedies for clear violations of law or uncompelled efforts to integrate schools. One who is trying to develop a coherent approach to the ethical and legal problems of reverse discrimination must, therefore, come to terms with the ethical and legal problems that accompany remedies for specific breaches of law and decisions on how to respond to de facto segregation.

A. RACIAL SEGREGATION

For too many years, *Brown v. Board of Education* was simply disregarded altogether by most southern school districts, although the Supreme Court's opinion on implementation had approved only brief delay (see Materials, pp. 126–128). Inaction represented a kind of accommodation to public resistance in the South, but unfortunately it contributed to that resistance by encouraging some people to believe that the day of reckoning could be indefinitely postponed. Even in those districts where remedies were applied, they were rather halting, allowing students to transfer to schools of their choice and producing little real change in segregated school systems. Approximately a decade after *Brown*, the Supreme Court made it clear that effective integration of a school system was the only acceptable remedy for school segregation, and that effective integration meant racially mixed schools, to be achieved by redesigning school zones or by busing if that was necessary to accomplish the goal.

If we are to ask whether this remedial requirement is ethically and constitutionally defensible, it helps to consider first what has come to be called de facto segregation. In many northern cities, the school system has not been administered with a segregative purpose, or at least no such purpose has been provable in court. Yet because of housing patterns, school attendance zones drawn by geographical area produce schools whose students are entirely or almost entirely of one race. Typically, past government action of various sorts may have contributed to the housing patterns; but such patterns are mostly the product of private discrimination, and in any event, school administrators are not to blame for them.

What are the responsibilities of the school officials in such a setting? Part of the legal answer is that according to the Supreme Court, the Constitution has not been violated unless there has been intentional discrimination; and courts have generally declined to require school boards to remedy the indirect effect of housing patterns for which other government bodies may have borne some responsibility. So school boards are not constitutionally required to do anything about de facto segregation, even if action by other government agencies has helped cause that segregation. But a few school districts have thought that even in the absence of prior discrimination more integrated schools would be desirable, and they have voluntarily taken steps in that direction, sometimes using racial categorizations of pupils for purposes of school assignment. In some states it is, or was, part of the general policy of the state education department that school districts should try to achieve "racial balance."

What is the ethical status of these attempts? We should first draw a distinction. One way of integrating schools is by redrawing or combining attendance zones. A line between zones is redrawn to bring more whites into a school that was previously mostly black and to bring more blacks into a school that was previously mostly white. Or, say, in the instance of two elementary schools, zones are combined so that all children go to grades 1–3 at one school and grades 4–6 at the other school. When administrators redraw lines and combine zones, they will have the racial composition of the neighborhoods in mind, and to that extent, they are not acting in a color-blind way; but no individual pupil is assigned to a particular school because of his or her race. Busing programs are typically race-conscious in a stronger sense. Suppose one school is 90 percent white and 10 percent black, and another is 90 percent black and 10 percent white. Only white students will be bused from the "white" school to the "black" one, and only black students will be bused in the other direction. Thus the treatment of these individual students is determined by their race. Because this practice comes much closer to reverse discrimination, we shall consider attempts to achieve racial balance in this most controversial form.

A busing program is, of course, likely to involve some extra degree of inconvenience for pupils who are sent away from their neighborhoods. For this reason and perhaps others—such as the possible benefits of having school friends who can be playmates away from school—deviations from the idea of neighborhood schools involve costs, and at some point these costs will become so great they will outweigh possible benefits. No one, for example, has suggested busing small children two hours each way in order to achieve integration. But the fundamental moral question is most sharply posed if we imagine a program that is relatively cost-free in these terms.

Against such a program, it may be said that the district is distinguishing pupils on the arbitrary ground of race. One pupil is sent to school A because he is black; another pupil, alike in every relevant respect except for his whiteness, is sent to school B. Assuming that the white pupil is dissatisfied with his assignment, he may argue that he is being denied what he or his parents consider a benefit on no ground other than his race, and that this practice both directly violates principles of distributive justice and involves the state in perpetuating distinctions based on race.

In favor of the program, it may be said that blacks will benefit from being educated in a setting where they encounter whites, who make up by far the largest racial group in society. Indeed, if the Court was right in *Brown v. Board of Education* that blacks do not learn as effectively in segregated schools, blacks in schools that are segregated de facto may suffer about as much as those segregated by the design of school authorities. Moreover, it is desirable for whites also to learn in an integrated setting, since they should realize early in their lives that they live in a multiracial society. There is a twofold response to the claim of the white pupil that he is being denied a benefit on the basis of the arbitrary characteristic of race. First, it may be said that since he is being sent to a school of comparable quality and receiving what the school board regards as the value of an integrated education, he is not, whatever his own perceptions may be, being denied a significant benefit. Even if the quality of schooling is by some standard less good than in his neighborhood school, he may have no special claim to receive schooling of that quality. Second, it can be argued that because the arbitrary characteristic of race has played such a crucial role in our society, persons, black and white, now think largely in racial terms; and the only way to ameliorate the effects of centuries of unjust treatment of members of minority races and to moderate the possibility of future discrimination is now to recognize race temporarily to achieve racially mixed education and contribute to a truly integrated society.

You will have to decide for yourself which position you find more compelling. My own view is that, assuming a race-conscious classification can accomplish integrated schools without great cost and that other techniques will not be effective, the use of such classification is justified. In *Swann v. Charlotte-Mecklenburg Board of Education* (Materials, pp. 128–135), a case not actually presenting this issue, the entire membership of the Supreme Court indicated that as far as the Constitution is concerned a school board can, if it chooses, use racial categorizations to integrate schools that are segregated de facto. Thus the Constitution neither requires nor forbids race-conscious programs to correct de facto segregation and promote integration.

It is time now to return to the remedies for de jure segregation. The Supreme Court, in the *Swann* opinion, insisted that districts previously segregated de jure—whether by law or by the actions of school officials—must be genuinely integrated by whatever steps are required, including busing if necessary. The practical effect of this ruling is that southern school districts, and the many northern districts found to have engaged in de jure segregation, must attain a degree of integration considerably greater than that which exists in most northern cities and greater than would have existed had the district never had segregated schools. We can assume that housing patterns alone would have produced a good bit of racial division in southern schools as well as northern ones. But southern districts are not permitted now simply to draw school assignments on geographical nonracial lines, as may most northern districts; they must actually accomplish integration. Not surprisingly, the scope of the remedies for prior segregation, typically requiring race-conscious action, has caused some people to think the respective treatment of de jure and de facto segregation is itself unjust.

If we believe that race-conscious action is warranted to correct de facto segregation, we will not object to its use to cure de jure segregation, although we may still question whether a court should demand it. But whatever our views about de facto segregation, there are strong reasons supporting the Supreme Court's position on de jure systems. We know that housing patterns would have produced some segregation of southern schools regardless of school policies, but how much? That is the rub. Actual housing patterns are, of course, linked to the historical locations of segregated schools, so there is no way of knowing what the housing patterns would now be if schools had been integrated. A court is simply not in a position to say how far de facto segregation would have occurred in any event. So it imposes a remedy that will do as much as is feasible to correct segregation caused by the actions of school authorities. An order of as full integration as seems practical is the only remedy that can assuredly be said to do so.

B. EMPLOYMENT DISCRIMINATION

The remedies in employment discrimination cases raise more directly the central issues of reverse discrimination. The Supreme Court has interpreted the federal statute (Materials, pp. 153–154) to bar the use of tests for employment that have a disproportionate impact on a minority group unless they are justified by "business necessity." Say, for example, an employer has used a general aptitude test to screen for all jobs in his firm, and blacks tend to do worse on the test than whites. If an applicant's test results have little bearing on his or her ability to perform a certain job, then as to that job, the employer has "discriminated" against blacks under the meaning of the statute, whether or not that was the intention. In order to comply with the statute, employers thus have a burden that goes beyond refraining from intentional discrimination. If they use tests to screen for employment or promotions, they must first ascertain whether there is any disproportionate impact; whether certain groups—for example, blacks, women, or Catholics—score worse on the tests than do other groups and are, therefore, disproportionately excluded from the positions in question. If there is a disproportionate impact, the employer must determine if the test serves "business necessity," that is, if there is a demonstrable correlation between performance on the test and performance on the job. If there is such a correlation, continued use of the test is acceptable, the theory being that the group whose members score less well on the test really has fewer members qualified for the position. If the test does not serve business necessity, the employer must stop relying on it, its use being viewed as an indirect way of excluding members of a group from jobs for which they may well be qualified.

Assuming that the law properly forbids intentional discrimination in employment, is this disproportionate impact–business necessity standard also proper? If what were involved were criminal penalties, penalizing an employer for guessing wrong about whether a test serves business necessity might be thought unfair. But that problem is much less significant when only civil remedies are involved. If the sole standard for administration of the statute were intentional discrimination, many employers who used tests intentionally as a method to discriminate would go undetected, for it would be hard to prove an employer's bad motive for using a test neutral on its face. Other powerful reasons support attacking the tests. The poor performance of blacks on many tests is largely the product of previous educational disadvantage, much of it caused by intentional discrimination. Part of the purpose of fair employment laws is to avoid perpetuation of prior discrimination and to bring disadvantaged groups more nearly into the mainstream of the economy. These aims warrant the prohibition of tests that hurt members of disadvantaged groups and serve no real need of the employers. Since employers must decide what tests to use, they may fairly bear the burden of ensuring that tests with a disproportionate impact are genuinely needed. The point is not so much that employers who intend no discrimination are necessarily to blame for using improper tests, although they might be accused of insufficient sensitivity to a social problem; rather, their slight interest in choosing methods of screening is required to give way to the broader need for equal opportunity.

When courts have determined that employers have discriminated, either intentionally or by the use of unjustified tests, they have not ordered employers to fire existing white employees; but they have sometimes, in addition to other remedies, required that in the future a certain percentage of the group discriminated against be hired and that identifiable victims of discrimination be put, when possible, in the position they would have had but for discrimination. Thus a black employee improperly denied seniority may be placed on the seniority scale in the position that he or she would have had but for being a victim of discrimination.

Each of these remedies incorporates the possibility that the best-qualified applicant for a position at a particular point in time will not get the job. Does that applicant have a good argument that he or she is being unjustly treated? (I assume here and throughout the following discussion that the original discrimination was intentional. You may want to consider how far the analysis holds for unintentional discrimination.)

Let us first take the narrowest remedy: only blacks who earlier applied and would have gotten the job had there not been illegal discrimination are now given jobs; and a white who is better qualified than some of those blacks is denied a job. Each black who is given a job is put in no better a position than he or she would have been in had the employer acted correctly in the first place. Such treatment seems minimally appropriate compensation for the original wrong (perhaps the employer should also pay him back something for the years when he did not have the job), and distributive justice may also call for a person to occupy the position he or she would have occupied had no wrong to him or her been done. Whatever the strength of a general claim to be considered on the basis of one's qualifications, it does not override the claim for redress for past wrongs by the employer. Employers must take care of such wrongs before they can be viewed as having positions open to new applicants.

Still, the present white applicant appears to be an innocent victim of the employer's original wrong. The beneficiary is another white, the white who was earlier hired because of discrimination; but by now this employee may be an experienced and skilled worker who has built up strong expectations based on years at the job. Firing that worker to satisfy the claim of justice of the new white applicant would defeat his or her own claim of justice not to have reasonably formed expectations frustrated; and from the utilitarian perspective it would be highly undesirable both to productivity and to psychological security to replace such experienced workers with novices. (Indeed if he or she could now compete freshly for the job, the experienced worker might well be the best qualified; or would his or her qualifications have to be disregarded because earned as a result of the employer's original discrimination?) However one approaches the issue, the possible claims of the well-qualified white applicant seem weaker than the claims of the victims of discrimination and of those presently employed.

Note that when remedies are given only to the very persons who suffered illegal discrimination, reverse discrimination by race is not really involved. These people are now favored only because a denial of their rights has been established, not (except indirectly) because they are black.

The analysis becomes more complicated, and the conclusion less clear, if the remedy requires an employer to hire or advance a certain percentage of blacks, plainly benefiting some blacks who were not previously victimized by this employer. To respond to the question whether excluded white applicants have a legitimate claim that they are not being accorded distributive justice, we need to consider what purposes an order to hire a specific percentage of blacks might serve. First, the percentage requirement may be the most accurate way of redressing the wrongs of those who suffered from the employer's past discrimination. Often blacks will not even have bothered to apply to employers who were known to refuse to hire blacks; their claim to compensatory and distributive justice hardly seems weaker than that of the unsuccessful applicant, if it is a fact that they would have applied and been chosen had there been no discrimination. Once the class of victims is broadened in this way, the impossibility of designating each one accurately is plain. Many of those who seek a job may well be among those who previously failed to apply because of discrimination. Forcing the employer to hire a set percentage of blacks makes it more likely that those who suffered will be hired, without their having to face competition with all present applicants.

Second, a set percentage may constitute a guarantee against continued discrimination. Identifying intentional discrimination is not always easy, especially in respect to jobs that require complex qualifications. If an employer has been proved to have discriminated, it may be prudent to establish objective goals in hiring that will effectively preclude further discrimination against the same group. Of course, such goals *may* be an unnecessary or unwise way to try to stop discrimination; but if they are the best society can do to ensure nondiscrimination, a "best-qualified" white who happens on one occasion to lose out does not have a well-founded objection, since any alternative scheme will do a worse job overall of choosing the best qualified.

Third, the effects of prior discrimination may not have exhausted themselves. Awareness of jobs is often by word-of-mouth, and hiring is frequently affected by the recommendations of present employees. If most employees are now white because of prior discrimination, these influences may serve to diminish the chances of blacks for jobs, even if the employer ceases to discriminate. These concerns may be met to a degree by minimizing the role of employee recommendations in hiring decisions and by widely publicizing available jobs; but the requirement to hire a specified percentage may arguably be a way to ensure that the lingering influences of past discrimination do not defeat fair employment opportunity in the present. Whether any particular percentage really satisfies these purposes will be questionable; but if the order to hire a percentage of minority employees is actually necessary to accomplish them, it seems a legitimate corrective of past discrimination and a safeguard against future wrongdoing. It is a form of reverse discrimination, because persons are favored on the basis of their membership in a minority group; but it is covered by the same corrective justification that applies most clearly when the individual victim of discrimination is preferred.

Suppose the percentage of minority group members to be hired is justified on a different theory: that the minority group should have the proportion of persons in the work force that it would have had if there had never been discrimination. We shall consider here a police force whose discrimination was unconstitutional even before any fair employment statutes were passed. Imagine that there has been systematic discrimination against black applicants for a period of thirty years and that, as a consequence, 5 percent of the police force is black instead of 25 percent. Suppose the court orders that half of those hired must be black until the representation of blacks on the force has reached 25 percent. Since only relatively recent black victims of past discrimination will actually now be qualified and interested in becoming police officers, a job that attracts young persons, the percentage of blacks to be hired appears too high even for the combined purposes of correcting past discrimination for actual victims of that discrimination and ensuring future nondiscriminatory hiring free of the effects of prior discrimination. One justification that

might be offered is that since blacks as a group suffered discrimination, the remedy properly applies to blacks as a group. As stated, this
justification appears to be based on fallacious reasoning. Because
some blacks at an earlier period were victimized by discrimination is
not a good reason to grant undeserved benefits to other blacks at a
later period simply because they are black. The justification could
become plausible only if some greater connection were asserted
between the blacks who lost out and the blacks who now benefit. A
second possible justification is that the community needs a police
force that is 25 percent black. It might be urged, for example, that
black citizens will respond better to black officers and will respect the
force as a whole more if they see a reasonable proportion of black
police. Each of these general justifications is also advanced for
reverse discrimination that does not respond to specific violations;
and they will be discussed more fully in that context. The important
point to note here, however, is that unless some version of the group
redress justification is persuasive, the hypothetical remedy goes
beyond what can legitimately be considered corrective of previous
discrimination; and unless either that or the desirable proportion
justification holds, the white applicant's claim that he or she has been
unjustly deprived of a benefit because the remedy exceeds the scope
of the violation appears to be valid.

VIII.

Broader Efforts to Stop Discrimination and the
Encouragement of Reverse Discrimination

Corrective measures against illegal discrimination are not always
based on a determination that a particular organization has discriminated. Rather, a whole class of organizations may be subject to
remedial devices imposed by the nonjudicial branches of government, and these may include specified percentages of minority group
members and women to be chosen. Using reported instances of
individual discrimination and general statistical data about potential
applicants and successful applicants, the executive branch, or possibly the legislature, concludes that discrimination, say in employment,
occurs frequently. Rather than simply telling all employers to refrain

from discriminating, the agency requires that employers set targets or "goals" if their present number of minority or female employees falls below that which would generally be appropriate in that area. The federal government has instituted such goals for government contractors under its power to determine how public money is spent. If the government contractors fail to satisfy the Office of Federal Contract Compliance Programs (OFCCP), under the Labor Department, that they are not engaging in discrimination, federal financial support is terminated. One controversial government effort of this sort has concerned universities. Since virtually all major universities receive a substantial amount of their budget from various federal government sources, the threat of a cutoff of funds has been virtually equivalent to compulsion. In addition to mandating open hiring practices, including advertising, and elaborate reporting techniques to uncover possible discrimination, the government (until late 1978 the Department of Health, Education, and Welfare but now the OFCCP) has directed universities to set goals for how many minority group members and women should be hired. The precise status of these goals has been a matter of acute controversy. Officials have said that they are not rigid quotas and that their only aim is nondiscriminatory hiring: if a university does not meet its goals, it will not be penalized if it can prove that it has not discriminated. Nevertheless, it is obvious that if the goals are met, university officials will have a lot less explaining to do than if they are not met, and the risks of meeting the goals seem far fewer than the risks of not meeting them. The goals thus operate as something considerably more significant than a rough statistical projection of what nondiscriminatory hiring would be expected to yield. Since academic appointments turn on a host of subtle and essentially unmeasurable factors, such as potential for creative scholarship and ability to communicate effectively to students, saying in any particular instance whether discrimination against or in favor of a minority group member has occurred is very hard. A university may thus perceive that if it does not meet, or come very close to meeting, its goals, establishing that it did not discriminate will be difficult. Whatever the theory of the goals, they can place pressure on some universities, and their branches, to engage in reverse discrimination. Programs such as the guidelines for universities may be justified as more effective, less narrowly focused, efforts to stop discrimination by institutions that have discriminated and might otherwise continue to discriminate. They may also be a way of combating the influence of past discriminatory practices on present hiring. If, for example, white males have acquired superior academic "credentials" through past discrimination, present nondiscriminatory hiring that gives heavy emphasis to those credentials may be unfair to blacks and women who are actually better qualified but can present less sparkling resumes. Seen in this light, the goals are not dissimilar to the corrective orders given by courts, save that in particular instances some employers may be required, or encouraged, to hire a proportion of minorities or women even though they have never discriminated in the past and would not discriminate in the future. As to such employers, and as to the white male applicants to such employers who do not get jobs because of the goals, the setting of goals might be justified as a perhaps unfortunate but necessary concomitant of having an effectively administrable approach. Whether goals of this sort really are needed to prevent discrimination and the unfair effects of past discrimination is sharply disputed. If other more modest techniques would suffice, these justifications alone do not override the claims of white males to be evaluated fairly on the basis of their qualifications.

Other qualifications might be offered for hiring goals that operate in the fashion described. It might be claimed that for some reason having more minority and women employees is socially desirable, or that advancing the positions of members of groups that have suffered previous discrimination is appropriate even when that advancement exceeds what would occur under nondiscriminating hiring policies. I have already mentioned such possible justifications in connection with corrective court orders, and we shall examine them more fully in the next section.

IX.

Reverse Discrimination That Does Not Correct Specified Violations and That Plainly Goes Beyond Guarantees of Nondiscriminatory Choice

The most controversial instances of reverse discrimination are ones in which preferential treatment is given to members of minority groups by organizations that are not engaging, and have not recently engaged, in illegal discrimination and for purposes other than to prevent possible discrimination by these organizations. Indeed, when the problem of reverse discrimination or preferential treatment is debated, these are the instances that people usually have in mind. At the time of this writing, the Supreme Court has addressed such practices on five occasions. First it upheld employment preferences for Indians in the Bureau of Indian Affairs (*Morton v. Mancari,* 417 U.S. 535, 94 S. Ct. 2474, 41 L.Ed.2d 290 [1979]), relying on the unique status of Indian tribes and the need to make the bureau more responsive to its constituents. The next two cases involved graduate school admissions policies favoring minority group members. A majority of the Court did not reach the substantive issues in the *DeFunis* case (Materials, pp. 165–173), involving law school admissions; but in *University of California Regents v. Bakke* (Materials, pp. 174–205), four justices said that preferences were not legally appropriate, four said that they were appropriate even if a fixed number of places was set aside for minority group members, and one justice said that only more flexible preferences were appropriate. The fourth case, *United Steelworkers v. Weber* (Materials, pp. 206–208), involved an agreement by a union and a private company to give black employees half of the places in an in-plant craft-training program until the percentage of black craftworkers in the plant reached that of blacks in the local labor force. The Court held that private companies might prefer blacks in order to correct racial imbalances whether or not those companies had previously engaged in illegal discrimination. Finally, in *Fullilove v. Klutznick* (Materials, pp. 208–218), the Court sustained a "set-aside" statute under which 10 percent of federal funds granted for local works projects had to be used to obtain services or supplies from businesses owned and controlled by minority groups.

In the discussion that follows, I concentrate mainly on the issues of graduate school admissions presented by *DeFunis* and *Bakke.* My strategy is to examine first the ethical problems that preferential admissions raise and then to proceed to the legal dimensions treated in *Bakke.* Only when the comparisons seem especially illuminating do I refer to the related problems of employment preferences and financial set-asides.

A bit of summary factual background is useful. Although blacks constitute about 11 percent of the population, they have made up only about 2 percent of the nation's doctors and an even lower percentage of the nation's lawyers. In the relatively recent past, at least, major universities have not intentionally discriminated against blacks in admission to medical and law schools. The main, but not sole, criteria for admissions have been undergraduate grades, and aptitude and achievement tests. These are thought to correlate with performance in professional school, and to a lesser extent with performance ultimately in the profession. Although some people have argued that both correlations are so weak such criteria should not survive a business necessity standard, we shall assume that substantial reliance on them is the best that professional schools can do right now. Blacks, American Indians, Mexican-Americans, and Puerto Ricans do not generally do as well by these criteria as white Americans, and if no special accommodation were made, comparatively few of them would now get into medical schools and the more prestigious law schools, for which there is great competition. No one, of course, questions the appropriateness of discounting the criteria to some extent in particular cases. For example, a poor black who worked forty hours a week during college and maintained a B average may thereby have demonstrated more potential than a rich white without any extensive nonacademic activities who achieved a B+ average. But so long as the basic standard is performance in professional school, it seems clear that even once all appropriate adjustments of this sort are made, few blacks and other minority group members would be admitted to these highly competitive institutions. The question posed is whether some special admissions preference should be given in order to have a higher percentage of minority group members in these schools. Most schools have recently given such a preference, either in the form of setting aside a fixed or somewhat flexible number of places for blacks and others, or by weighing substantially in an applicant's favor the fact that he or she is a member of a minority group. Most institutions do their weighing with some eye toward how many minority group members they aim to admit to a typical class, so there is no clear distinction between institutions that set a goal and those that do not. The admissions program of the Medical School of the University of California at Davis, challenged in *Bakke*, set aside a specified number of places for minority group members; the program of the University of Washington Law School, challenged in *DeFunis*, was less rigid. Since the Davis practice was terminated by the Supreme Court decision in

Bakke, and since in some fundamental respects the flexible programs are not so different from it, we shall discuss them together, except when the need for a distinction is clearly indicated.

A. ETHICAL ARGUMENTS

On each side of the reverse discrimination debate are arguments of justice and utility. The task is to assess these and to place them in some coherent whole in order to make judgments about the moral justifiability of particular practices. In the discussion that follows, I treat claims of justice as being made by those who have suffered injustice in the past or by those who assert that some proposed policy will directly deprive them of justice. The consequentialist considerations that are advanced are cast in terms of general social welfare. As the earlier analysis of moral standards suggests, one can also make consequentialist claims about justice, namely that a particular course of action will promote or retard realization of valid claims of justice in the future. That possibility is not developed specifically here with respect to reverse discrimination; but the reader should keep in mind that some of the asserted consequences of practices of reverse discrimination—for example, resentment of those who lose out in the competition for desired positions, or amelioration of racial stereotypes—may have long-term implications for justice as well as for welfare.

1. Justice

The mere fact that blacks are underrepresented in the medical and legal professions, and in other well-paying and prestigious jobs, does not by itself establish any injustice. Members of a group with a sense of self-identity and cultural values different from those of the majority might be less interested in certain kinds of rewards than are other people, or their value systems might place less emphasis on developing the traits (e.g., hard work and denying self-discipline) that are necessary to get those rewards. We know that Jews are substantially overrepresented in the medical and legal professions, but we do not leap to the conclusion that non-Jews have suffered discrimination or have failed to have fair equality of opportunity. Indeed, it is possible that had Jews not suffered discrimination, they would have an even larger representation in the professions than they do now; and so they may be able to construct an argument of injustice on their own behalf despite the fact of overrepresentation. Like overrepresentation, the underrepresentation of some groups could be the product of cultural factors that do not indicate injustice.

Of course, it is *logically* possible to argue that each "group" in society simply deserves its share of choice spots, and that anything less is distributive injustice. But this would be a strange argument, at least in our society. It would be hard to say what relevant groups would count; but even if that could be done, why, as a *matter of justice*, should each group have its share of choice spots, regardless of the particular interests and developed skills of members of that group? To allocate places to groups would fly in the face of the widely shared social value that generally individuals should be judged on their own merits. So something more than present underrepresentation must be shown for an argument of justice to work.

The two main arguments from justice for favoring minority group members and redressing underrepresentation are that preferences are needed to place blacks and others in the position they would have had but for discrimination and that preferences serve the ideal of equal opportunity. When the argument is based on the need to correct the effects of prior discrimination, the threads of compensatory and distributive justice are difficult to separate. The claim of individuals to be placed in the positions they would have enjoyed but for some original wrong can be seen either as a compensatory claim to have the wrongs appropriately remedied or as a distributive claim to be given (somewhat late) the positions they would have attained under fair conditions.

If preferences were defended simply as a way of paying back minority group members for grievous harms done them or their ancestors, then we would have a more purely compensatory rationale. But such a rationale seems unpersuasive. Initially, we might question the wisdom of government programs designed to reimburse broad classes of victims of social wrongs, unless the wrongs are extreme and specific (such as the German slaughter of Jews during the World War II period). Although earlier American treatment of blacks and Indians might qualify under this standard, that treatment alone would not warrant compensation to descendants decades later. The injustices of recent generations are more amorphous, less obvious candidates for compensation, except of course when concrete denials of legal right have occurred. Even supposing wide compensation to be appropriate, admissions, job, and set-aside preferences are peculiar compensatory devices. They reach only a portion of those who have suffered injury and often are likely to reach those who are probably least harmed by earlier discrimination, that is, those who have done well enough to be applicants for admission to educational institutions or for relevant jobs or who have built up business enterprises. Moreover, one aspect of ordinary principles of compensatory justice is that the wrongdoer pays the compensation; yet the main burden of preferences falls on the, quite possibly innocent, persons who would have received the benefits had it not been for the preferences. It can be argued, of course, that when some blacks receive preferences other blacks benefit, but presumably they benefit less than if some direct compensation had come their way. Perhaps some distinctively compensatory justification can provide limited support on behalf of preferential programs designed for other objectives, but the main justification must be found elsewhere. I shall not discuss the compensatory rationale further, except as it merges with the distributive rationale and undergirds the claim to positions minority members would have gotten but for original discrimination.

(a) Redressing the Effects of Past Injustice

No reasonable person doubts that past immoral and illegal discrimination is largely responsible for the present underrepresentation of blacks and American Indians in desired positions. Applicants to professional schools have themselves suffered discrimination in schooling or have at least suffered the more pervasive and subtle discrimination directed at blacks in a self-consciously white society. If, as a consequence of such unjust discrimination, blacks are now hindered in the competition to enter the professions, their underrepresentation reflects injustice. This is perhaps most obvious in the case of blacks who have lived their lives in one state, have been systematically denied an equal education in the schools of that state, and are now unable to present educational qualifications as good as those of whites competing for admission to state professional schools. We could say with some confidence that if all those blacks fail to become doctors and lawyers, injustice has occurred.

We shall shortly examine variations, but we should first consider three possible objections to employing preferential admissions as a corrective to injustice even in this strongest case. First, it might be said that no one can identify which blacks would have applied to and been admitted at professional schools in the absence of discrimination. Since inadequate educational opportunity will hurt some students more than others, and will affect aspirations as well as achievement, perfect identification is obviously impossible. But at least if one treats graduate educational institutions as a group, rather than focusing on a single school or profession, it is reasonable to assume a substantial correlation between the minority applicants who would now be admitted with the aid of a moderate preference and those who would have been admitted without a preference had they received the same earlier education as most whites. That substantial correlation is sufficient to answer this identification objection. Second, it might be urged that government policy should be forward-looking, taking people as they presently are rather than seeking to undo harms committed long ago. Understandably, governments cannot continually look back and try to eliminate all the effects of past injustices. There is a kind of utilitarian restraint on the pursuit of compensatory and distributive justice. But if the government has caused a substantial and clear harm, efforts to rectify it are certainly among the proper aims of public policy. Granting this point, the critic might still argue that the only proper rectification is to give persons what they have actually been deprived of, not to favor them in a competition for limited positions. Here the idea would be to devote resources to preparing blacks for professional school, rather than admitting them over better-qualified whites. On examination, it is hard to know what to make of this contention. Suppose the real deprivation was in primary school; one certainly does not send a college graduate back to second grade to get a better education in that grade. Moreover, if only blacks are to get the special pre-professional educational supplements, they are still being preferred to whites in having that opportunity. Thus it seems more a question of efficiency than principle whether preferences for professional schools should be employed or some other device. Any of these three objections to preferential policies may look stronger if linked to some claim of right of the better-qualified white applicants who will be excluded; that possible claim is discussed in section (d).

Now it is time to suggest some variations and ask if they weaken the justice argument in favor of preference.

Suppose that the discrimination has taken place in another state. Say, for example, that a black as a result of growing up in Mississippi and receiving an inadequate education there is less well prepared than he would otherwise have been to get into medical school in Minnesota, to which state he has moved. If Minnesota has never practiced discrimination of this sort, it has not caused distributive injustice. But we could say that nationally, distributive injustice exists; and we might say that Mississippi has caused distributive injustice that is manifested in Minnesota. The analytical problem is similar to instances in which persons who suffer discrimination in one country migrate to another, where they are treated fairly but without preference. Then we might hesitate to say that distributive *injustice* exists in the second society, even though as a consequence of action in the first country, victims of discrimination still do not have the places in life they would otherwise have achieved. In my judgment, there is in the United States enough self-consciousness as a national society and enough mobility and interdependence so that it is proper to take a national view. Moreover, if discrimination has occurred in most states but its victims move from place to place, it may not matter whether failure to become a doctor in one state is a consequence of actions taken in that state or in another.

Suppose the discrimination causing disadvantage is mostly private, rather than governmental, and perhaps not even illegal. Certainly, illegality of original discrimination need not be the touchstone of an argument of distributive injustice, since slavery itself was legal at the time it occurred. And if a pervasive pattern of immoral discrimination by the majority of society against a minority determines the distribution of goods, we may speak of distributive injustice in that society even if the government is not responsible. In actuality, a society rife with private discrimination is highly unlikely to be free of government discrimination, and at the least, the government may bear responsibility for not acting against many forms of private discrimination. But quite apart from these points, it seems proper to speak of a society's distribution as unjust if it is the product of an immoral and general social practice engaged in by private persons. Governmental efforts to correct the injustice are proper, although the government's responsibility may be less compelling than if the government itself had been its cause.

Suppose that the discrimination, instead of being against present applicants, was against earlier generations of blacks. If those earlier blacks were deprived of a decent education and relegated to the lowest positions in society, this generation of blacks will be handicapped, since poor and broken families do not themselves provide the best setting for social achievement, and fewer opportunities are available to the poor. This generation of blacks can claim that they suffer from distributive injustice because the consequences of earlier systematic injustice are still working themselves out to their disadvantage. The present generation of whites may not be to blame for the disadvantages that are suffered, but blacks do suffer present disadvantage because of immoral discrimination by a "different" society—here a past society, rather than a society in a different state or country. The claim of distributive injustice seems even stronger because the descendants of those who did the discriminating will themselves, although innocent, benefit from the earlier discrimination. Perhaps in some respects everyone would be better off if there had never been discrimination; but certainly as to choice and limited positions, the descendants of the discriminators are aided in their competition by the disadvantages to others caused by their forefathers.

The identification problem becomes much more serious as the unjust discrimination recedes in time from the present; and if the injury was done to ancestors, no one can be confident about the degree of effect on particular members of the present generation. Indeed, because of the nature of biological laws, it is only in a somewhat extended sense that a member of this generation can say that *he* or *she* would have benefited from better treatment of an ancestor. (The genetic make-up of any person depends on the identity of his or her biological parents and the moment at which they had sexual intercourse. Any broad social practices so alter these circumstances that someone who now exists would almost certainly not have existed—unless one imports a concept of Divine intervention—if the lives of his or her actual ancestors had varied significantly.) We may be willing to assume that for purposes of ethical analysis this last worry should be disregarded; but even so the problem of tracing effects makes the justice argument weaker than if the discrimination has occurred against the present generation itself. Still, in my judgment, if the discrimination has been pervasive and grave against the ancestors and has detrimentally affected the life chances of most members of the current generation, these are substantial reasons for society to try to redress its influences in part by preferential policies.

In any event, the claims of blacks and other minority groups will, in actuality, rarely if ever rest only on injustices done to past generations; they will rest on a combination of the lingering effects of those injustices and more recent discrimination.

(b) Fair or Equal Opportunity

The second broad justice argument for preferential treatment is that it serves an ideal of fair opportunity or equal opportunity. This argument, if detached from the argument based on prior discrimination, must rest on a theory that all individuals should have adequate opportunity or roughly the same opportunity as others to fulfill their potential, with the government assigned the responsibility to ensure the conditions for such opportunity. Genuinely equal opportunity in this sense cannot be taken as a practical goal for government action. No one can distinguish precisely between native endowment and the effects of social influence, so one can rarely be sure whether superior performance is a consequence of superior genes or superior opportunity (or superior determination, which itself may be a combination of genes and social influence). And so long as society preserves an important role for families in raising children, equalizing social environments is impossible. Barring extremely radical changes in social life, the most that government can be expected to do is to ensure minimal opportunity and to counter gross environmental disadvantage, attempting to give persons something like the life chances they would otherwise have had if they had not suffered such disadvantage. Many members of minority groups do have substantially worse earlier opportunities than most other persons, and preferential policies might be viewed as a method for redressing those disadvantages.

This justification for preferential policies also raises problems of identification, although perhaps it is simpler to show the likely effects of various environmental deprivations on present qualifications than to trace the connection to acts of discrimination. The discrimination justification need not rest on a widely expansive view of the role of government; the government is correcting wrongs done by itself or by the general society. A fair or equal opportunity justification, even in its more modest versions, gives government a duty to correct conditions for which neither it nor its general citizenry may be to blame. That justification is correspondingly more controversial; but I believe the government properly does try to guarantee minimally adequate opportunity and to assist those who have suffered extreme environmental deprivation. Although such a justification *alone* may rarely warrant preferential admission to graduate school or preferential hiring to an especially desirable job, it might lend some support to other justifications for those practices, and could play a more important role in justifying preferential hiring to lower-level jobs.

(c) The Practical Reach of Justice Arguments

Before examining the justice argument against reverse discrimination, we can pause briefly over the dimensions of the programs that the arguments so far discussed would justify. A preference based on disadvantage from prior discrimination should not include blacks who have apparently suffered little from this country's discrimination—for example, recent immigrants and perhaps those whose positions from birth have been highly advantageous. But the preference would properly extend to American Indians and might cover members of other groups that have suffered serious discrimination. It might extend to some whites who could demonstrate that illegal or immoral discrimination had affected them (although whites might be excluded on the ground that few or none of them have suffered discrimination as acute as that directed at minority groups). The preference would not reach groups whose disadvantage is not the fault of American society, for example, poor immigrants who did not speak English on arrival and whose dire plight is not the consequence of American foreign policy. A program justified to counteract early deprivation should not reach most blacks who come from affluent families and good schools; it should reach many members of disadvantaged groups whatever the cause of their disadvantage, and it should reach substantial numbers of whites whose early environment was demonstrably unsatisfactory.

(d) Claims of the Better Qualified

I turn now to possible claims of the better-qualified white applicants that they are denied justice if blacks and members of other minorities are preferred. An argument on their behalf may be cast in terms of a right not to be discriminated against on arbitrary grounds, or in terms of the injustice of innocent persons having to bear the burdens of redress.

The first argument begins with the premise that part of the right of fair or equal opportunity is the right to be chosen for a desirable position if one is the best-qualified applicant for it. If preferences are given to blacks and members of other minorities, better-qualified whites do not get the positions. We need initially to ask whether a supposed right of the most qualified to be awarded positions is indeed a right, and if so, what its strength is. The most skeptical position is that the best qualified are awarded positions only because things work best that way, and that their choice is dictated only by utilitarian considerations, not by any right they have to the positions. (Indeed, because of the solid esteem and financial rewards that accompany many desired positions, it may be thought that meritocratic choice is *unfair* to the less qualified.) Under this view, one of the best-qualified applicants to professional school might have a legitimate objection if he or she were excluded arbitrarily but would have no legitimate personal complaint if the grounds of choice were wholly other than merit, say a lottery. One can certainly imagine a society organized on the principle that nothing more than usefulness warrants giving desirable positions to the best qualified; but I do not believe our society is so organized. People are encouraged to work hard and develop their capabilities partly on the basis that if they do so they will win desirable positions and will have *deserved* to do so. Part of their sense of satisfaction and self-respect in the positions they do obtain derives from their feeling that they achieved them through *merit*. Although the pervasive effects of seniority systems are a strong countervailing influence, the notion that the best qualified should get positions is more deeply woven into our moral fabric than as a usually applicable corollary of a principle of utility. Whether this is healthy is another question; such attitudes may promote too much competitiveness in many people and a sense of defeat in those who stumble. My own judgment is that, on balance, the belief that the best qualified *deserve* to get the positions to which they aspire is salutary. Those who reject this conclusion should at least recognize that their own position deviates from the presently dominant view.

Not having rejected altogether the claimed right of the best qualified, I must proceed to consider its application and strength. In the discussion of remedies for violations of law, I have already suggested that correction of an original wrong by the organization responsible for it must be considered prior to choice among new applicants for an available job. Thus the better-qualified white applicant plainly has no legitimate complaint if a person who was once denied a position illegally is given the position ahead of him. In much the same manner, if preference satisfies broader claims of redress for wrongful discrimination or unequal opportunity, and is necessary to satisfy those claims, then the asserted right of the best qualified may yield.

In support of this conclusion is the insight that when a justice argument genuinely supports preference, many of the whites who are barely well enough qualified to have gained admission in the absence of preference may have that position only because initial conditions of opportunity were unfair. Assume, for example, that a law school sets aside 30 of its 300 freshman places for minority group applicants. Suppose that in the absence of previous discrimination or unequal opportunity, about that many minority group applicants would have gained admission without any preference. Suppose further that 10 of the 30 minority group admittees qualify for places without preference. The number of white applicants who are excluded because of the preference is then 20. But if there had never been discrimination or unequal opportunity, these 20 applicants would not have been among the first 300. Obviously this example grossly oversimplifies, since we can never be sure who would have been what if the course of history had been significantly altered; but the example illustrates an added reason, sometimes applicable, why the duty to correct wrongs takes precedence over any right of the best qualified to succeed.

The primary significance of any right of the best qualified would be to counter utilitarian arguments for preference, the contention being that their rights should not be overridden in pursuit of the general welfare. The problem with this position is that it is vastly overstated. If there is any right of the best qualified to succeed, and I think there is, it is a relatively weak right, which often yields, and properly so, to other considerations. Given a shortage of doctors in a farming community, it would plainly be acceptable for a medical school to pick a slightly less qualified applicant from that community who had expressed a wish to return there, in preference to a slightly better qualified applicant from a large city with too many doctors. In this example, willingness to practice in the farming community might be treated as a special kind of qualification, but other deviations from merit selection cannot be so explained. Universities have, in their admissions policies, taken much into account besides academic qualifications, preferring out-of-state residents to give the school a national character, and preferring family members of alumni and faculty to keep those bonds strong. Many employers prefer family, friends, and acquaintances to strangers. The government affords veterans significant preferences in employment that are, perhaps, only partly grounded in claims of justice.

Room exists for disagreement over how powerful the reasons should have to be to depart from merit selection, but we must conclude that the right of the best qualified to be chosen is a relatively weak one. It has some claim on our attention and should not be overridden for slight reason; but it properly gives way when substantial utilitarian considerations (or claims of liberty) support deviation from it.

The excluded applicant may argue that whatever other shifts from merit selection are appropriate, he has been treated unjustly because choice was made on the arbitrary ground of race. That race is *ordinarily* an arbitrary ground of selection does not, of course, suffice to establish its arbitrariness in connection with reverse discrimination. If the aim is, for example, to redress racial discrimination, then the race of those to be preferred is one crucial factor. The strength of the excluded applicant's complaint will depend on how closely the preference is tailored to its legitimate objectives. That an otherwise deserving applicant will be denied a position is, however, one good reason for not accepting lightly pleas that preference be much broader in scope than its underlying justification simply to serve adminstrative convenience.

Finally, the excluded applicant may complain that he unfairly bears the burden of redressing wrongs committed by others. I pass over the point, already made, that even if innocent he may owe to those wrongs the fact that his present qualifications are comparatively better. The discussion so far has revealed that better-qualified applicants bear the burden of preferences of all sorts, and the policies behind preferences for disadvantaged persons are as substantial as those that underlie other preferences. Yet when society as a whole, or the government, has committed a wrong, it would be desirable to make the burden of a remedy fall more evenly (although placing it on excluded applicants may be more painless politically). If a choice is to be made between admissions and hiring preferences or some remedy that spreads the burden across the whole society, the broader impact of the burden is one good moral reason for the latter alternative. If, however, preferences are a necessary part of a remedy or other important social goal, the impact of the burden is not a strong reason for rejecting them.

2. Utility

(a) In Favor of Reverse Discrimination

There are strong utilitarian arguments for and against reverse discrimination. We shall first consider arguments that admissions preferences for minorities will have desirable consequences. (Some of these arguments obviously have little or no application to hiring preferences for ordinary jobs; others have more.)

(i) Service to Minority Groups. It is argued that one reason members of minority groups are underserved by doctors and lawyers is because there are so few minority doctors and lawyers. Of course, not every black will serve the black community, and some whites will do so, so there is a far from perfect correlation between the number of black doctors and the amount of medical service available to blacks. Perhaps professional schools, if service to minorities is their objective, should use some more individualized criteria than race to determine how likely it is that an applicant will perform such service. But this may be difficult. Most students when they enter professional school are not sure what they will do when they get out. Many who honestly believe at entry that they will devote their lives to public service find as they grow older that their ambitions become more personal and that lucrative private practice seems less reprehensible than it once did. Moreover, if it once became known that a desire to practice in deprived areas could win admission to medical school, many applicants would not only color their statements about likely future practice but would build up a list of undergraduate extracurricular activities to support their statements. An alternative would be to condition entrance to medical school upon a binding agreement to serve in deprived areas, or to compel young doctors to serve there; but these restraints on liberty carry their own drawbacks. The point of choosing by race is not, as Justice Powell mischaracterizes the argument in *Bakke*, that blacks are assumed to be less selfish than whites. Rather it is that the likelihood is greater that a black will live in and serve the black community than that a white will do so.

Apart from the fact of service to the black community, blacks may actually be able to perform more usefully there than whites, because of their understanding of and rapport with the people they serve. And in positions in which the helpful response of community members is important, as with police jobs, black officers may be able to elicit more cooperation than whites. Insofar as these observations are apt, being black may actually be perceived as one kind of desirable qualification for certain sorts of jobs, and as a potential qualification for some positions for which professional schools might wish to groom students. (Indeed, since my initial definition of discrimination was in terms of criteria of choice not closely related to the benefit in question, choice of blacks made mainly because they can actually perform jobs better might not even be reverse discrimination in the strict sense.)

(ii) Professional School Diversity. Professional school is an education, and education takes place in contacts with other students as well as with teachers. Students will learn more if their fellow students are diverse, sharing the insights of their varied experience. It is a fact, unfortunate perhaps, that race is in American society a substantial determinant of experience. Black students may have different perspectives from white students on particular legal issues or on the provision of health services for the community. Were white students to miss gaining these perspectives because few blacks were admitted to professional school, their own education would be to that extent impoverished.

(iii) Role Models for Those in the Minority Community. If blacks and other members of minority groups are to strive to become doctors and lawyers, it is important that they see members of their own groups in those roles. Otherwise they are likely to accept their consignment to less prestigious, less demanding roles in society. Thus an important aspect of improving the motivations and education of black youths is to help put blacks into positions where blacks are not often now found so that they can serve as effective role models.

(iv) Destruction of Stereotyping and Participation of Minorities in Community Life. For whites as well as blacks, it may be important to see a substantial percentage of blacks in important positions. When whites have extensive contact with black doctors, lawyers, professors, and businessmen, their stereotypes about blacks, if they have them, are likely to be affected. And blacks of all ages may take pride in the achievements of professional blacks. Thus reverse discrimination may help to shatter prejudices that have exercised a tenacious hold on American society.

Moreover, when some blacks are in positions of power and influence, the interests of all blacks are likely to be better perceived and protected.

Most of these utilitarian arguments for reverse discrimination have somewhat different implications for the appropriate reach of a preferential program than do the justice arguments. These arguments could support including members of minority groups who had themselves not suffered disadvantage, and excluding whites who were victims of discrimination or unequal opportunity. These arguments can also support preferences for clearly identifiable groups that are now socially depressed, whether or not that depression results from wrongs committed in the United States.

(b) Against Reverse Discrimination

(i) Racial Lines and Racial Thought.   Any organization engaging in preferential treatment must stand ready to identify who is a member of the preferred group. This is a rather simple task if women are to be preferred, but it is less self-evident who counts as black or Mexican-American. It may be thought objectionable for any organ of government ever to be in the business of deciding who belongs to which race, although, of course, such designations are also necessary when specific instances of prior discrimination are corrected by means of general remedies.

Second, by drawing racial lines, the government may help perpetuate thinking in racial terms. Both blacks and whites may regard differently those classmates whom they assume were admitted only because of a special preference; and even after the education is complete, those who deal with graduates and lack easy access to school records (for example, potential patients considering whether to consult a doctor) may view minority graduates with some unease, wondering if they are now really as well qualified as other graduates. Such attitudes will affect even those minority applicants who would have been admitted without preference.

More important, preferences may cause resentment among those who are excluded. One thing that apparently has happened in university hiring is that many more people think they are victims of reverse discrimination than are. Suppose a philosophy department has a place available and hires a black who would not have been the choice but for the fact that he is a black. Fifteen well-qualified whites may be told that they would "probably have gotten the job" if there had not been a felt need to hire a black, it being much easier to tell a disappointed applicant this than that he would not have been hired in any event.

When people realize or mistakenly believe they are losing jobs or are failing to be admitted because of thier race, they may begin to think in racial terms, and a risk of racial division is created. People may organize around their racial identity to promote or fight extensions of reverse discrimination. Further, once the principle of racial selection is carried beyond remedies for specific violations of law, some fear it will be very hard to stop. Even when the need for racial categorization disappears, dismantling programs that ensure positions for members of minority groups may be difficult.

In sum, the argument is that the long-term damage of introducing race as an important criterion for decision is likely to outweigh any short-term benefits, that it will reinforce rather than ameliorate racial sterotypes and that it will produce divisiveness among members of different races. Thus it is urged that the color-blind principle is the appropriate one to govern the allocation of benefits and burdens.

(ii) Risks to Quality.   The most obvious objection to any preferential program is that the choice of persons who are less well qualified than those who are excluded may mean a sacrifice in quality. If a less able carpenter is picked in preference to a more able one, he is likely to build a worse table. Doctors and lawyers are not only persons who have prestige and power and earn a lot of money; they also render important services to society, and the quality of that service matters.

There are two important points to note at the outset about the quality argument against reverse discrimination. The first is that it applies to any program to benefit the disadvantaged by giving them preferences, not only to programs framed in racial terms. If veterans, or all educationally and economically disadvantaged persons, are preferred for positions, the positions will not be occupied by those who are best able to fill them at that moment in time. The second point about the quality argument is that its strength varies tremendously depending on the sort of preference that is involved. For some positions, a modicum of extra education or training may quickly bring those who are initially less qualified up to the level of performance of those who are initially more qualified. For some positions, fairly small sacrifices in the level of performance may not matter a great deal. In respect to other positions, the initial difference in qualifications may be much more difficult to overcome, and even slight sacrifices from attainable quality may be regarded as unacceptable.

The quality argument in relation to educational preferences is complex. One must consider both the quality of education and the quality of professional service. One danger is that less well qualified students will "drag down" the level of instruction, as teachers are forced to go over elementary matters more deliberately than would otherwise be necessary. Or, if the teacher disregards the needs of the less well qualified students, there is the danger that they will actually learn less than they might have at a less "high-powered" institution. It is only a partial answer to this problem to say that schools using preferences admit only qualified applicants, because there are still large differences in competence among "qualified applicants," and the level of an educational program depends significantly on how far above the minimum qualification most students are. It is also only a partial answer to respond that law school and medical school applicants are much better qualified than they were a generation ago. We are, of course, reassured to learn that reverse discrimination is not producing admittees who fail to measure up to the standards of previous times; but we may still be concerned that reverse discrimination is slowing acceleration in the quality of educational programs.

What effect admissions preferences have on the quality of professional services is impossible to say, and even determining how one would acquire reliable information to make that judgment is difficult. One could estimate with a fair degree of accuracy the extent to which initial disadvantage in educational qualification is overcome by the end of professional training. But the qualities of able professionals are so much more rich and varied than the qualities of able professional students, it would be hard to establish standards of performance against which to measure the levels of professional competence reached by those who years before had received admissions preferences. And if the ultimate concern is the general quality of medical and legal service, where the services are performed may matter as much as how they are performed. That is to say, a slightly less competent doctor who practices in an area without enough doctors may contribute more to the quality of medical service than a more competent doctor who hangs out his shingle where there is an overabundance of highly skilled physicians. Since there are so many law schools, preferential policies in law schools are much less likely to bar excluded applicants' access to the profession than are their counterpart policies in medical schools; and this fact would bear significantly on worries that the quality of the legal profession is disserved by reverse discrimination.

The assumption of most educators in professional schools is that preferences for a limited number of disadvantaged students will not significantly affect educational quality, and that those admitted on this basis are capable of becoming highly competent professionals. Nevertheless, when the pros and cons of reverse discrimination are weighed, substantial utilitarian reasons for merit selection should not be disregarded.

(iii) The Undesirability of Backward-Looking Policies. In discussing arguments of justice for reverse discrimination, I have already mentioned the objection that a government should ordinarily look forward to improving the lot of all its citizens, rather than looking backward to identify wrongs that need to be corrected. The latter endeavor, the critic may assert, costs too much and is potentially divisive. The point is, as I have suggested, a sensible one, but it should not block attempts to remedy gross injustice. In any event, a policy of preferential treatment based on utilitarian considerations is much less subject to this objection, grounded as it is on the premise that the general welfare will be served. Of course in the immediate present, what is given to one person is denied to another, so there may be no net gain; but if policies of preference can help change attitudes that frustrate and defeat large and identifiable segments of the community, the long-term consequence should be a society that is more productive and harmonious.

3. The Dimensions of a Sensible Preferential Program

The dilemma in formulating a policy of preference can be put as follows: A policy that is limited solely to minority groups and includes even those members of the preferred minorities who are not personally disadvantaged may smack of injustice and arbitrariness; but one that is directed at all those who fall below a certain economic level may not catch enough minority members to achieve the special purposes of redress and advancement of disadvantaged minority groups. There can be no single formula for designing programs that respond to variant needs. When preference is to be given in hiring or training for ordinary jobs of manual labor, a simple racial criterion, such as the one employed in the *Weber* case, may be appropriate. But something more complex is called for in professional school admissions. The utilitarian reasons for preference are great enough, in my judgment, to include members of deprived minority groups who are not themselves deprived. But within the group to be preferred, there is room for giving greater preference to individuals who have actually suffered themselves in significant ways, both because of their special claims of justice and because some of the utilitarian aims of preferences are better served when individuals from deprived backgrounds are chosen. Preference should be extended to whites who can show not only that they are from relatively poor families but that they have suffered the kind of pervasive deprivation, and perhaps the discrimination, that characterizes the life of many members of minority groups. Even then, however, giving greater preference on the basis of membership in a minority group is acceptable, since some of the reasons for preference apply only to minorities. Although a professional school may have a rough idea how many applicants it plans to choose on bases partly different from its ordinary criteria, having any rigid number of places to be filled is ill-advised. Such an approach draws a sharp distinction between classes of admitted persons and leaves no room for accommodation if in a particular year the number of applicants who fall within the rationales for preference is particularly large or particularly small.

4. Preferences Based on Gender

As far as professional school admissions are concerned, women in general are about as well qualified as men in general, and large numbers of women have been applying, so there has seemed no need for preference. (At at least one law school, comparatively fewer women students than men have achieved the very highest grades, and the possibility of some gender preference for the prestigious positions on the school's law review has been discussed.)

Whether women should be preferred for certain jobs has been a more significant issue. Preferences might be given to help encourage other women to seek jobs in areas previously closed to them. For teaching positions in colleges and universities in general, the argument can be made that women faculty are effective role models for women students and can be more sensitive to some of the special concerns of those students. In such places as law and medical schools, in which the faculty has traditionally been entirely or almost entirely male, acceptance of this argument might lead to preferences for women in faculty hiring. But this conclusion might be resisted if it were thought that within a short period of time a sufficient number of women would be hired without any preference. The contention that minorities need representatives in positions of power and influence also has its parallel for women, who have long been underrepresented in such positions. Gender-based preferences for major jobs (such as high government offices), and for lesser positions in which public power is exercised, might be justified on this rationale.

So long as women in American society bear the main burdens of child care, what may be more important for them than admissions and hiring preferences is provision for part-time employment and generous long-term leaves for persons (males as well as females) who bear primary responsibility for raising children.

B. THE LEGAL ARGUMENTS

We are now ready to take a look at the Supreme Court's disposition of cases involving the use of racial preferences by organizations that have not been found to have discriminated in the past. Again, the discussion will be mainly directed at the *Bakke* case, with reference to the training program preferences of *Weber* and the set-aside provision involved in *Fullilove*. Our purpose in looking at the opinions is not mainly to learn the law of reverse discrimination. Rather, it is to see how legal evaluation in the constitutional context differs from straightforward ethical evaluation, and how, nevertheless, ethical concerns intertwine with legal ones and influence judicial decisions.

In the *Bakke* case, the job of the Supreme Court was not to decide whether reverse discrimination is, on balance, ethically desirable. It was to determine whether the specific program employed by the medical school at Davis—the setting aside of 16 places (in an entering class of 100) for disadvantaged minority students, who were selected by a separate admission process—either violated a federal statute barring discrimination in institutions receiving federal grants or violated the equal protection clause of the Fourteenth Amendment. On these issues, the Court split badly. Briefly, four justices believed that the statute bars race-conscious hiring or admissions programs, so they concluded that the Davis program violated it. Since for them the statute disposed of the case, they did not need to discuss the constitutional question, and they did not—the custom of the Court being not to discuss constitutional questions except when that is required for decision. The other five justices determined that the statute precludes only the kind of discrimination that itself would be unconstitutional, so they were compelled to address the constitutional question. Four justices thought that the Constitution broadly permits reverse discrimination in favor of groups previously victimized by discrimination and presently disadvantaged. Justice Powell took a much narrower view of what could be done by a state educational institution, insisting that generally the law must treat blacks and whites equally and that, from this perspective, most arguments for reverse discrimination advanced by the university were insufficient. But he thought that the power of universities to select their own students was part of their power to decide what kind of education would be best and was closely linked to the constitutionally protected right of freedom of speech. He thus concluded that universities can take race into account in deciding whom to admit. But since this justification would not by itself support the allocation of a fixed number of places for members of minority groups, he declared the Davis program to be illegal. So by two different 5-to-4 margins, the Court invalidated fixed-allocation reverse discrimination in the admissions process but upheld the principle of using race in that process. Table 1 shows the disposition of the various justices.

The Constitution is framed in broad generalities and is very difficult to amend, so the Supreme Court has felt relatively free to reconsider and alter prior interpretations it now believes are wrong. Statutes, on the other hand, can be changed by Congress if it is discontented with Supreme Court interpretation, and the tradition has been that only in rare cases will the Court overrule a previous interpretation of a statute. What the Court would do in a future Title VI case may depend partly upon whether justices who interpreted the statute to bar reverse discrimination accept the majority view that the statute prohibits only discrimination that would be constitutionally impermissible, and if so, on their view of the constitutionality of racial preferences. Thus after *Bakke,* it was not certain (even apart from changes in Court personnel) that Justice Powell would continue to occupy the middle position in Title VI cases. (In *Fullilove*, Justices Stewart and Rehnquist adopted a color-blind view of the equal protection aspect of the Fifth Amendment's due process clause, so we know they would not have accepted the racial preferences that

Table 1

	Justices Brennan, White, Marshall, Blackmun	Justice Powell	Justice Stevens, with Chief Justice Burger, Justice Stewart, and Justice Rehnquist	Totals
Meaning of Section 601 of 1964 Civil Rights Act	Bars only unconstitutional discrimination	Bars only unconstitutional discrimination	Bars racial preferences	5—bars only unconstitutional discrimination 4—bars racial preferences
Constitutionally sufficient reasons, if any, for racial preference by university	Permissible to redress disadvantages caused by societal discrimination; did not discuss other possibilities	Only academic diversity a proper reason for considering race	Did not discuss	4—can redress disadvantage caused by discrimination 1—can give preference only for diversity
Acceptability of Davis rigid quotas	Constitutionally acceptable and permitted by statute	Not constitutionally acceptable	Not acceptable under statute	5—rigid quota not acceptable 4—rigid quota acceptable
Acceptability of taking race into account in admissions on more flexible basis	Acceptable	Acceptable to promote diversity	Not acceptable under statute	5—flexible regard for race acceptable 4—race not a proper criterion for admissions

Justice Powell rejects; and given his opinion in that case, Justice Stevens seems unlikely to do so. Whether Chief Justice Burger, whose *Fullilove* opinion Powell joined, or Justice O'Connor, Justice Stewart's replacement, will find the Constitution more permissive of racial preference than did Justice Powell is still uncertain.)

Although in *Bakke* and the other cases dealing with preferential treatment the Supreme Court did not directly decide ethical questions, the opinions show that the ethical considerations carried great weight.

The following discussion of the legal issues is only summary, meant to clarify the issues that divided the Court in *Bakke* so as to indicate the significance of subsequent cases, and to relate the legal questions to the ethical concerns we have considered.

1. The Statutory Issues

Section 601 of the Civil Rights Act of 1964 provides:

> No person in the United States shall on the ground of race, color, or national origin, be excluded from participation in, be denied the benefits of, or be subjected to discrimination under any program or activity receiving Federal financial assistance.

Title VI was part of a larger civil rights package adopted in 1964 that included bans on discrimination in public accommodations and in employment as well. It seems agreed that the major aims of this title were to bar discrimination against blacks by private institutions that were spending federal money and to give federal agencies a statutory basis for withholding funds from institutions that were discriminating. Although reverse discrimination had yet to become a serious issue of public policy, some of the major supporters of the act did state in Congress that it would bar discrimination in favor of blacks as well as against blacks. For Justice Stevens and the three justices who joined him, this legislative history, coupled with the language of the statute, which seems on its face to bar racial categorization, were sufficient to require that the statute be interpreted to bar reverse discrimination.

The other five justices rejected that conclusion. First, they argued that "discrimination" was meant to be an open-ended term, to be interpreted in accord with what the Constitution forbids. One problem with this approach as an interpretation of the statutory language is that the act also bars persons being "excluded from participation in" or being "denied the benefits of" programs on the ground of race, and "discrimination" is not a term that appears in these clauses. Thus Bakke said that he was excluded from participation at Davis medical school on the ground of race, and that claim would seem to bring him squarely within the actual language of the statute.

The main emphasis of the five justices was on the history of passage of the act. They stressed all the occasions on which it was said that the aim of the provision was to bar discrimination that would be unconstitutional if engaged in by the government, suggesting that the real purpose was to reach only such uses of racial categorization, and that comments about discrimination in favor of blacks were isolated and peripheral. They also argued that the Court should defer to the interpretations of agencies administering the act, which have not thought it precluded reverse discrimination. And they pointed to subsequent legislative programs that require reverse discrimination, such as the set-aside statute challenged in *Fullilove,* as strong indications that Congress did not mean to bar that practice. Finally, they asserted that it would be anomalous to require race-conscious decisions when organizations had previously discriminated and to preclude them altogether when the particular organization had not discriminated or it was unclear whether it had discriminated.

The statutory question posed is a difficult one, and it is not surprising that it divided the Court. Justice Stevens's position is strongly supported by the language of the section and by explicit comments in the course of legislative consideration. In favor of the contrary position, however, is the dubious wisdom of barring a major technique for attempting to promote racial justice that Congress did not address in a considered way in 1964 and has approved in other, albeit much more limited, contexts since then.

When a court interprets a statute, it is in some sense seeking to give effect to the intention of the legislature that wrote it; the court is not, in theory, deciding what it thinks would be the optimal manner in which to handle a social problem. But divining the intention of the legislature is difficult when it is not obvious what most of those voting for a measure would have perceived as its application to the problem at hand. This dilemma can occur and often does when the language of the statute is ambiguous in a crucial respect or when, as in the *Bakke* case, the language points in one direction but it is doubtful whether legislators seriously addressed the consequences that would follow. Legal philosophers disagree whether judges are properly influenced by their own evaluations of the practices that are subject to challenge. To oversimplify somewhat, one view is that judges should strive to remain detached and to implement the purposes of the legislature, however murky those purposes may be and however hard it may be to discount one's own "legislative" judgment. The contrasting view, with which I agree, is that if the legislature has not spoken with clarity, judges properly are influenced by their own judgment about what would be desirable legislation. Especially in a highly charged case such as *Bakke*, few judges when they interpret a statute will be able to discount entirely their own personal views about the morality and social desirability of the practice being challenged, whatever their general views about the proper functions of judges; and one suspects that the disagreement over the application of Title VI was in substantial part a submerged disagreement over the acceptability and necessity of special preferences for minority groups.

The *Weber* case involved interpretation of the Title VII prohibition on employment discrimination, the crucial issue of statutory interpretation being closely similar to the one that divided the court in *Bakke*. With respect to Title VII, the division was 5 to 2 against the color-blind view, the majority holding that firms and unions could agree to engage in preferential treatment for members of disadvantaged groups that had suffered broadly from discrimination.

2. *The Constitutional Issues*

Once five justices decided in *Bakke* that the Davis admissions program was not barred by Title VI unless the discrimination was also unconstitutional, they had to reach the constitutional issue. The equal protection clause permits some kinds of classifications but bars others, and they had to determine into which category the Davis program fell.

Since it was the main purpose of the equal protection clause to protect the newly freed slaves, the Supreme Court has consistently been hesitant to accept classifications that it perceives as harming blacks and the other minority groups. Even when it approved segregation, the theory was that separation works no legally significant harm. The doctrine as it has developed in this century is that racial classifications are "suspect," requiring "strict scrutiny" by the Court, and legitimate only if shown to be necessary to accomplish a "compelling state interest." Race is not the only suspect basis of classification; religion and national origin would be suspect, and so in some circumstances at least would be alienage, poverty, and illegitimacy. The Court has expanded the compelling interest test to apply also to classifications that impair fundamental rights, such as voting, speech, and travel. When such classifications are presented, the chances of invalidation have been very high. By contrast, when the Supreme Court reviews ordinary economic and social classifications, it asks only whether the classification is "rationally related" to a legitimate state purpose. This is a much more relaxed test, demanding only that the state's purpose be any legitimate purpose, and accepting any plausible connection between the purpose and the classification. Thus when New York City banned advertising on trucks except advertising by owners on their own trucks, the Court said that traffic safety might plausibly warrant a restriction on truck advertising and that the city council might have perceived a significant difference between owner advertising and rental advertising.

What, if anything, supports such a vast difference in the level of review the Court applies to legislative actions? In part, the explanation is historical; the Court reviews most carefully the kinds of classifications at which the Fourteenth Amendment was directed and those that interfere with other constitutional values. But that is far from a total explanation.

It is sometimes said that race and other similar classifications are "suspect," and therefore warrant strict scrutiny, because they are based on immutable characteristics; and it is undoubtedly relevant that no one can freely change his race. But a classification in terms of intelligence or height is also based on an immutable characteristic, or at least a characteristic not easily altered. The point must be that race is not only immutable but also is perceived as being irrelevant to one's capacities, opportunities, and deserts as a human being. Thus a legislative classification in terms of race requires very careful review.

Also reflected in some judicial opinions, and advanced more explicitly in scholarly writings, is a conception of the comparative competence of courts and legislatures, and a notion that the legislature is likely to deal more fairly with some problems than others. It is assumed, though not always true, that competing forces are fairly represented in the political process when the legislature deals with ordinary economic matters; and it is believed that the legislature is well suited to the process of adjustment and compromise that is required. However, if the legislature acts adversely with respect to underrepresented and unpopular minorities, there is much less reason to be confident that it has acted fairly. Of course the courts, like the legislatures, are mostly white and male, but they at least are further removed from the play of political pressures, and they have time to act reflectively on the basis of important principles. Moreover, if the courts excercise stricter review when legislatures classify in a manner that harms minority groups, judicial intervention cannot make things worse for those groups, only better. Thus the varying tests under the equal protection clause reflect an implicit political theory about the roles of legislatures and courts under the American constitutional framework.

For some years, the issue of whether gender should be a suspect classification was unresolved by Court decision and debated by scholars. On the one hand it was urged that women, although a majority of voters, are perennially underrepresented in the political process and that legislative distinctions drawn on the basis of sex are every bit as arbitrary as those drawn on the basis of race. On the other hand it was said that women are not a politically isolated minority and that, at the time the Fourteenth Amendment was adopted, the framers certainly approved gender classificatons, since the law of all states was full of restrictions on the legal rights of women. Moreover, the ostensible purpose of much modern legislation distinguishing men from women was to protect women, and it seemed doubtful to some jurists that all classifications drawn in terms of gender, including those relating to military service, alimony, and child custody, were ill-advised. Some justices expressed their willingness to declare gender classifications suspect, but that view never won a majority. Finally, in 1976 in *Craig v. Boren* (Materials, pp. 146–149), a majority did agree on an intermediate level of scrutiny. A classification in terms of gender "must serve important governmental objectives and must be substantially related to the achievement of those objectives." This test demands an important objective—something less than a compelling purpose but more than any legitimate state purpose. And it asks if the classification is substantially related to the achievement of those objectives—something less than being necessary for their achievement but something more than being rationally related to their achievement. The Court has employed this test when a gender classification favors women as well as when one favors men.

During the time of doubt about the appropriate level of review for gender classifications, some opinions, most notably one by Justice Marshall in a case attacking the financing of schools by local taxes, suggested that the sharp dichotomy between strict scrutiny and rational basis was generally too rigid, not openly permitting the varying levels of review appropriate for a vast variety of cases.

The status of racial classifications favoring minority groups was uncertain. One view among legal writers was that since discrimination in favor of a minority by representatives of the majority presented none of the dangers of classifications hurting minorities, "rational basis" was the appropriate level of review. The contrary view was that racial classifications have historically been disfavored and are always to be regarded with distaste; that with many classifications (e.g., preserving places in a housing development for whites in order to encourage integration), it is hard to say whether members of the minority group are harmed or helped, and that, therefore, either all racial classifications should be per se invalid, or strict scrutiny and the compelling interest test should be applicable. The intermediate view, to which I subscribed, was that racial classifications do always have some undesirable aspects but that discrimination in favor of disadvantaged minorities is less dangerous and less at odds with Fourteenth Amendment values than discrimination against them; therefore, an intermediate level of scrutiny is desirable. An approach similar in practical consequence but different in conception was to continue to use a version of the "compelling interest" test as applicable to all racial classifications, but to treat the improvement of the position of disadvantaged minorities as compelling.

In *Bakke*, Justices Brennan, White, Marshall, and Blackmun, in an unusual opinion signed by all four justices, opt for an intermediate standard, explicitly adopting the formulation employed in recent cases of gender differentiation. Another passage in the opinion requires an "important and articulated" purpose, indicating that the justices will not, as they have done in older rational basis cases, hypothesize purposes that have not been suggested by those defending a classification of this sort. The opinion is less clear about how closely the Court should examine whether a nonracial classification would accomplish the objectives of a challenged racial classification. It does say that "there are no practical means by which [Davis] could achieve its ends in the foreseeable future without the use of race-conscious measures." But the manner in which the opinion formulates the issue is "whether race is reasonably used in light of the program's objectives"—a relatively relaxed inquiry. Sometimes race-conscious measures may be employed as a convenient shortcut, let us say for general economic and educational disadvantage, when a somewhat more burdensome nonracial screening process might possibly accomplish the same objective. In my view, the Court should look very carefully at whether a nonracial classification would be adequate, and it should reject race-conscious criteria when they do not appear genuinely necessary to accomplish the purposes for which they are introduced.

Justice Powell strongly rejects the intermediate level of review, arguing that racial classifications have consistently been viewed as highly objectionable by the Court; that the presence or absence of the imposition of a stigma through a racial classification, on which his four brethren place so much emphasis, is too elusive a concept to be central for equal protection interpretation; that the line between benign and perverse discrimination is too difficult to draw; that whatever its original intent, the clause has come to be interpreted as equally protective of members of all races; that it is inappropriate to have a varying standard of review that depends on whether a group is a minority and disadvantaged at a particular point in history; and that, therefore, the same strict scrutiny of review should apply to all racial classifications.

When they turn to applying their standard of review to the Davis program, Justices Brennan, White, Marshall, and Blackmun say the "articulated purpose of remedying the effects of past societal discrimination is . . . sufficiently important to justify the use of race-conscious admissions programs where there is a sound basis for concluding that minority underrepresentation is substantial and chronic, and that the handicap of past discrimination is impeding access of minorities to the medical school." The opinion does not tell us whether, alone, either the fact of prior discrimination or the fact of present substantial disadvantage would be enough to sustain such a program, but in combination they pass muster.

Much of the opinion is devoted to demonstrating the consistency of this conclusion with prior law. The justices, for example, note the Court's unanimous approval of the voluntary use of race-conscious classifications to integrate schools, and they then point out that in employment cases, employers free of intentional discrimination have been required to hire members of minority groups at the expense of "innocent" white applicants. They conclude that a state government may adopt a program to correct the effects of prior societal discrimination as well as its own, and that the educational discrimination against blacks and their gross underrepresentation in the medical profession indicate the appropriateness of such a program. The opinion states that any racial classification that stigmatizes persons or groups is unconstitutional, but it determines that the Davis program stigmatizes neither members of the benefited minorities nor members of the remaining majority. Finally, it concludes that any admissions preference cast broadly in terms of economic and educational disadvantage would benefit relatively few members of minority groups and that, therefore, racial classification is needed to accomplish the purpose of combating the pervasively harmful effects of racial discrimination. Certainly, one of the major weaknesses of the opinion is its virtually exclusive concentration on the preference for blacks. For the entire program of Davis to have been valid, there had to have been adequate justification for preferences for Asians, Chicanos, and American Indians as well, yet the opinion does not stop to establish the reasons why Davis could prefer members of those groups.

Justices Marshall and Blackmun each wrote separate opinions, as well as joining the one just discussed. Justice Marshall places much more emphasis on the historical intent of the Fourteenth Amendment to improve the position of blacks, noting the passage at that time of the Freedmen's Bureau Act, many of whose benefits were available only to blacks. Justice Blackmun stresses the necessity of race-conscious classifications: "In order to get beyond racism we must first take account of race. There is no other way."

In these two opinions, as well as in that written by the four justices, we see that members of the Court accept the moral arguments for reverse discrimination as powerful reasons supporting the Davis program.

Justice Powell takes a different view. He argues that the goal of remedying "societal discrimination" is not sufficiently comparable to correcting identified discrimination to warrant racial classification that harms innocent victims. He thus creates a sharp dichotomy between what may be done if a court or administrative body determines that racial discrimination has occurred, in which event race-conscious remedies are acceptable, and what may be done in the absence of such determination. Justice Powell also talks of legislative findings of discrimination, and his position in the *Fullilove* case shows that he does accept the use of race-conscious classifications by the federal legislature even if not every entity that is covered has actually discriminated. In *Bakke*, Powell does not clearly indicate whether the state legislature can direct one sort of public body, the state university system, to take action remedying the discrimination of other public bodies and of private individuals; but he does assert that those running the university system may not themselves do so, since their mission is neither adjudication nor legislative policy, but education. Justice Powell next rejects the purpose of improving medical service in minority areas as being inadequate to support the Davis program, because a more individualized screening of applicants would better serve this purpose.

The only justification for race-conscious decisions in professional school admissions that he regards as adequate is that relating to the benefits of diversity in the educational environment, an interest he finds "compelling" because the right of universities to select their students and determine the content of their education is closely connected to the First Amendment value of freedom of speech. Although universities may take race into account in selecting students, they cannot allocate a fixed number of places for any minority group because, in any given year, individual applicants should be considered to see which of them will promote the most desirable educational environment. Justice Powell indicates that universities will, save with this restriction, continue to have wide discretion to decide admissions policies.

Like the opinion of the four justices, that of Justice Powell is responsive to the moral arguments about reverse discrimination. The three that move him most are the importance of treating all people equally regardless of race, the unfairness to innocent victims of reverse discrimination, and the utilitarian argument about the benefits of diversity in legal education.

In my view, there are substantial theoretical and practical problems with Justice Powell's approach, and I shall summarize these briefly. First, not every interest that bears some relation to a constitutional value is necessarily compelling. For years, state and private universities have been forbidden to discriminate on various grounds, yet apart from the special case of the religious university that wants to discriminate on religious grounds, no one seriously argues that such limitations invade the First Amendment. The tie between admissions policy and freedom of expression exists, but it is tenuous. And the reasons Justice Powell discards seem much more powerful social justifications than the one he accepts.

Second, the achievement of educational diversity has not been the main goal of reverse discrimination in admissions; the aim has been much broader. If Justice Powell's approach were followed, conscientious university policymakers would have to ask themselves to what extent race should be taken into account if educational diversity is the only legitimate goal. They might also have to emphasize much more heavily than they do now whether a particular minority group applicant communicates effectively with those of different background. It is unlikely that many universities would undertake this reexamination; and the result would be that programs entered into mostly for one set of reasons, and tailored to those reasons, would be continued intact although now legally supportable only for another, originally subsidiary, reason, to which those programs are not well tailored. This is a prospect of hypocrisy that is disturbing for institutions of higher education.

Of course, the relatively few institutions with a fixed allocation of places would have to alter their programs, but most schools have a general sense of the number of minority students their policies will admit in each year, and the abandonment of rigid allocations is unlikely to make a great practical difference.

Third, it seems doubtful if Justice Powell would really adhere to the logic of his opinion in a different circumstance. Suppose a university said that in its experience most blacks do not communicate effectively with the majority of their fellow students and that in the absence of demonstrated ability and willingness to communicate with whites, being black would count against an applicant in the admissions process. Or the university decided that commonality of background and feeling, producing a sense of security and openness to the comments of colleagues, was more important for education than diversity, and again, now viewing blacks as "outsiders" who disturb the tranquility that promotes learning, the university discriminated against them in admissions. It seems highly doubtful, indeed almost inconceivable, that such programs would, if subjected to the same level of scrutiny as that of Davis, be approved; yet a faithful application of Justice Powell's position would make these cases hard to distinguish from permissible discrimination in university admissions policies.

Fourth, absent a judicial, legislative, or adminstrative finding of discrimination, Justice Powell's position seems to allow reverse discrimination only by educational institutions. This, of course, is acceptable if the legitimate justifications are restricted to educational institutions, but if they are not, the limitation is unfortunate.

Fifth, the position would greatly interfere with efforts by institutions that believe they have discriminated but are not certain that they would be found to have done so, to remedy that discrimination. Voluntary efforts to correct discrimination might subsequently be declared to be impermissible reverse discrimination, so prudent organizations would wait for a judicial or administrative determination before doing anything. If universities did prefer minority group applicants and offered as their justification the fact of their earlier discrimination against these groups, courts would have to pass on the adequacy of that justification. Justice Powell suggests that some prior authoritative finding of discrimination is necessary to support such programs; but it would be a strange posture for the law to condemn a remedy voluntarily granted when that precise remedy could have been imposed on the same facts by a judicial or adminstrative order. But if the appropriateness of the voluntary remedy is conceded, then courts would have the troublesome task of evaluating whether a university's own protestations of prior discrimination were accurate. Thus in addition to its other defects, Justice Powell's approach may not yield a standard that is judicially administrable. No doubt similar problems are part of the explanation as to why in *Weber* a majority of the Court did not read Title VII to forbid preferential programs voluntarily undertaken by unions and employers.

You will want to consider, after reading the excerpts from Justice Powell's opinion, whether you find these criticisms fair. You will want to keep in mind not only your own ethical evaluation of reverse discrimination but also a theory about the Court's appropriate role in constitutional decisions, and a sense of what sorts of standards can be managed by judges as various sorts of cases arise.

Fullilove v. Klutznick reveals the constitutional views of the justices who had rested on interpretation of the statute in *Bakke*. Since Congress had explicitly approved a provision to set aside 10 percent of the funds for public works projects for businesses owned and controlled by members of designated minority groups, the constitutional question had to be squarely faced. Justices Stewart and Rehnquist urge that all racial classifications should be constitutionally barred. Justice Stevens says that the group-oriented provision was not well tailored to redress past discrimination, and he would demand more careful consideration by Congress and a plainer showing of necessity before approving any preference of this sort. Three justices approve the provision on the broad remedial theory they employed in defending the Davis preference in *Bakke*. The crucial opinion is by Chief Justice Burger, joined by Justices Powell and White. Emphasizing Congress's legitimate role in identifying practices of discrimination and its purpose to remedy discrimination in public contracting, his opinion upholds the provision as remedial. Justice Powell joined the Burger opinion but also wrote separately to stress his continued adherence to a compelling interest test, his belief that the illegality of prior discrimination is crucial if a remedy is to be justified, and his acceptance of a much wider role for Congress than for educational institutions in identifying and remedying discrimination.

Fullilove establishes a fairly solid block of six justices who will look sympathetically on racial preferences if they are adopted by legislatures and bear a reasonably close relationship to prior discrimination, although perhaps somewhat less deference will be shown to state legislative efforts than to those of Congress.

IX.

The Future of Reverse Discrimination

American society has now reached a substantial consensus that government agencies should not discriminate against members of minorities or women, and that legal bars against such discrimination by major private enterprises are also appropriate. Disagreement still exists about the precise boundaries of permissible differentiation, as evidenced by debate over subjecting women to a military draft and over the Equal Rights Amendment, about exactly what constitutes discriminatory action and about apropriate remedies. Disagreement also exists about the priority that should be given to efforts to eliminate discrimination. Thus ample room exists for future weakening or strengthening of techniques to combat discrimination, and one must expect some ebb and flow in the years to come; but what one would not expect is a major challenge to the basic principles of nondiscrimination.

The situation is different with respect to reverse discrimination, which in major aspects remains anathema to many thoughtful citizens. More precisely, the fundamental dispute is over the use of racial and gender preferences, absent strong evidence that the enterprise granting the preferences has itself discriminated. How widely such preferences are employed in the future will depend largely on how people weigh claims based on past injustices against claims grounded on equal treatment for equally qualified applicants, and on how they conceive American society can best move away from its terrible history of racism to a more tolerant multiracial society.

The *Bakke, Weber* and *Fullilove* decisions afford considerable latitude for government and private entities to grant preference to members of minorities, and presumably also to women. But the decisions do not compel such preferences. Ethical evaluation of their status by those who are to decide whether or not to use them remains critical; and their future use will be largely determined by a social sense of their acceptability. Even had the legal decisions turned out differently, ethical evaluation would remain important as a possible basis for alteration of existing statutes or of decisional law, and perhaps even of the Constitution. Determinations of legality or illegality obviously cannot conclusively settle the morality of a practice. Moral judgment stands not only as an ingredient in the development of new legal doctrines but as a perspective from which to criticize established law. Thus while examining the development of the law can illuminate our perspectives on reverse discrimination, it cannot absolve us from making our own moral judgments about it; these judgments, multiplied many times over, will influence its use in the future and the fate of the legal doctrines that now affect it.

Materials

I.

The Declaration of Independence and the Original Constitution

The Declaration of Independence (1776) ═══════════════

We hold these truths to be self-evident, that all men are created equal, that they are endowed by their Creator with certain unalienable Rights, that among these are Life, Liberty and the pursuit of happiness.

The Constitution of the United States (proposed 1787, adopted 1789) ═══════════════

ARTICLE I, SECTION 2

Representatives and direct Taxes shall be apportioned among the several States which may be included within this Union, according to their respective Numbers, which shall be determined by adding to the whole Number of free Persons, including those bound to Service for a Term of Years, and excluding Indians not taxed, three fifths of all other Persons.

ARTICLE I, SECTION 9

The Migration or Importation of such Persons as any of the States now existing shall think proper to admit, shall not be prohibited by the Congress prior to the Year one thousand eight hundred and eight, but a Tax or duty may be imposed on such Importation, not exceeding ten dollars for each Person.

ARTICLE IV, SECTION 2

No Person held to Service or Labour in one State, under the Laws thereof, escaping into another, shall, in Consequence of any Law or Regulation therein, be discharged from such Service or Labour, but shall be delivered up on Claim of the Party to whom such Service or Labour may be due.

ARTICLE V

. . . no Amendment which may be made prior to the Year One thousand eight hundred and eight shall in any Manner affect the first and fourth Clauses in the Ninth Section of the first Article; and . . . no State, without its Consent, shall be deprived of its equal Suffrage in the Senate.

NOTE

Although the word "slave" does not appear in the United States Constitution, the institution of slavery is there recognized and protected. As a compromise between northern and southern states, it was agreed that each slave would count as three-fifths of a person for the purposes of apportioning representatives and direct taxes. Another compromise was that Congress was forbidden to abolish the importation of slaves before 1808. And this restriction, which was adopted despite the prohibition by most slave states of further importation within their own boundaries, was insulated from the amendment process—one of three provisions in the Constitution to receive that special form of protection. Finally, state officials and courts in "free" states were constitutionally required to deliver up escaped slaves to owners who claimed enforcement of property rights created in other states. Under the constitutional order, slaves obviously were not among those who were "free and equal" under the law; and the institution of slavery as practiced in the United States was blatantly at odds with any belief that God had created all men "free and equal" and endowed them with "unalienable rights." (For further comment, see Essay, pp. 26–27.)

QUESTIONS

1. Could compromises in respect to slavery reached in order to create a closer federal union than existed under the Articles of Confederation be morally defensible? Were northern legislators who believed slavery wrong but nevertheless approved the Constitution morally blameworthy for doing so?

2. Was it proper for any person to accept the position of a federal or state judge knowing that one of his legal obligations would be to enforce fugitive slave laws? What should a judge have done when presented with the claim of an owner against an escaped

slave, a claim that was supported by fugitive slave statutes that were valid under the Constitution? Should he have rendered judgment for the owner? Disregarded the law and rendered judgment against the owner? Resigned to avoid having to make that choice? Is a judge's ultimate responsibility in such circumstances to enforce the laws in the system in which he is an official or to do what he believes to be morally right?

II.

The Post–Civil War Constitutional Amendments and Civil Rights Legislation

Amendment XIII (1865)

Section 1. Neither slavery nor involuntary servitude, except as a punishment for crime whereof the party shall have been duly convicted, shall exist within the United States, or any place subject to their jurisdiction.

Section 2. Congress shall have power to enforce this article by appropriate legislation.

Amendment XIV (1868)

Section 1. All persons born or naturalized in the United States, and subject to the jurisdiction thereof, are citizens of the United States and of the State wherein they reside. No State shall make or enforce any law which shall abridge the privileges or immunities of citizens of the United States; nor shall any State deprive any person of life, liberty, or property, without due process of law; nor deny to any person within its jurisdiction the equal protection of the laws.

Section 5. The Congress shall have power to enforce, by appropriate legislation, the provisions of this article.

Amendment XV (1870)

Section 1. The right of citizens of the United States to vote shall not be denied or abridged by the United States or by any State on account of race, color, or previous condition of servitude.

Section 2. The Congress shall have power to enforce this article by appropriate legislation.

Amendment XIX (1920)

The right of citizens of the United States to vote shall not be denied or abridged by the United States or by any State on account of sex.

Congress shall have power to enforce this article by appropriate legislation.

Civil Rights Act of 1866

SECTION 1

Be it enacted by the Senate and House of Representatives of the United States of America in Congress assembled, That all persons born in the United States and not subject to any foreign power, . . . are hereby declared to be citizens of the United States; and such citizens, of every race and color, without regard to any previous condition of slavery or involuntary servitude, . . . shall have the same right, in every State and Territory in the United States, to make and enforce contracts, to sue, be parties, and give evidence, to inherit, purchase, lease, sell, hold, and convey real and personal property, and to full and equal benefit of all laws and proceedings for the security of person and property, as is enjoyed by white citizens, and shall be subject to like punishment, pains, and penalties, and to none other, any law, statute, ordinance, regulation, or custom, to the contrary notwithstanding.

SECTION 2

That any person who, under color of any law, statute, ordinance, regulation, or custom, shall subject, or cause to be subjected, any inhabitant of any State or Territory to the deprivation of any right secured or protected by this act, or to different punishment, pains, or penalties on account of such person having at any time been held in a condition of slavery or involuntary servitude, except as a punishment for crime whereof the party shall have been duly convicted, or by reason of his color or race, than is prescribed for the punishment of white persons, shall be deemed guilty of a misdemeanor, and, on conviction, shall be punished by fine not exceeding one thousand dollars, or imprisonment not exceeding one year, or both, in the discretion of the court.

Civil Rights Act of 1875

SECTION 1

. . . [A]ll persons within the jurisdiction of the United States shall be entitled to the full and equal enjoyment of the accommodations, advantages, facilities, and privileges of inns, public conveyances on land or water, theatres, and other places of public amusement; subject only to the conditions and limitations established by law, and applicable alike to citizens of every race and color, regardless of any previous condition of servitude.

NOTES

The Thirteenth, Fourteenth, and Fifteenth amendments were designed to ensure equality of rights for newly freed blacks. The Thirteenth Amendment raised a constitutional bar against slavery and involuntary servitude. The Fourteenth ensured that blacks were citizens of the states where they resided as well as of the United States, and guaranteed all persons equal protection of the laws and the right not to be deprived by a state of life, liberty, and property without due process of law. The Fifteenth forbade racial discrimination in voting.

During the period in which it was proposing these amendments, Congress also passed civil rights statutes, the most important of which has proved to be the Civil Rights Act of 1866, passed by the Republican Congress over Andrew Johnson's veto. There are some interesting points concerning the relationships among the three constitutional provisions, and between them and the civil rights statutes. First, the Fourteenth and Fifteenth amendments are restrictions on state activities; but the Thirteenth Amendment directly prohibits certain relationships between persons, whether or not those relationships enjoy the support of state law. It is an unusual provision of the Constitution that can be violated by the actions of purely private persons. Second, it was obviously not assumed during the Reconstruction period that the Fourteenth Amendment by itself guaranteed legal equality for blacks in all respects, because, had that been assumed, the Fifteenth Amendment would have been unnecessary. Third, all three amendments give Congress power to enforce their provisions, and this may permit Congress to reach somewhat beyond the actual activities that violate the amendments. Fourth, the Civil Rights Act of 1866 assured the newly freed slaves of many legal rights. At the time, the powers of Congress to regulate interstate commerce were far from fully developed, so the apparent source of Congress's power had to be the Thirteenth Amendment. This suggests that at least as far as legislative power was concerned, that amendment was perceived as going beyond a simple abolition of slavery and involuntary servitude. Nevertheless, there were doubts about the constitutional support for this legislation, and they were an important reason for passage of the Fourteenth Amendment. Fifth, the 1875 Civil Rights Act clearly reached some kinds of racial discrimination by one private person against another, and on one interpretation the 1866 act did so as well. An important question of constitutional interpretation, but one to which we shall devote only slight attention, is how far the three amendments allow Congress to forbid private discrimination. Sixth, during the period of all this activity, Congress enacted programs specifically directed at former slaves. For example, the 1866 Freedmen's Bureau Act included educational assistance for newly freed blacks, and protected blacks who had occupied specified abandoned lands. The act was passed over Johnson's veto and despite arguments that it was improper for Congress "to take under its charge a portion of the people, discriminating against all others. . . ." (For further comment, see Essay, pp. 26–28.)

QUESTIONS

1. In your judgment, does the language of the Thirteenth Amendment provide adequate constitutional support for the rights guaranteed by the 1866 Civil Rights Act? Should a judge deciding this and similar questions be consciously influenced by his judgment as to whether the rights that the act provides are morally required and socially desirable?

2. Insofar as it provided benefits limited to freed blacks, was the Freedmen's Bureau Act of 1866 consistent with the equal protection

of the laws guarantee subsequently made part of the Fourteenth Amendment? Was such legislation morally defensible? How much of a bearing does the moral defensibility and possible constitutionality of such legislation have on the moral defensibility and constitutionality of modern preferences for blacks?

III.

Nineteenth-Century Interpretations of the Thirteenth and Fourteenth Amendments

Slaughter-House Cases * ══════════════════

In this case, the granting by a state of a monopoly of slaughterhouses was challenged by butchers who were not included in the monopoly. They claimed that the grant of a monopoly violated their rights under both the Thirteenth and the Fourteenth amendments. The Supreme Court rejected both these challenges. Most significantly, it gave a very narrow reading to the Fourteenth Amendment guarantee that "No state shall make or enforce any law which shall abridge the privileges or immunities of citizens of the United States. . . ." It interpreted the guarantee to include only a narrow class of privileges of federal citizenship, an interpretation that has effectively eliminated this provision as a source of constitutional rights. In the course of his lengthy majority opinion, Justice Miller wrote the following about the amendments in general and about the equal protection clause in particular.

The institution of African slavery, as it existed in about half the States of the Union, and the contests pervading the public mind for many years, between those who desired its curtailment and ultimate extinction and those who desired additional safeguards for its security and perpetuation, culminated in the effort, on the part of most of the States in which slavery existed, to separate from the Federal government, and to resist its authority. This constituted the war of the rebellion, and whatever auxiliary causes may have contributed to bring about this war, undoubtedly the overshadowing and efficient cause was African slavery.

In that struggle slavery, as a legalized social relation, perished. It perished as a necessity of the bitterness and force of the conflict. When the armies of freedom found themselves upon the soil of

---

* 83 (16 Wall.) U.S. 36, 21 L.Ed. 394 (1873). (Most case citations are omitted in this and subsequent cases.)

slavery they could do nothing less than free the poor victims whose enforced servitude was the foundation of the quarrel. And when hard pressed in the contest these men (for they proved themselves men in that terrible crisis) offered their services and were accepted by thousands to aid in suppressing the unlawful rebellion, slavery was at an end wherever the Federal government succeeded in that purpose. The proclamation of President Lincoln expressed an accomplished fact as to a large portion of the insurrectionary districts, when he declared slavery abolished in them all. But the war being over, those who had succeeded in re-establishing the authority of the Federal government were not content to permit this great act of emancipation to rest on the actual results of the contest or the proclamation of the Executive, both of which might have been questioned in after times, and they determined to place this main and most valuable result in the Constitution of the restored Union as one of its fundamental articles. Hence the thirteenth article of amendment of that instrument. . . .

The process of restoring to their proper relations with the Federal government and with the other States those which had sided with the rebellion, undertaken under the proclamation of President Johnson in 1865, and before the assembling of Congress, developed the fact that, notwithstanding the formal recognition by those States of the abolition of slavery, the condition of the slave race would, without further protection of the Federal government, be almost as bad as it was before. Among the first acts of legislation adopted by several of the States in the legislative bodies which claimed to be in their normal relations with the Federal government, were laws which imposed upon the colored race onerous disabilities and burdens, and curtailed their rights in the pursuit of life, liberty, and property to such an extent that their freedom was of little value, while they had lost the protection which they had received from their former owners from motives both of interest and humanity.

They were in some States forbidden to appear in the towns in any other character than menial servants. They were required to reside on and cultivate the soil without the right to purchase or own it. They were excluded from any occupations of gain, and were not permitted to give testimony in the courts in any case where a white man was a party. It was said that their lives were at the mercy of bad men, either because the laws for their protection were insufficient or were not enforced.

These circumstances, whatever of falsehood or misconception may have been mingled with their presentation, forced upon the statesmen who had conducted the Federal government in safety through the crisis of the rebellion, and who supposed that by the thirteenth article of amendment they had secured the result of their labors, the conviction that something more was necessary in the way of constitutional protection to the unfortunate race who had suffered so much. They accordingly passed through Congress the proposition for the fourteenth amendment, and they declined to treat as restored to their full participation in the government of the Union the States which had been in insurrection, until they ratified that article by a formal vote of their legislative bodies . . . .

A few years' experience satisfied the thoughtful men who had been the authors of the other two amendments that, notwithstanding the restraints of those articles on the States, and the laws passed under the additional powers granted to Congress, these were inadequate for the protection of life, liberty, and property, without which freedom to the slave was no boon. They were in all those States denied the right of suffrage. The laws were administered by the white man alone. It was urged that a race of men distinctively marked as was the negro, living in the midst of another and dominant race, could never be fully secured in their person and their property without the right of suffrage.

Hence the fifteenth amendment, which declares that "the right of a citizen of the United States to vote shall not be denied or abridged by any State on account of race, color, or previous condition of servitude." The negro having, by the fourteenth amendment, been declared to be a citizen of the United States, is thus made a voter in every State of the Union.

We repeat, then, in the light of this recapitulation of events, almost too recent to be called history, but which are familiar to us all; and on the most casual examination of the language of these amendments, no one can fail to be impressed with the one pervading purpose found in them all, lying at the foundation of each, and without which none of them would have been even suggested; we mean the freedom of the slave race, the security and firm establishment of that freedom, and the protection of the newly-made freeman and citizen from the oppressions of those who had formerly exercised unlimited dominion over him. It is true that only the fifteenth amendment, in terms, mentions the negro by speaking of his color and his slavery. But it is just as true that each of the other articles was addressed to the grievances of that race, and designed to remedy them as the fifteenth.

We do not say that no one else but the negro can share in this protection. Both the language and spirit of these articles are to have their fair and just weight in any question of construction. Undoubtedly while negro slavery alone was in the mind of the Congress which proposed the thirteenth article, it forbids any other kind of slavery, now or hereafter. If Mexican peonage or the Chinese coolie labor system shall develop slavery of the Mexican or Chinese race within our territory, this amendment may safely be trusted to make it void. And so if other rights are assailed by the States which properly and necessarily fall within the protection of these articles, that protection will apply, though the party interested may not be of African descent. But what we do say, and what we wish to be understood is, that in any fair and just construction of any section or phrase of these amendments, it is necessary to look to the purpose which we have said was the pervading spirit of them all, the evil which they were designed to remedy, and the process of continued addition to the Constitution, until that purpose was supposed to be accomplished, as far as constitutional law can accomplish it. . . .

"Nor shall any State deny to any person within its jurisdiction the equal protection of the laws."

In the light of the history of these amendments, and the pervading purpose of them, which we have already discussed, it is not difficult to give a meaning to this clause. The existence of laws in the States where the newly emancipated negroes resided, which discriminated with gross injustice and hardship against them as a class, was the evil to be remedied by this clause, and by it such laws are forbidden.

If, however, the States did not conform their laws to its requirements, then by the fifth section of the article of amendment Congress was authorized to enforce it by suitable legislation. We doubt very much whether any action of a State not directed by way of discrimination against the negroes as a class, or on account of their race, will ever be held to come within the purview of this provision. It is so clearly a provision for that race and that emergency, that a strong case would be necessary for its application to any other. . . .

QUESTIONS

1.   Given the history of the Reconstruction amendments recited by the Court, is it proper for a court to use the equal protection clause to protect the interests of groups, such as women, that the framers clearly did not have in mind?

2.   Can it ever be proper for a court to use the equal protection clause to defeat programs designed to improve the position of blacks?

*Strauder v. West Virginia** ===================

A black man, convicted of murder, claimed that he had been denied equal protection of the laws because West Virginia law made blacks ineligible for jury duty.

This is one of a series of constitutional provisions having a common purpose; namely, securing to a race recently emancipated, a race that through many generations had been held in slavery, all the civil rights that the superior race enjoy. The true spirit and meaning of the amendments, as we said in the *Slaughter-House Cases* (16 Wall. 36), cannot be understood without keeping in view the history of the times when they were adopted, and the general objects they plainly sought to accomplish. At the time when they were incorporated into the Constitution, it required little knowledge of human nature to antici- pate that those who had long been regarded as an inferior and subject race would, when suddenly raised to the rank of citizenship, be looked upon with jealousy and positive dislike, and that State laws might be enacted or enforced to perpetuate the distinctions that had before existed. Discriminations against them had been habitual. It was well known that in some States laws making such discriminations then existed, and others might well be expected. The colored race, as a race, was abject and ignorant, and in that condition was unfitted to command the respect of those who had superior intelligence. Their training had left them mere children, and as such they needed the protection which a wise government extends to those who are unable to protect themselves. They especially needed protection against unfriendly action in the States where they were resident. It was in

* 100 U.S. 303, 25 L.Ed. 664 (1880).

view of these considerations that the Fourteenth Amendment was framed and adopted. It was designed to assure to the colored race the enjoyment of all the civil rights that under the law are enjoyed by white persons, and to give to that race the protection of the general government, in that enjoyment, whenever it should be denied by the States. It not only gave citizenship and the privileges of citizenship to persons of color, but it denied to any State the power to withhold from them the equal protection of the laws. . . .

What is this but declaring that the law in the States shall be the same for the black as for the white; that all persons, whether colored or white, shall stand equal before the laws of the States, and, in regard to the colored race, for whose protection the amendment was primarily designed, that no discrimination shall be made against them by law because of their color? The words of the amendment, it is true, are prohibitory, but they contain a necessary implication of a positive immunity, or right, most valuable to the colored race,—the right to exemption from unfriendly legislation against them distinctively as colored,—exemption from legal discriminations, implying inferiority in civil society, lessening the security of their enjoyment of the rights which others enjoy, and discriminations which are steps towards reducing them to the condition of a subject race.

That the West Virginia statute respecting juries—the statute that controlled the selection of the grand and petit jury in the case of the plaintiff in error—is such a discrimination ought not to be doubted. Nor would it be if the persons excluded by it were white men. If in those States where the colored people constitute a majority of the entire population a law should be enacted excluding all white men from jury service, thus denying to them the privilege of participating equally with the blacks in the administration of justice, we apprehend no one would be heard to claim that it would not be a denial to white men of the equal protection of the laws. Nor if a law should be passed excluding all naturalized Celtic Irishmen, would there be any doubt of its inconsistency with the spirit of the amendment. The very fact that colored people are singled out and expressly denied by a statute all right to participate in the administration of the law, as jurors, because of their color, though they are citizens, and may be in other respects fully qualified, is practically a brand upon them, affixed by the law, an assertion of their inferiority, and a stimulant to that race prejudice which is an impediment to securing to individuals of the race that equal justice which the law aims to secure to all others.

NOTE

Strauder v. West Virgina states a proposition to which the Supreme Court has consistently adhered: that the Fourteenth Amendment bars discrimination against blacks as to *civil rights*. The significance of the decision is in classing jury service as a civil right, rather than treating it as a "political" right, which was not considered to be covered by the amendment. The questions raised by *Plessy v. Ferguson*, the decision sustaining racial segregation, are about what constitutes "discrimination" and whether the claim to social equality concerns a "civil right."

QUESTIONS

1.   Was the decision in *Strauder* wrong if the men who wrote and adopted the Fourteenth Amendment did not suppose that it would guarantee blacks "political" rights, such as the right to jury service? What role should the actual language of the provision, the apparent intent of those who wrote it, and the moral justice of possible outcomes play in a judge's deliberations?

2.   Was the Court correct in *Strauder* to suggest that the Fourteenth Amendment protects whites against racial discrimination? Is discrimination against whites morally different from discrimination against blacks? Does that depend on previous historical conditions? On whether whites or blacks represent a majority in the legislature?

3.   Was the Court correct to suggest that the amendment bars other forms of arbitrary classification, such as an exclusion of all naturalized Celtic Irishmen?

*Yick Wo v. Hopkins**

The San Francisco Board of Supervisors, acting under an ordinance that required its approval for any laundry not operated in a brick or stone building, had granted permits to non-Chinese applicants to operate laundries in wooden buildings but had denied permits to Chinese applicants. The Court held that the administrative practice violated the equal protection clause.

For the cases present the ordinances in actual operation, and the facts shown establish an administration directed so exclusively against a particular class of persons as to warrant and require the conclusion,

* 118 U.S. 356, 6 S. Ct. 1064, 30 L.Ed. 220 (1886).

that, whatever may have been the intent of the ordinances as
adopted, they are applied by the public authorities charged with
their administration, and thus representing the State itself, with
a mind so unequal and oppressive as to amount to a practical denial by the State of that equal protection of the laws which is secured to the petitioners, as to all other persons, by the broad and
benign provisions of the Fourteenth Amendment to the Constitution of the United States. Though the law itself be fair on its
face and impartial in appearance, yet, if it is applied and administered by public authority with an evil eye and an unequal hand,
so as practically to make unjust and illegal discriminations between
persons in similar circumstances, material to their rights, the denial
of equal justice is still within the prohibition of the Constitution.

NOTE

Yick Wo is significant in using the equal protection clause on behalf
of a racial minority other than blacks and in establishing that equal
protection may be denied by discriminatory practices under neutral
laws as well as by discriminatory laws.

Civil Rights Cases*

*The Supreme Court passed on the constitutional validity of the Civil Rights
Act of 1875, which prohibited racial discrimination in respect to public accommodations, theaters, and transportation facilities. The Court held the act
invalid, on the basis that the Reconstruction amendments did not give Congress the power to regulate racial discrimination by private persons and enterprises.*

Has Congress constitutional power to make such a law? Of course,
no one will contend that the power to pass it was contained in the
Constitution before the adoption of the last three amendments. The
power is sought, first, in the Fourteenth Amendment, and the views
and arguments of distinguished Senators, advanced whilst the law
was under consideration, claiming authority to pass it by virtue of
that amendment, are the principal arguments adduced in favor of the
power. . . .

* 109 U.S. 3, 3 S. Ct. 18, 27 L.Ed. 835 (1883).

The first section of the Fourteenth Amendment (which is the one relied on), after declaring who shall be citizens of the United States, and of the several States, is prohibitory in its character, and prohibitory upon the States. It declares that:

"No State shall make or enforce any law which shall abridge the privileges or immunities of citizens of the United States; nor shall any State deprive any person of life, liberty, or property without due process of law; nor deny to any person within its jurisdiction the equal protection of the laws."

It is State action of a particular character that is prohibited. Individual invasion of individual rights is not the subject-matter of the amendment. It has a deeper and broader scope. It nullifies and makes void all State legislation, and State action of every kind, which impairs the privileges and immunities of citizens of the United States, or which injures them in life, liberty or property without due process of law, or which denies to any of them the equal protection of the laws. It not only does this, but, in order that the national will, thus declared, may not be a mere *brutum fulmen,* the last section of the amendment invests Congress with power to enforce it by appropriate legislation. To enforce what? To enforce the prohibition. To adopt appropriate legislation for correcting the effects of such prohibited State laws and State acts, and thus to render them effectually null, void, and innocuous. This is the legislative power conferred upon Congress, and this is the whole of it. It does not invest Congress with power to legislate upon subjects which are within the domain of State legislation; but to provide modes of relief against State legislation, or State action, of the kind referred to. It does not authorize Congress to create a code of municipal law for the regulation of private rights; but to provide modes of redress against the operation of State laws, and the action of State officers executive or judicial, when these are subversive of the fundamental rights specified in the amendment. . . .

But the power of Congress to adopt direct and primary, as distinguished from corrective legislation, on the subject in hand, is sought, in the second place, from the Thirteenth Amendment, which abolishes slavery. . . .

It is true, that slavery cannot exist without law, any more than property in lands and goods can exist without law: and, therefore, the Thirteenth Amendment may be regarded as nullifying all State laws which establish or uphold slavery. But it has a reflex character also, establishing and decreeing universal civil and political freedom throughout the United States; and it is assumed, that the power vested in Congress to enforce the article by appropriate legislation, clothes Congress with power to pass all laws necessary and proper for abolishing all badges and incidents of slavery in the United States: and upon this assumption it is claimed, that this is sufficient authority for declaring by law that all persons shall have equal accommodations and privileges in all inns, public conveyances, and places of amusement; the argument being, that the denial of such equal accommodations and privileges is, in itself, a subjection to a species of servitude within the meaning of the amendment. . . .

After giving to these questions all the consideration which their importance demands, we are forced to the conclusion that such an act of refusal has nothing to do with slavery or involuntary servitude, and that if it is violative of any right of the party, his redress is to be sought under the laws of the State; or if those laws are adverse to his rights and do not protect him, his remedy will be found in the corrective legislation which Congress has adopted, or may adopt, for counteracting the effect of State laws, or State action, prohibited by the Fourteenth Amendment. It would be running the slavery argument into the ground to make it apply to every act of discrimination which a person may see fit to make as to the guests he will entertain, or as to the people he will take into his coach or cab or car, or admit to his concert or theatre, or deal with in other matters of intercourse or business.

NOTE

The *Civil Rights Cases* are one historical reflection of the Supreme Court's refusal to give a generous interpretation to the post–Civil War amendments. Insofar as the opinion indicates that there is no direct violation of the Fourteenth Amendment unless the state has acted in some way, its principles are still followed; although "state action" may now be found in judicial enforcement of a private contract to discriminate or in some supportive relationship between the government and a private discriminator.

The opinion's comments on congressional power are no longer of practical importance. In recent years the Supreme Court has indicated that Congress, in enforcing the Fourteenth Amendment, can prohibit some activities that do not themselves violate the amendment. Even more significant for these purposes, it has given a very broad interpretation to Congress's power under the commerce clause and under the Thirteenth Amendment. As a consequence, Congress can now prohibit virtually any form of racial discrimination that a state can prohibit.

QUESTION

Should a judge's interpretation of whether the Thirteenth or Fourteenth Amendment authorized enactment of the 1875 Civil Rights Act have been influenced by his view on the social desirability of the constraints imposed by the act? By his view on whether such constraints would best come from the states or from the central government?

Plessy v. Ferguson*

MR. JUSTICE BROWN, after stating the case, delivered the opinion of the court.

This case turns upon the constitutionality of an act of the General Assembly of the State of Louisiana, passed in 1890, providing for separate railway carriages for the white and colored races. Acts 1890, No. 111, p.152.

The first section of the statute enacts "that all railway companies carrying passengers in their coaches in this State, shall provide equal but separate accommodations for the white, and colored races, by providing two or more passenger coaches for each passenger train, or by dividing the passenger coaches by a partition so as to secure separate accommodations. . . . No person or persons, shall be admitted to occupy seats in coaches, other than, the ones, assigned, to them on account of the race they belong to."

By the second section it was enacted "that the officers of such passenger trains shall have power and are hereby required to assign each passenger to the coach or compartment used for the race to which such passenger belongs; any passenger insisting on going into a coach or compartment to which by race he does not belong, shall be

---

* 163 U.S. 537, 16 S. Ct. 1138, 41 L.Ed. 256 (1896).

liable to a fine of twenty-five dollars, or in lieu thereof to imprisonment for a period of not more than twenty days in the parish prison. . . .

The information filed in the criminal District Court charged in substance that Plessy, being a passenger between two stations within the State of Louisiana, was assigned by officers of the company to the coach used for the race to which he belonged, but he insisted upon going into a coach used by the race to which he did not belong. Neither in the information nor plea was his particular race or color averred.

The petition for the writ of prohibition averred that petitioner was seven eighths Caucasian and one eighth African blood; that the mixture of colored blood was not discernible in him, and that he was entitled to every right, privilege and immunity secured to citizens of the United States of the white race; and that, upon such theory, he took possession of a vacant seat in a coach where passengers of the white race were accommodated, and was ordered by the conductor to vacate said coach and take a seat in another assigned to persons of the colored race, and having refused to comply with such demand he was forcibly ejected with the aid of a police officer, and imprisoned in the parish jail to answer a charge of having violated the above act.

The constitutionality of this act is attacked upon the ground that it conflicts both with the Thirteenth Amendment of the Constitution, abolishing slavery, and the Fourteenth Amendment, which prohibits certain restrictive legislation on the part of the States.

1. That it does not conflict with the Thirteenth Amendment, which abolished slavery and involuntary servitude, except as a punishment for crime, is too clear for argument. . . .

A statute which implies merely a legal distinction between the white and colored races—a distinction which is founded in the color of the two races, and which must always exist so long as white men are distinguished from the other race by color—has no tendency to destroy the legal equality of the two races, or reëstablish a state of involuntary servitude. . . .

2. By the Fourteenth Amendment, all persons born or naturalized in the United States, and subject to the jurisdiction thereof, are made citizens of the United States and of the State wherein they reside; and the States are forbidden from making or enforcing any law which shall abridge the privileges or immunities of citizens of the

United States, or shall deprive any person of life, liberty or property without due process of law, or deny to any person within their jurisdiction the equal protection of the laws.

The proper construction of this amendment was first called to the attention of this court in the *Slaughter-house cases,* 16 Wall. 36, which involved, however, not a question of race, but one of exclusive privileges. The case did not call for any expression of opinion as to the exact rights it was intended to secure to the colored race. . . .

The object of the amendment was undoubtedly to enforce the absolute equality of the two races before the law, but in the nature of things it could not have been intended to abolish distinctions based upon color, or to enforce social, as distinguished from political equality, or a commingling of the two races upon terms unsatisfactory to either. Laws permitting, and even requiring, their separation in places where they are liable to be brought into contact do not necessarily imply the inferiority of either race to the other, and have been generally, if not universally, recognized as within the competency of the state legislatures in the exercise of their police power. The most common instance of this is connected with the establishment of separate schools for white and colored children, which has been held to be a valid exercise of the legislative power even by courts of States where the political rights of the colored race have been longest and most earnestly enforced.

One of the earliest of these cases is that of *Roberts* v. *City of Boston*, 5 Cush. 198, in which the Supreme Judicial Court of Massachusetts held that the general school committee of Boston had power to make provision for the instruction of colored children in separate schools established exclusively for them, and to prohibit their attendance upon the other schools. . . .

We consider the underlying fallacy of the plaintiff's argument to consist in the assumption that the enforced separation of the two races stamps the colored race with a badge of inferiority. If this be so, it is not by reason of anything found in the act, but solely because the colored race chooses to put that construction upon it. The argument necessarily assumes that if, as has been more than once the case, and is not unlikely to be so again, the colored race should become the dominant power in the state legislature, and should enact a law in precisely similar terms, it would thereby relegate the white race to an inferior position. We imagine that the white race, at least, would not acquiesce in this assumption. The argument also assumes that social prejudices may be overcome by legislation, and that equal rights cannot be secured to the negro except by an enforced commingling of the two races. We cannot accept this proposition. If the two races are to meet upon terms of social equality, it must be the result of natural affinities, a mutual appreciation of each other's merits and a voluntary consent of individuals. As was said by the Court of Appeals of New York in *People* v. *Gallagher,* 93 N.Y. 438, 448, "this end can neither be accomplished nor promoted by laws which conflict with the general sentiment of the community upon whom they are designed to operate. When the government, therefore, has secured to each of its citizens equal rights before the law and equal opportunities for improvement and progress, it has accomplished the end for which it was organized and performed all of the functions respecting social advantages with which it is endowed." Legislation is powerless to eradicate racial instincts or to abolish distinctions based upon physical differences, and the attempt to do so can only result in accentuating the difficulties of the present situation. If the civil and political rights of both races be equal one cannot be inferior to the other civilly or politically. If one race be inferior to the other socially, the Constitution of the United States cannot put them upon the same plane.

It is true that the question of the proportion of colored blood necessary to constitute a colored person, as distinguished from a white person, is one upon which there is a difference of opinion in the different States, some holding that any visible admixture of black blood stamps the person as belonging to the colored race, *(State* v. *Chavers,* 5 Jones, [N.C.] 1, p.11; others that it depends upon the preponderance of blood, *(Gray* v. *State,* 4 Ohio, 354; *Monroe* v. *Collings*, 17 Ohio St. 665); and still others that the predominance of white blood must only be in the proportion of three fourths. *(People* v. *Dean,* 14 Michigan, 406; *Jones* v. *Commonwealth,* 80 Virginia, 538.) But these are questions to be determined under the laws of each state and are not properly put in issue in this case. Under the allegations of his petition it may undoubtedly become a question of importance whether, under the laws of Louisiana, the petitioner belongs to the white or colored race.

The judgment of the court below is, therefore,

Affirmed.

MR. JUSTICE HARLAN DISSENTING.

In respect of civil rights, common to all citizens, the Constitution of the United States does not, I think, permit any public authority to know the race of those entitled to be protected in the enjoyment of such rights. Every true man has pride of race, and under appropriate circumstances when the rights of others, his equals before the law, are not to be affected, it is his privilege to express such pride and to take such action based upon it as to him seems proper. But I deny that any legislative body or judicial tribunal may have regard to the race of citizens when the civil rights of those citizens are involved. Indeed, such legislation, as that here in question, is inconsistent not only with that equality of rights which pertains to citizenship, National and State, but with the personal liberty enjoyed by everyone within the United States.

The Thirteenth Amendment does not permit the withholding or the deprivation of any right necessarily inhering in freedom. It not only struck down the institution of slavery as previously existing in the United States, but it prevents the imposition of any burdens or disabilities that constitute badges of slavery or servitude. It decreed universal civil freedom in this country. This court has so adjudged. But that amendment having been found inadequate to the protection of the rights of those who had been in slavery, it was followed by the Fourteenth Amendment, which added greatly to the dignity and glory of American citizenship, and to the security of personal liberty. . . . These two amendments, if enforced according to their true intent and meaning, will protect all the civil rights that pertain to freedom and citizenship.

It was said in argument that the statute of Louisiana does not discriminate against either race, but prescribes a rule applicable alike to white and colored citizens. But this argument does not meet the difficulty. Every one knows that the statute in question had its origin in the purpose, not so much to exclude white persons from railroad cars occupied by blacks, as to exclude colored people from coaches occupied by or assigned to white persons. Railroad corporations of Louisiana did not make discrimination among whites in the matter of accommodation for travellers. The thing to accomplish was, under the guise of giving equal accommodation for whites and blacks, to compel the latter to keep to themselves while travelling in railroad passenger coaches. No one would be so wanting in candor as to assert the contrary.

The white race deems itself to be the dominant race in this country. And so it is, in prestige, in achievements, in education, in wealth and in power. So, I doubt not, it will continue to be for all time, if it remains true to its great heritage and holds fast to the principles of constitutional liberty. But in view of the Constitution, in the eye of the law, there is in this country no superior, dominant, ruling class of citizens. There is no caste here. Our Constitution is color-blind, and neither knows nor tolerates classes among citizens. In respect of civil rights, all citizens are equal before the law. The humblest is the peer of the most powerful. The law regards man as man, and takes no account of his surroundings or of his color when his civil rights as guaranteed by the supreme law of the land are involved. It is, therefore, to be regretted that this high tribunal, the final expositor of the fundamental law of the land, has reached the conclusion that it is competent for a State to regulate the enjoyment by citizens of their civil rights solely upon the basis of race.

NOTE

Although *Plessy v. Ferguson* dealt with racial separation in railway carriages, the opinion approved the principle of segregation more broadly, and the case was taken as deciding that school segregation and other forms of racial segregation were constitutionally permissible. Contrary to what is often supposed, the practices approved by *Plessy* were not then firmly entrenched throughout the South. For some years after the withdrawal of federal troops in 1877, which ended the era of Reconstruction, rules against racial mixing were sporadic, and many influential southern leaders opposed strict segregation. Only in the last years of the century were rigid and pervasive segregation laws adopted. During the same period, systematic and largely successful efforts were made to disenfranchise blacks.

Note that the majority opinion in *Plessy* does not deny that the Fourteenth Amendment guaranteed to blacks equality of civil rights, but it does deny that the amendment protects equality of social rights and that legally imposed separation amounts to legally imposed inequality. In at least one respect, the majority opinion in *Plessy* is actually more congenial to proposals for reverse discrimination than Justice Harlan's dissent. The majority finds no particular constitutional difficulty in the state's engaging itself in the unpalatable task of determining the race of its citizens, whereas Justice Harlan says that legislative bodies and judicial tribunals may not "have regard to the race of citizens when the civil rights of those citizens are involved."

QUESTIONS

1. Is the majority right in maintaining that enforced separation of the races did not by itself stamp "the colored race with a badge of inferiority"? Should it be relevant whether a racial classification reflects the legislators' view that one race is inferior to another or will create the impression of inferiority in the public generally? How is a court to determine what the legislators' motives were or how most of the public will react to a racial classification? Suppose white administrators at a state university accede to the demand of some blacks for an "all-black" dormitory. Should the legality of what they have done turn on whether they think blacks are inferior, or on whether most students will perceive acceptance of a black dormitory as a reflection of belief in black inferiority?

2. Is "color blindness" the appropriate position for all governmental concerns? What of adoption of children of a different race; should state adoption services disregard the race of prospective parents? Would "color blindness" be an appropriate long-term goal for governmental action? If so, what deviations from that principle are acceptable in the short run?

IV.

Discrimination and Law in the First Half of the Twentieth Century

NOTE: RACIAL DISCRIMINATION

The constitutional principles that emerged in the last part of the nineteenth century remained controlling through the first half of the twentieth century. Most notably, the basic doctrine of *Plessy v. Ferguson* was not overturned. The Supreme Court had, however, insisted that facilities for blacks must be genuinely equal to those for whites, and that a black could not be excluded from a major state law school that afforded opportunities superior to those at a law school created for blacks. Some northern states had passed laws forbidding racial discrimination in various spheres; but there was no important federal legislation and so no occasion for review of the ambit of federal power to deal with discrimination. The Supreme Court continued to hold that state denials of rights on the ground of race were impermissible.

NOTE: THE EQUAL PROTECTION CLAUSE IN OTHER CONTEXTS, AND GENDER CLASSIFICATIONS

During the late nineteenth and early twentieth centuries, the Supreme Court had used the Fourteenth Amendment, mainly the due process clause, to protect claims of liberty and property by business enterprises against the effects of modern social legislation. A statute providing for maximum hours was held, for example, to violate the liberty of the employer and employee to bargain over hours. The equal protection clause played a decidedly subsidiary role, rarely being relied on by the courts in other than racial contexts. By the late 1930s the Supreme Court had abandoned its active use of the due process clause to strike down social legislation, and allowed legislatures to engage in any sort of social legislation that was rational. The doctrine as far as equal protection was concerned was that if a classification was "rationally related" to any proper legislative purpose, it was permissible; and courts did not look very carefully at the reasons that might support a classification. In *Railway Express Agency v. New York*, 336 U.S. 106, 69 S. Ct. 463, 93 L.Ed. 533 (1949), for example, it considered a city ordinance that generally barred advertising on cars and trucks but permitted owners of cars and trucks used for business to advertise their own businesses on their vehicles. Railway Express, which wished to sell advertising space on its trucks, complained that there was no reasonable basis for forbidding rental advertising and permitting owner advertising. The Court responded to this equal protection challenge: "The local authorities may well have concluded that those who advertise their own wares on their trucks do not present the same traffic problem in view of the nature or extent of the advertising which they use." This willingness in ordinary economic cases to accept at face value asserted justifications for classifications, and even to make up possible justifications, has carried down to the present.

During the first half of the twentieth century, state legislatures had begun to dismantle many of the legal disabilities under which women had suffered, but legislative distinctions between men and women were still pervasive. Many of these were purportedly protective of women, but they had the consequence of denying desired opportunities for women. When these distinctions came before the Court, they were treated like other nonracial classifications; any rational argument in defense of the legislative differentiation sufficed to meet a constitutional challenge. For example, in *Goesaert v. Cleary* 335 U.S. 464, 69 S. Ct. 198, 93 L.Ed. 163 (1948), the Court upheld a Michigan law that forbade any woman from being a bartender unless she was the wife or daughter of a male owner.

V.

The Modern Law of Discrimination: Race

*Korematsu v. United States**

MR. JUSTICE BLACK delivered the opinion of the Court.

The petitioner, an American citizen of Japanese descent, was convicted in a Federal district court for remaining in San Leandro, California, a "Military Area," contrary to Civilian Exclusion Order No. 34 of the Commanding General of the Western Command, U.S. Army, which directed that after May 9, 1942, all persons of Japanese ancestry should be excluded from that area. No question was raised as to petitioner's loyalty to the United States. . . .

It should be noted, to begin with, that all legal restrictions which curtail the civil rights of a single racial group are immediately suspect. That is not to say that all such restrictions are unconstitutional. It is to say that courts must subject them to the most rigid scrutiny. Pressing public necessity may sometimes justify the existence of such restrictions; racial antagonism never can.

In the instant case prosecution of the petitioner was begun by information charging violation of an Act of Congress, of March 21, 1942, . . . which provides that ". . . whoever shall enter, remain in, leave, or commit any act in any military area or military zone prescribed, under the authority of an Executive order of the President, by the Secretary of War, or by any military commander designated by the Secretary of War, contrary to the restrictions

* 323 U.S. 214, 65 S. Ct. 193, 89 L.Ed. 194 (1944).

applicable to any such area or zone or contrary to the order of the Secretary of War or any such military commander, shall, if it appears that he knew or should have known of the existence and extent of the restrictions or order and that his act was in violation thereof, be guilty of a misdemeanor and upon conviction shall be liable to a fine of not to exceed $5,000 or to imprisonment for not more than one year, or both, for each offense."

Exclusion Order No. 34, which the petitioner knowingly and admittedly violated, was one of a number of military orders and proclamations, all of which were substantially based upon Executive Order No. 9066, 7 Fed Reg 1407. That order, issued after we were at war with Japan, declared that "the successful prosecution of the war requires every possible protection against espionage and against sabotage to national-defense material, national-defense premises, and national-defense utilities. . . ."

One of the series of orders and proclamations, a curfew order, which like the exclusion order here was promulgated pursuant to Executive Order 9066, subjected all persons of Japanese ancestry in prescribed West Coast military areas to remain in their residences from 8 p.m. to 6 a.m. As is the case with the exclusion order here, that prior curfew order was designed as a "protection against espionage and against sabotage." In *Hirabayashi v. U.S.*, 320 US 81, . . . we sustained a conviction obtained for violation of the curfew order. The Hirabayashi conviction and this one thus rest on the same 1942 Congressional Act and the same basic executive and military orders, all of which orders were aimed at the twin dangers of espionage and sabotage.

The 1942 Act was attacked in the *Hirabayashi* Case as an unconstitutional delegation of power; it was contended that the curfew order and other orders on which it rested were beyond the war powers of the Congress, the military authorities and of the President, as Commander in Chief of the Army; and finally that to apply the curfew order against none but citizens of Japanese ancestry amounted to a constitutionally prohibited discrimination solely on account of race. To these questions, we gave the serious consideration which their importance justified. We upheld the curfew order as an exercise of the power of the government to take steps necessary to prevent espionage and sabotage in an area threatened by Japanese attack.

In the light of the principles we announced in the *Hirabayashi* Case, we are unable to conclude that it was beyond the war power of Congress and the Executive to exclude those of Japanese ancestry from the West Coast war area at the time they did. True, exclusion from the area in which one's home is located is a far greater deprivation than constant confinement to the home from 8 p.m. to 6 a.m. Nothing short of apprehension by the proper military authorities of the gravest imminent danger to the public safety can constitutionally justify either. But exclusion from a threatened area, no less than curfew, has a definite and close relationship to the prevention of espionage and sabotage. The military authorities, charged with the primary responsibility of defending our shores, concluded that curfew provided inadequate protection and ordered exclusion. They did so, as pointed out in our *Hirabayashi* opinion, in accordance with congressional authority to the military to say who should, and who should not, remain in the threatened areas.

In this case the petitioner challenges the assumptions upon which we rested our conclusions in the *Hirabayashi* Case. He also urges that by May 1942, when Order No. 34 was promulgated, all danger of Japanese invasion of the West Coast had disappeared. After careful consideration of these contentions we are compelled to reject them.

Here, as in the *Hirabayashi* Case, . . . "we cannot reject as unfounded the judgment of the military authorities and of Congress that there were disloyal members of that population, whose number and strength could not be precisely and quickly ascertained. We cannot say that the war-making branches of the Government did not have ground for believing that in a critical hour such persons could not readily be isolated and separately dealt with, and constituted a menace to the national defense and safety, which demanded that prompt and adequate measures be taken to guard against it."

Like curfew, exclusion of those of Japanese origin was deemed necessary because of the presence of an unascertained number of disloyal members of the group, most of whom we have no doubt were loyal to this country. It was because we could not reject the finding of the military authorities that it was impossible to bring about an immediate segregation of the disloyal from the loyal that we sustained the validity of the curfew order as applying to the whole group. In the instant case, temporary exclusion of the entire group was rested by the military on the same ground. The judgment that exclusion of the whole group was for the same reason a military imperative answers the contention that the exclusion was in the nature of group punishment based on antagonism to those of Japanese origin.

In *Korematsu* and its predecessor case, *Hirabayashi*, the Supreme Court upheld regulations that it acknowledges in *Korematsu* were directed at a "single racial group" and that undoubtedly resulted in denial of equality of right for members of that group as compared with other citizens. In *Hirabayashi*, what was sustained was a nighttime curfew applicable only to persons of Japanese ancestry. In *Korematsu*, it was the much more drastic measure of excluding persons of Japanese ancestry from their homes in the West Coast area, to be followed by detention in centers established by the government. It is perhaps ironic that in a decision sustaining a racial classification, the Court first used phrases, such as "rigid scrutiny," "suspect legal restrictions," and "pressing public necessity," that suggested a rigorous standard of review for classifications that disadvantaged racial minorities. (For further comment, see Essay, p. 31.)

1.   Can a classification that disadvantages a racial minority ever be morally acceptable? Are the reasons provided in *Korematsu* the kinds of reasons that could justify such a classification? Does the Constitution permit such reasons to be taken into account? In *Hirabayashi*, the Court indicated that if only persons of Japanese ancestry posed a serious threat of sabotage on the West Coast, the government should not be forced to choose between having no curfew and having a curfew applicable to everyone. Is that reasoning persuasive? If there is a series of killings by an unidentified white or whites or by an unidentified black or blacks, should a municipality be able to impose a curfew only on whites or only on blacks? Is *Korematsu* significantly different from a purely racial case because the controlling criterion was national origin?

2.   Do you think the examination of the supporting reasons in *Korematsu* was demanding enough, or should the Court, as the dissenters claimed, have looked more closely at the supposed military

need for exclusion? Should it have mattered to the result that racial prejudice undoubtedly played a part in the decision as to what to do about Japanese nationals and Japanese-Americans, and that, whatever the motives for curfew, exclusion, and detention, those measures tended to stigmatize Japanese-Americans in the eyes of much of the general public?

*Shelley v. Kraemer**

MR. CHIEF JUSTICE VINSON delivered the opinion of the Court.

I

Whether the equal protection clause of the Fourteenth Amendment inhibits judicial enforcement by state courts of restrictive covenants based on race or color is a question which this Court has not heretofore been called upon to consider.

It is well, at the outset, to scrutinize the terms of the restrictive agreements involved in these cases. In the Missouri case, the covenant declares that no part of the affected property shall be "occupied by any person not of the Caucasian race, it being intended hereby to restrict the use of said property . . . against the occupancy as owners or tenants of any portion of said property for resident or other purpose by people of the Negro or Mongolian Race." Not only does the restriction seek to proscribe use and occupancy of the affected properties by members of the excluded class, but as construed by the Missouri courts, the agreement requires that title of any person who uses his property in violation of the restriction shall be divested. The restriction of the covenant in the Michigan case seeks to bar occupancy by persons of the excluded class. It provides that "This property shall not be used or occupied by any person or persons except those of the Caucasian race."

It is . . . clear that restrictions on the right of occupancy of the sort sought to be created by the private agreements in these cases could not be squared with the requirements of the Fourteenth Amendment if imposed by state statute or local ordinance. Here the particular patterns of discrimination and the areas in which the restrictions are to operate, are determined, in the first instance, by

* 334 U.S. 1, 68 S. Ct. 836, 92 L.Ed. 1161 (1948).

the terms of agreements among private individuals. Participation of the State consists in the enforcement of the restrictions so defined. The crucial issue with which we are here confronted is whether this distinction removes these cases from the operation of the prohibitory provisions of the Fourteenth Amendment.

Since the decision of this Court in the *Civil Rights Cases*, 109 U.S. 3 (1883), the principle has become firmly embedded in our constitutional law that the action inhibited by the first section of the Fourteenth Amendment is only such action as may fairly be said to be that of the States. That Amendment erects no shield against merely private conduct, however discriminatory or wrongful.

We conclude, therefore, that the restrictive agreements standing alone cannot be regarded as violative of any rights guaranteed to petitioners by the Fourteenth Amendment. So long as the purposes of those agreements are effectuated by voluntary adherence to their terms, it would appear clear that there has been no action by the State and the provisions of the Amendment have not been violated.

But here there was more. These are cases in which the purposes of the agreements were secured only by judicial enforcement by state courts of the restrictive terms of the agreements. The respondents urge that judicial enforcement of private agreements does not amount to state action: or, in any event, the participation of the State is so attenuated in character as not to amount to state action within the meaning of the Fourteenth Amendment. Finally, it is suggested, even if the States in these cases may be deemed to have acted in the constitutional sense, their action did not deprive petitioners of rights guaranteed by the Fourteenth Amendment. We move to a consideration of these matters.

II

That the action of state courts and judicial officers in their official capacities is to be regarded as action of the State within the meaning of the Fourteenth Amendment, is a proposition which has long been established by decisions of this Court . . . .

One of the earliest applications of the prohibitions contained in the Fourteenth Amendment to action of state judicial officials occurred in cases in which Negroes had been excluded from jury service in criminal prosecutions by reason of their race or color. These cases demonstrate, also, the early recognition by this Court that state action in violation of the amendment's provisions is equally repugnant to the constitutional commands whether directed by state statute or taken by a judicial official in the absence of statute. Thus, in *Strauder* v. *West Virginia*, 100 U.S. 303 (1880), this Court declared invalid a state statute restricting jury service to white persons as amounting to a denial of the equal protection of the laws to the colored defendant in that case. In the same volume of the reports, the Court in *Ex parte Virginia, supra*, held that a similar discrimination imposed by the action of a state judge denied rights protected by the Amendment, despite the fact that the language of the state statute relating to jury service contained no such restrictions.

III

We have no doubt that there has been state action in these cases in the full and complete sense of the phrase. The undisputed facts disclose that petitioners were willing purchasers of properties upon which they desired to establish homes. The owners of the properties were willing sellers; and contracts of sale were accordingly consummated. It is clear that but for the active intervention of the state courts, supported by the full panoply of state power, petitioners would have been free to occupy the properties in question without restraint.

These are not cases, as has been suggested, in which the States have merely abstained from action, leaving private individuals free to impose such discriminations as they see fit. Rather, these are cases in which the States have made available to such individuals the full coercive power of government to deny to petitioners, on the grounds of race or color, the enjoyment of property rights in premises which petitioners are willing and financially able to acquire and which the grantors are willing to sell. The difference between judicial enforcement and nonenforcement of the restrictive covenants is the difference to petitioners between being denied rights of property available to other members of the community and being accorded full enjoyment of those rights on an equal footing.

The enforcement of the restrictive agreements by the state courts in these cases was directed pursuant to the common-law policy of the States as formulated by those courts in earlier decisions. . . . State action, as that phrase is understood for the purposes of the Fourteenth Amendment, refers to exertions of state power in all forms.

And when the effect of that action is to deny rights subject to the protection of the Fourteenth Amendment, it is the obligation of this Court to enforce the constitutional commands.

We hold that in granting judicial enforcement of the restrictive agreements in these cases, the States have denied petitioners the equal protection of the laws and that, therefore, the action of the state courts cannot stand.

NOTE

This case marked an important extension of the situations in which the courts would find state action that violated the Fourteenth Amendment. Another significant extension occurred in cases that invalidated "white primaries" in southern states, even when the exclusion of blacks was by the local Democratic party, or by a supposedly private club within the party, rather than by the state. By stretching the boundaries of state action, the Supreme Court was able to give blacks somewhat greater protection against racial discrimination. Although it did not say that restrictive covenants were themselves illegal, it did say that courts could not enforce them, and it said in a later case that one party to such a covenant could not recover damages from another party who had sold his home to a black in violation of the covenant.

The opinion in *Shelley* was hotly debated, even by those sympathetic with the social policy of forbidding racial discrimination in the housing market. The objection was raised that the Supreme Court had not come up with a "neutral principle" justifying the result. The Court apparently said that judicial enforcement of a private decision to discriminate is forbidden state action; but applied to other cases, this would mean that a writer of a will could not condition his generosity on discriminatory distinctions forbidden to the state, and that a private homeowner who asked someone to leave his house because he did not like members of that race in his home could not get the state's assistance to remove the undesired guest or have him treated as a trespasser in the courts. Critics concluded that in some situations it must be constitutionally permissible for courts to enforce private wishes to discriminate and that the Court had not afforded a reasoned basis for treating enforcement of the discriminatory covenant differently. Some critics doubted whether such a basis could be found; others supplied what they regarded as acceptable reasons for the decision.

QUESTIONS

1. Should homeowners be able to discriminate on racial grounds in the sale of property? Should they be able to agree to discriminate? Should a homeowner be able to force someone to leave his or her home because he or she is offended by the race, religion, or national origin of the visitor? Should people be able to write wills drawing racial or religious lines, for example, "$10,000 to my daughter Sheila when she gets married, but only if she marries a Roman Catholic"? When judicial enforcement is involved, are there plausible distinctions of constitutional relevance among these situations?

2. Should the Court always come up with a "neutral principle" of decision before it holds action illegal under the Constitution? Is the search for "neutral principles" characteristic of all moral judgment? Of all rational judgment?

*Brown v. Board of Education**

MR. CHIEF JUSTICE WARREN delivered the opinion of the Court.

These cases come to us from the States of Kansas, South Carolina, Virginia, and Delaware. They are premised on different facts and different local conditions, but a common legal question justifies their consideration together in this consolidated opinion.

In each of the cases, minors of the Negro race, through their legal representatives, seek the aid of the courts in obtaining admission to the public schools of their community on a nonsegregated basis. In each instance, they had been denied admission to schools attended by white children under laws requiring or permitting segregation according to race. This segregation was alleged to deprive the plaintiffs of the equal protection of the laws under the Fourteenth Amendment. . . .

The plaintiffs contend that segregated public schools are not "equal" and cannot be made "equal," and that hence they are deprived of the equal protection of the laws. Because of the obvious importance of the question presented, the Court took jurisdiction. Argument was heard in the 1952 Term, and reargument was heard this Term on certain questions propounded by the Court.

* 347 U.S. 483, 74 S. Ct. 686, 98 L.Ed. 873 (1954).

Reargument was largely devoted to the circumstances surrounding the adoption of the Fourteenth Amendment in 1868. It covered
exhaustively consideration of the Amendment in Congress, ratification by the states, then existing practices in racial segregation, and
the views of proponents and opponents of the Amendment. This
discussion and our own investigation convince us that, although these
sources cast some light, it is not enough to resolve the problem with
which we are faced. At best, they are inconclusive. The most avid
proponents of the post-War Amendments undoubtedly intended
them to remove all legal distinctions among "all persons born or
naturalized in the United States." Their opponents, just as certainly,
were antagonistic to both the letter and the spirit of the Amendments
and wished them to have the most limited effect. What others in
Congress and the state legislatures had in mind cannot be determined
with any degree of certainty.

An additional reason for the inconclusive nature of the Amendment's history, with respect to segregated schools, is the status of
public education at that time. In the South, the movement toward
free common schools, supported by general taxation, had not yet
taken hold. Education of white children was largely in the hands of
private groups. Education of Negroes was almost nonexistent, and
practically all of the race were illiterate. In fact, any education of
Negroes was forbidden by law in some states. Today, in contrast,
many Negroes have achieved outstanding success in the arts and
sciences as well as in the business and professional world. It is true
that public school education at the time of the Amendment had
advanced further in the North, but the effect of the Amendment on
Northern States was generally ignored in the congressional debates.
Even in the North, the conditions of public education did not
approximate those existing today. The curriculum was usually rudi-
mentary; ungraded schools were common in rural areas; the school
term was but three months a year in many states; and compulsory
school attendance was virtually unknown. As a consequence, it is not
surprising that there should be so little in the history of the Fourteenth Amendment relating to its intended effect on public education.

In the first cases in this Court construing the Fourteenth Amendment, decided shortly after its adoption, the Court interpreted it as
proscribing all state-imposed discriminations against the Negro race.
The doctrine of "separate but equal" did not make its appearance in

this Court until 1896 in the case of *Plessy* v. *Ferguson, supra,* involving not education but transportation. American courts have since labored with the doctrine for over half a century. In this Court, there have been six cases involving the "separate but equal" doctrine in the field of public education. In *Cumming* v. *County Board of Education,* 175 U.S. 528, and *Gong Lum* v. *Rice,* 275 U.S. 78, the validity of the doctrine itself was not challenged. In more recent cases, all on the graduate school level, inequality was found in that specific benefits enjoyed by white students were denied to Negro students of the same educational qualifications. *Missouri ex rel. Gaines* v. *Canada,* 305 U.S. 337; *Sipuel* v. *Oklahoma,* 332 U.S. 631; *Sweatt* v. *Painter,* 339 U.S. 629; *McLaurin* v. *Oklahoma State Regents,* 339 U.S. 637. In none of these cases was it necessary to re-examine the doctrine to grant relief to the Negro plaintiff. And in *Sweatt* v. *Painter, supra,* the Court expressly reserved decision on the question whether *Plessy* v. *Ferguson* should be held inapplicable to public education.

In the instant cases, that question is directly presented. Here, unlike *Sweatt* v. *Painter,* there are findings below that the Negro and white schools involved have been equalized, or are being equalized, with respect to buildings, curricula, qualifications and salaries of teachers, and other "tangible" factors. Our decision, therefore, cannot turn on merely a comparison of these tangible factors in the Negro and white schools involved in each of the cases. We must look instead to the effect of segregation itself on public education.

In approaching this problem, we cannot turn the clock back to 1868 when the Amendment was adopted, or even to 1896 when *Plessy* v. *Ferguson* was written. We must consider public education in the light of its full development and its present place in American life throughout the Nation. Only in this way can it be determined if segregation in public schools deprives these plaintiffs of the equal protection of the laws.

Today, education is perhaps the most important function of state and local governments. Compulsory school attendance laws and the great expenditures for education both demonstrate our recognition of the importance of education to our democratic society. It is required in the performance of our most basic public responsibilities, even service in the armed forces. It is the very foundation of good citizenship. Today it is a principal instrument in awakening the child to cultural values, in preparing him for later professional training, and in helping him to adjust normally to his environment. In these days, it is doubtful that any child may reasonably be expected to succeed in life if he is denied the opportunity of an education. Such an opportunity, where the state has undertaken to provide it, is a right which must be made available to all on equal terms.

We come then to the question presented: Does segregation of children in public schools solely on the basis of race, even though the physical facilities and other "tangible" factors may be equal, deprive the children of the minority group of equal educational opportunities? We believe that it does.

In *Sweatt* v. *Painter, supra*, in finding that a segregated law school for Negroes could not provide them equal educational opportunities, this Court relied in large part on "those qualities which are incapable of objective measurement but which make for greatness in a law school." In *McLaurin* v. *Oklahoma State Regents, supra*, the Court, in requiring that a Negro admitted to a white graduate school be treated like all other students, again resorted to intangible considerations: ". . . his ability to study, to engage in discussions and exchange views with other students, and, in general, to learn his profession." Such considerations apply with added force to children in grade and high schools. To separate them from others of similar age and qualifications solely because of their race generates a feeling of inferiority as to their status in the community that may affect their hearts and minds in a way unlikely ever to be undone. The effect of this separation on their educational opportunities was well stated by a finding in the Kansas case by a court which nevertheless felt compelled to rule against the Negro plaintiffs:

> "Segregation of white and colored children in public schools has a detrimental effect upon the colored children. The impact is greater when it has the sanction of the law; for the policy of separating the races is usually interpreted as denoting the inferiority of the negro group. A sense of inferiority affects the motivation of a child to learn. Segregation with the sanction of law, therefore, has a tendency to [retard] the educational and mental development of negro children and to deprive them of some of the benefits they would receive in a racial[ly] integrated school system."

Whatever may have been the extent of psychological knowledge at the time of *Plessy* v. *Ferguson*, this finding is amply supported by modern authority. Any language in *Plessy v. Ferguson* contrary to this finding is rejected.

We conclude that in the field of public education the doctrine of "separate but equal" has no place. Separate educational facilities are inherently unequal. Therefore, we hold that the plaintiffs and others similarly situated for whom the actions have been brought are, by reason of the segregation complained of, deprived of the equal protection of the laws guaranteed by the Fourteenth Amendment. This disposition makes unnecessary any discussion whether such segregation also violates the Due Process Clause of the Fourteenth Amendment.

NOTE

Brown v. Board of Education was perhaps the most controversial and the most important decision the Supreme Court has ever made. It led to a new stage in race relations in the United States and to an immense expansion in the coverage of the equal protection clause. Although for a decade the dictates of the opinion had to be enforced against stiff southern resistance and without congressional aid, eventually school districts largely complied with its mandate and Congress began to bear a large part of the burden of ensuring equality of treatment for black Americans. In the meantime, the Court struck down state segregation of libraries, beaches, swimming pools, and other facilities. It did so in brief opinions, without mentioning the possible relevance of the sociological conclusions it relied on in *Brown* to those other settings. (For further comment, see Essay, pp. 29–30.)

QUESTIONS

1.   The Court says that the history of the Fourteenth Amendment is inconclusive on the subject of school segregation. If that history indicates, as is widely believed, that the framers of the amendment did not believe it would outlaw school segregation, would it follow that the Court's decision in *Brown* was unjustified? Would that depend on whether the framers meant to leave open the possibility that the broad language of the equal protection clause might *later* be interpreted to forbid such practices? What role should the intention of the draftsmen play in the decision of such cases?

2.   Should the Court have relied so heavily on sociological evidence? To put the point differently, should the Court have accepted racial segregation if there had been no evidence that blacks fare worse in segregated schools? How could the Court know whether blacks would learn better in segregated schools or in integrated schools with a hostile white majority? Should it have asked that question? Since it relied so heavily in *Brown* on the evidence that segregation impedes the educational opportunity of blacks, should the Court have disposed of other kinds of segregation without reference to sociological evidence and without explanation of why they are also unconstitutional?

3.   Should the Court have examined the supposed reasons for school segregation? In *Korematsu*, it sustained a racial classification that undeniably disadvantaged Japanese-Americans; why, having first determined that school segregation worked to the detriment of blacks, did it not ask if there were powerful enough reasons to impose that detriment?

4.   Should the Court simply have said that racial divisions that work to the disadvantage of blacks, and perhaps other minority groups, are illegal? Should it have followed the first Justice Harlan and said that the Constitution requires states to be color-blind?

*Brown   II—The   Implementation Decision**

MR. CHIEF JUSTICE WARREN delivered the opinion of the Court.

These cases were decided on May 17, 1954. The opinions of that date, declaring the fundamental principle that racial discrimination in public education is unconstitutional, are incorporated herein by reference. . . .

Full implementation of these constitutional principles may require solution of varied local school problems. School authorities have the primary responsibility for elucidating, assessing, and solving these problems; courts will have to consider whether the action of school authorities constitutes good faith implementation of the governing constitutional principles. Because of their proximity to local conditions and the possible need for further hearings, the courts which

* Brown v. Board of Education, 349 U.S. 294, 75 S. Ct. 753, 99 L.Ed. 1083 (1955).

originally heard these cases can best perform this judicial appraisal. Accordingly, we believe it appropriate to remand the cases to those courts.

In fashioning and effectuating the decrees, the courts will be guided by equitable principles. Traditionally, equity has been characterized by a practical flexibility in shaping its remedies and by a facility for adjusting and reconciling public and private needs. These cases call for the exercise of these traditional attributes of equity power. At stake is the personal interest of the plaintiffs in admission to public schools as soon as practicable on a nondiscriminatory basis. To effectuate this interest may call for elimination of a variety of obstacles in making the transition to school systems operated in accordance with the constitutional principles set forth in our May 17, 1954, decision. Courts of equity may properly take into account the public interest in the elimination of such obstacles in a systematic and effective manner. But it should go without saying that the vitality of these constitutional principles cannot be allowed to yield simply because of disagreement with them.

While giving weight to these public and private considerations, the courts will require that the defendants make a prompt and reasonable start toward full compliance with our May 17, 1954, ruling. Once such a start has been made, the courts may find that additional time is necessary to carry out the ruling in an effective manner. The burden rests upon the defendants to establish that such time is necessary in the public interest and is consistent with good faith compliance at the earliest practicable date. To that end, the courts may consider problems related to administration, arising from the physical condition of the school plant, the school transportation system, personnel, revision of school districts and attendance areas into compact units to achieve a system of determining admission to the public schools on a nonracial basis, and revision of local laws and regulations which may be necessary in solving the foregoing problems. They will also consider the adequacy of any plans the defendants may propose to meet these problems and to effectuate a transition to a racially nondiscriminatory school system. During this period of transition, the courts will retain jurisdiction of these cases.

The judgments below, except that in the Delaware case, are accordingly reversed and the cases are remanded to the District Courts to take such proceedings and enter such orders and decrees consistent with this opinion as are necessary and proper to admit to public schools on a racially nondiscriminatory basis with all deliberate speed the parties to these cases. . . . .

QUESTION

Should the Supreme Court have announced, as it did, principles under which some blacks who had sought an integrated education could be denied such an education during their remaining time in school? Was the "all deliberate speed" formulation a proper accommodation to southern feelings, or might it have encouraged resistance? Should courts ever take such considerations into account, or should they simply proceed on the proposition that their judgments about legal rights will be enforced?

*Swann   v.   Charlotte-Mecklenburg Board of Education**

MR. CHIEF JUSTICE BURGER delivered the opinion of the Court.

We granted certiorari in this case to review important issues as to the duties of school authorities and the scope of powers of federal courts under this Court's mandates to eliminate racially separate public schools established and maintained by state action. *Brown* v. *Board of Education,* 347 U.S. 483 (1954) (*Brown I*).

This case and those argued with it arose in States having a long history of maintaining two sets of schools in a single school system delberately operated to carry out a governmental policy to separate pupils in schools solely on the basis of race. That was what *Brown* v. *Board of Education* was all about. These cases present us with the problem of defining in more precise terms than heretofore the scope of the duty of school authorities and district courts in implementing *Brown I* and the mandate to eliminate dual systems and establish unitary systems at once. Meanwhile district courts and courts of appeals have struggled in hundreds of cases with a multitude and variety of problems under this Court's general directive. . . . Their efforts, of necessity, embraced a process of "trial and error," and our effort to formulate guidelines must take into account their experience.

* 402 U.S. 1, S. Ct. 1267, 28 L.Ed.2d 554 (1971).

I

The Charlotte-Mecklenburg school system, the 43d largest in the Nation, encompasses the city of Charlotte and surrounding Mecklenburg County, North Carolina. The area is large—550 square miles—spanning roughly 22 miles east-west and 36 miles north-south. During the 1968–1969 school year the system served more than 84,000 pupils in 107 schools. Approximately 71% of the pupils were found to be white and 29% Negro. As of June 1969 there were approximately 24,000 Negro students in the system, of whom 21,000 attended schools within the city of Charlotte. Two-thirds of those 21,000—approximately 14,000 Negro students—attended 21 schools which were either totally Negro or more than 99% Negro. . . .

III

The objective today remains to eliminate from the public schools all vestiges of state-imposed segregation. . . . Once a right and a violation have been shown, the scope of a district court's equitable powers to remedy past wrongs is broad, for breadth and flexibility are inherent in equitable remedies. . . .

This allocation of responsibility once made, the Court attempted from time to time to provide some guidelines for the exercise of the district judge's discretion and for the reviewing function of the courts of appeals. However, a school desegragation case does not differ fundamentally from other cases involving the framing of equitable remedies to repair the denial of a constitutional right. The task is to correct, by a balancing of the individual and collective interests, the condition that offends the Constitution.

In seeking to define even in broad and general terms how far this remedial power extends it is important to remember that judicial powers may be exercised only on the basis of a constitutional violation. Remedial judicial authority does not put judges automatically in the shoes of school authorities whose powers are plenary. Judicial authority enters only when local authority defaults.

School authorities are traditionally charged with broad power to formulate and implement educational policy and might well conclude, for example, that in order to prepare students to live in a pluralistic society each school should have a prescribed ratio of Negro to white students reflecting the proportion for the district as a whole. To do this as an educational policy is within the broad discretionary powers of school authorites; absent a finding of a constitutional violation, however, that would not be within the authority of a federal court. As with any equity case, the nature of the violation determines the scope of the remedy. In default by the school authorities of their obligation to proffer acceptable remedies, a district court has broad power to fashion a remedy that will assure a unitary school system.

IV

We turn now to the problem of defining with more particularity the responsibilities of school authorities in desegregating a state-enforced dual school system in light of the Equal Protection Clause.

V

The central issue in this case is that of student assignment, and there are essentially four problem areas:

(1) to what extent racial balance or racial quotas may be used as an implement in a remedial order to correct a previously segregated system;

(2) whether every all-Negro and all-white school must be eliminated as an indispensable part of a remedial process of desegregation;

(3) what the limits are, if any, on the rearrangement of school districts and attendance zones, as a remedial measure; and

(4) what the limits are, if any, on the use of transportation facilities to correct state-enforced racial school segregation.

(1) RACIAL BALANCES OR RACIAL QUOTAS

The constant theme and thrust of every holding from *Brown I* to date is that state-enforced separation of races in public schools is discrimination that violates the Equal Protection Clause. The remedy commanded was to dismantle dual school systems.

We are concerened in these cases with the elimination of the discrimination inherent in the dual school systems, not with myriad factors of human existence which can cause discrimination in a multitude of ways on racial, religious, or ethnic grounds. The target of the cases from *Brown I* to the present was the dual school system. . . .

Our objective in dealing with the issues presented by these cases is to see that school authorities exclude no pupil of a racial minority from any school, directly or indirectly, on account of race; it does not and cannot embrace all the problems of racial prejudice, even when those problems contribute to disproportionate racial concentrations in some schools.

In this case it is urged that the District Court has imposed a racial balance requirement of 71%–29% on individual schools. The fact that no such objective was actually achieved—and would appear to be impossible—tends to blunt that claim, yet in the opinion and order of the District Court of December 1, 1969, we find that court directing

> "that efforts should be made to reach a 71–29 ratio in the various schools so that there will be no basis for contending that one school is racially different from the others. . . . [t]hat no school [should] be operated with an all-black or predominantly black student body, [and] [t]hat pupils of all grades [should] be assigned in such a way that as nearly as practicable the various schools at various grade levels have about the same proportion of black and white students."

The District Judge went on to acknowledge that variation "from that norm may be unavoidable." This contains intimations that the "norm" is a fixed mathematical racial balance reflecting the pupil constituency of the system. If we were to read the holding of the District Court to require, as a matter of substantive constitutional right, any particular degree of racial balance or mixing, that approach would be disapproved and we would be obliged to reverse. The constitutional command to desegregate schools does not mean that every school in every community must always reflect the racial composition of the school system as a whole.

As the voluminous record in this case shows, the predicate for the District Court's use of the 71%–29% ratio was twofold: first, its express finding, approved by the Court of Appeals and not challenged here, that a dual school system had been maintained by the school authorities at least until 1969; second, its finding, also approved by the Court of Appeals, that the school board had totally defaulted in its acknowledged duty to come forward with an acceptable plan of its own, notwithstanding the patient efforts of the District Judge who, on at least three occasions, urged the board to submit plans. . . .

We see therefore that the use made of mathematical ratios was no more than a starting point in the process of shaping a remedy, rather than an inflexible requirement. . . . In sum, the very limited use made of mathematical ratios was within the equitable remedial discretion of the District Court.

(2) ONE-RACE SCHOOLS

The record in this case reveals the familiar phenomenon that in metropolitan areas minority groups are often found concentrated in one part of the city. In some circumstances certain schools may remain all or largely of one race until new schools can be provided or neighborhood patterns change. Schools all or predominately of one race in a district of mixed population will require close scrutiny to determine that school assignments are not part of state-enforced segregation.

In light of the above, it should be clear that the existence of some small number of one-race, or virtually one-race, schools within a district is not in and of itself the mark of a system that still practices segregation by law. The district judge or school authorities should make every effort to achieve the greatest possible degree of actual desegregation and will thus necessarily be concerned with the elimination of one-race schools. No *per se* rule can adequately embrace all the difficulties of reconciling the competing interests involved; but in a system with a history of segregation the need for remedial criteria of sufficient specificity to assure a school authority's compliance with its constitutional duty warrants a presumption against schools that are substantially disproportionate in their racial composition. Where the school authority's proposed plan for conversion from a dual to a unitary system contemplates the continued existence of some schools that are all or predominately of one race, they have the burden of showing that such school assignments are genuinely nondiscriminatory. The court should scrutinize such schools, and the burden upon the school authorities will be to satisfy the court that their racial composition is not the result of present or past discriminatory action on their part.

An optional majority-to-minority transfer provision has long been recognized as a useful part of every desegregation plan. Provision for optional transfer of those in the majority racial group of a particular school to other schools where they will be in the minority is an indispensable remedy for those students willing to transfer to other schools in order to lessen the impact on them of the state-imposed stigma of segregation. In order to be effective, such a transfer arrangement must grant the transferring student free transportation and space must be made available in the school to which he desires to move. . . .

(3) REMEDIAL ALTERING OF ATTENDANCE ZONES

The maps submitted in these cases graphically demonstrate that one of the principal tools employed by school planners and by courts to break up the dual school system has been a frank—and sometimes drastic—gerrymandering of school districts and attendance zones. An additional step was pairing, "clustering," or "grouping" of schools with attendance assignments made deliberately to accomplish the transfer of Negro students out of formerly segregated Negro schools and transfer of white students to formerly all-Negro schools. More often than not, these zones are neither compact nor contiguous; indeed they may be on opposite ends of the city. As an interim corrective measure, this cannot be said to be beyond the broad remedial powers of a court.

Absent a constitutional violation there would be no basis for judicially ordering assignment of students on a racial basis. All things being equal, with no history of discrimination, it might well be desirable to assign pupils to schools nearest their homes. But all things are not equal in a system that has been deliberately constructed and maintained to enforce racial segregation. The remedy for such segregation may be administratively awkward, inconvenient, and even bizarre in some situations and may impose burdens on some; but all awkwardness and inconvenience cannot be avoided in the interim period when remedial adjustments are being made to eliminate the dual school systems. . . .

We hold that the pairing and grouping of noncontiguous school zones is a permissible tool and such action is to be considered in light of the objectives sought. . . .

(4) TRANSPORTATION OF STUDENTS

The scope of permissible transportation of students as an implement of a remedial decree has never been defined by this Court and by the very nature of the problem it cannot be defined with precision. No rigid guidelines as to student transportation can be given for application to the infinite variety of problems presented in thousands of situations. Bus transportation has been an integral part of the public education system for years, and was perhaps the single most important factor in the transition from the one-room schoolhouse to the consolidated school. Eighteen million of the Nation's public school children, approximately 39%, were transported to their schools by bus in 1969–1970 in all parts of the country. The importance of bus transportation as a normal and accepted tool of educational policy is readily discernible in this and the companion case. . . .

[The] decree provided that . . . the trips for elementary school pupils average about seven miles and the District Court found that they would take "not over 35 minutes at the most." In these circumstances we find no basis for holding that the local school authorities must not be required to employ bus transportation as one tool of school desegregation.

NOTE

This case illustrates the Supreme Court's unanimous approval of drastic remedies to rectify de jure segregation by school authorities. The opinion explicitly supports race-conscious remedies. School attendance zones are, it indicates, properly drawn with the racial composition of various areas in mind; and approval of student requests for transfer, as well as the determination of who will be "bused" from one zone to another, can depend on the race of the students involved. The Supreme Court's elaboration of remedial guidelines in 1971 is in large part the product of the experience of the decade and a half since *Brown*, which showed that freedom of choice (students choosing their schools) and simple geographical zoning failed to produce anything approximating an integrated system in most southern school districts.

The *Swann* opinion also addresses the possibility of racial assignment in districts with de facto segregation resulting from housing patterns. It indicates that school boards are not constitutionally compelled to do anything about de facto segregation, but that they may assign students on a racial basis to promote racial balance if they choose to do so. Some states and local school districts had taken such steps despite the absence of demonstrable illegal segregation in the past.

One consequence of Swann is that districts previously segregated de jure are likely to end up more fully integrated than those in which housing patterns alone have produced racial imbalance. This is part of the objection made to busing and to other remedies that go beyond simple geographical assignment. (For further comment, see Essay, pp. 38–42.)

QUESTIONS

1.   Is the Court correct in *Swann* to reject arguments that in correcting previous racial discrimination, school boards should act in a color-blind manner? Was it right to permit the racial character of neighborhoods to influence the drawing and combining of attendance zones? To permit the assignment of individual pupils to be determined by their race? Is the corrective use of race ethically defensible?

2.   Should the Court have drawn such a sharp line between de jure and de facto segregation? Should it have required efforts to eliminate or ameliorate de facto segregation?

3.   Was the Court wrong to allow the use of racial criteria to alter patterns of de facto segregation? Is such use of race ethically defensible? Do whites who are sent away from the school closest to their home have a legitimate objection that they are innocent victims of the school board's policy? As a school board member, would you approve racial assignment to modify patterns of de facto segregation?

*Loving v. Virginia**

MR. CHIEF JUSTICE WARREN delivered the opinion of the Court.

This case presents a constitutional question never addressed by this Court: whether a statutory scheme adopted by the State of Virginia to prevent marriages between persons solely on the basis of racial classifications violates the Equal Protection and Due Process Clauses of the Fourteenth Amendment. For reasons which seem to us to reflect the central meaning of those constitutional commands, we conclude that these statutes cannot stand consistently with the Fourteenth Amendment.

In June 1958, two residents of Virginia, Mildred Jeter, a Negro woman, and Richard Loving, a white man, were married in the District of Columbia pursuant to its laws. Shortly after their marriage, the Lovings returned to Virginia and established their marital abode in Caroline County. At the October Term, 1958, of the

* 388 U.S. 1, 87 S. Ct. 1817, 18 L.Ed.2d 1010 (1967).

Circuit Court of Caroline County, a grand jury issued an indictment charging the Lovings with violating Virginia's ban on interracial marriages. On January 6, 1959, the Lovings pleaded guilty to the charge and were sentenced to one year in jail; however, the trial judge suspended the sentence for a period of 25 years on the condition that the Lovings leave the State and not return to Virginia together for 25 years. . . .

Virginia is now one of 16 States which prohibit and punish marriages on the basis of racial classifications. Penalties for miscegenation arose as an incident to slavery and have been common in Virginia since the colonial period. The present statutory scheme dates from the adoption of the Racial Integrity Act of 1924, passed during the period of extreme nativism which followed the end of the First World War. The central features of this Act, and current Virginia law, are the absolute prohibition of a "white person" marrying other than another "white person," a prohibition against issuing marriage licenses until the issuing official is satisfied that the applicant's statements as to their race are correct, certificates of "racial composition" to be kept by both local and state registrars, and the carrying forward of earlier prohibitions against racial inter-marriage.

Because we reject the notion that the mere "equal application" of a statute containing racial classifications is enough to remove the classifications from the Fourteenth Amendment's proscription of all invidious racial discriminations, we do not accept the State's contention that these statutes should be upheld if there is any possible basis for concluding that they serve a rational purpose.

. . . [We] deal with statutes containing racial classifications, and the fact of equal application does not immunize that statute from the very heavy burden of justification which the Fourteenth Amendment has traditionally required of state statutes drawn according to race.

The State argues that statements in the Thirty-ninth Congress about the time of the passage of the Fourteenth Amendment indicate that the Framers did not intend the Amendment to make unconstitutional state miscegenation laws. . . . As for the various statements directly concerning the Fourteenth Amendment, we have said in connection with a related problem, that although these historical sources "cast some light" they are not sufficient to resolve the problem; "[a]t best, they are inconclusive." . . .

There can be no question but that Virginia's miscegenation statues rest solely upon distinctions drawn according to race. The statutes proscribe generally accepted conduct if engaged in by members of different races. Over the years, this Court has consistently repudiated "[d]istinctions between citizens solely because of their ancestry" as being "odious to a free people whose institutions are founded upon the doctrine of equality." *Hirabayashi* v. *United States* 320 U.S. 81, 100 (1943). At the very least, the Equal Protection Clause demands that racial classifications, especially suspect in criminal statutes, be subjected to the "most rigid scrutiny," *Korematsu* v. *United States* 323 U.S. 214, 216 (1944), and, if they are ever to be upheld, they must be shown to be necessary to the accomplishment of some permissible state objective, independent of the racial discrimination which it was the object of the Fourteenth Amendment to eliminate. . . .

There is patently no legitimate overriding purpose independent of invidious racial discrimination which justifies this classification. The fact that Virginia prohibits only interracial marriages involving white persons demonstrates that the racial classifications must stand on their own justification, as measures designed to maintain White Supremacy. We have consistently denied the constitutionality of measures which restrict the rights of citizens on account of race. There can be no doubt that restricting the freedom to marry solely because of racial classifications violates the central meaning of the Equal Protection Clause.

NOTE

The Court, in *Loving*, does not say that racial classifications are automatically unconstitutional, but it demands a "legitimate overriding purpose independent of invidious racial discrimination." In other equal protection cases involving "suspect" classifications or classifications interfering with the exercise of fundamental rights, the Court has indicated that a classification must be "necessary to the achievement of a compelling state interest." This test represents "strict scrutiny," the higher level of review for equal protection cases. For most other equal protection issues, the Court asks only whether the classification is rationally related to a legitimate state purpose.

Are there any legitimate state purposes underlying a statute that forbids interracial marriages? Should the Court simply have said that all statutes that separate races are unconstitutional? Should prison authorities be allowed to segregate prisoners temporarily if there has been a race riot within the prison?

VI.

The Modern Law of Discrimination: Gender

Reed v. Reed*

MR.CHIEF JUSTICE BURGER delivered the opinion of the Court.

Richard Lynn Reed, a minor, died intestate in Ada County, Idaho, on March 29, 1967. His adoptive parents, who had separated sometime prior to his death, are the parties to this appeal. Approximately seven months after Richard's death, his mother, appellant Sally Reed, filed a petition in the Probate Court of Ada County, seeking appointment as administratix of her son's estate. Prior to the date set for a hearing on the mother's petition, appellee Cecil Reed, the father of the decedent, filed a competing petition seeking to have himself appointed administrator of the son's estate. The probate court held a joint hearing on the two petitions and thereafter ordered that letters of administration be issued to appellee Cecil Reed upon his taking the oath and filing the bond required by law. The court treated §§ 15–312 and 15–314 of the Idaho Code as the controlling statutes and read those sections as compelling a preference for Cecil Reed because he was a male.

Section 15–312 designates the persons who are entitled to administer the estate of one who dies intestate. In making these designations, that section lists 11 classes of persons who are so entitled and provides, in substance, that the order in which those classes are listed in the section shall be determinative of the relative rights of competing applicants for letters of administration. One of the 11 classes so enumerated is "[t]he father or mother" of the person dying intestate. Under this section, then, appellant and appellee, being members of the same entitlement class, would seem to have been

* 404 U.S. 71, 92 S. Ct. 251, 30 L.Ed.2d 225 (1971).

equally entitled to administer their son's estate. Section 15–314 provides, however, that

> "[o]f several persons claiming and equally entitled [under § 15–312] to administer, males must be preferred to females, and relatives of the whole to those of the half blood."

. . .

Section 15–314 is restricted in its operation to those situations where competing applications for letters of administration have been filed by both male and female members of the same entitlement class established by § 15–312. In such situations, § 15–314 provides that different treatment be accorded to the applicants on the basis of their sex; it thus establishes a classification subject to scrutiny under the Equal Protection Clause.

In applying that clause, this Court has consistently recognized that the Fourteenth Amendment does not deny to States the power to treat different classes of persons in different ways. . . . The Equal Protection Clause of that amendment does, however, deny to States the power to legislate that different treatment be accorded to persons placed by a statute into different classes on the basis of criteria wholly unrelated to the objective of that statute. A classification "must be reasonable, not arbitrary, and must rest upon some ground of difference having a fair and substantial relation to the object of the legislation, so that all persons similarly circumstanced shall be treated alike." *Royster Guano Co. v. Virginia*, 253 U.S. 412, 415 (1920). The question presented by this case, then, is whether a difference in the sex of competing applicants for letters of administration bears a rational relationship to a state objective that is sought to be advanced by the operation of §§ 15–312 and 15–314.

In upholding the latter section, the Idaho Supreme Court concluded that its objective was to eliminate one area of controversy when two or more persons, equally entitled under §15–312, seek letters of administration and thereby present the probate court "with the issue of which one should be named." The court also concluded that where such persons are not of the same sex, the elimination of females from consideration "is neither an illogical nor arbitrary method devised by the legislature to resolve an issue that would otherwise require a hearing as to the relative merits . . . of the two or more petitioning relatives. . . ." 93 Idaho, at 514, 465 P. 2d, at 638.

Clearly the objective of reducing the workload on probate courts by eliminating one class of contests is not without some legitimacy. The crucial question, however, is whether § 15–314 advances that objective in a manner consistent with the command of the Equal Protection Clause. We hold that it does not. To give a mandatory preference to members of either sex over members of the other, merely to accomplish the elimination of hearings on the merits, is to make the very kind of arbitrary legislative choice forbidden by the Equal Protection Clause of the Fourteenth Amendment; and whatever may be said as to the positive values of avoiding intrafamily controversy, the choice in this context may not lawfully be mandated solely on the basis of sex.

NOTE

Starting with *Reed*, the Supreme Court has used the equal protection clause to invalidate classifications based on gender. In *Reed*, the Court ostensibly uses the deferential rational basis test, and concludes that the state law is unjustifiable even under that relaxed level of scrutiny. In fact, the Court appears to be exercising a more stringent form of review than it has traditionally used for ordinary economic and social issues. (For further comment, see Essay, pp. 35–37.)

QUESTIONS

1.   Given the pervasive distinctions based on gender that were undoubtedly accepted by most of those who proposed and ratified the Fourteenth Amendment, is it proper for the Supreme Court to use that amendment to invalidate such distinctions?

2.   What gender classifications, if any, are morally defensible? Is it proper to afford divorced wives alimony without also giving alimony to similarly situated husbands? To give mothers a preference in disputes over child custody? If, in fact, men are usually more experienced in financial affairs than women, why was Idaho's scheme not reasonable? Because it foreclosed the possibility of a woman showing in any particular case that she was more experienced? But why could not the absolute preference for men be justified on the basis of administrative convenience if in most cases men were more experienced?

*Frontiero v. Richardson** ============================

MR. JUSTICE BRENNAN announced the judgment of the Court and an opinion in which MR. JUSTICE DOUGLAS, MR. JUSTICE WHITE, and MR. JUSTICE MARSHALL join.

The question before us concerns the right of a female member of the uniformed services to claim her spouse as a "dependent" for the purposes of obtaining increased quarters allowances and medical and dental benefits under 37 U.S.C. §§ 401, 403, and 10 U.S.C. §§ 1072, 1076, on an equal footing with male members. Under these statutes, a serviceman may claim his wife as a "dependent" without regard to whether she is in fact dependent upon him for any part of her support. 37 U.S.C. § 401 (1); 10 U.S.C. § 1072 (2) (A). A servicewoman, on the other hand, may not claim her husband as a "dependent" under these programs unless he is in fact dependent upon her for over one-half of his support. 37 U.S.C. § 401; 10 U.S.C. § 1072 (2) (C). Thus, the question for decision is whether this difference in treatment constitutes an unconstitutional discrimination against servicewomen in violation of the Due Process Clause of the Fifth Amendment. . . .

I

In an effort to attract career personnel through re-enlistment, Congress established, in 37 U.S.C. § 401 *et seq.*, and 10 U.S.C. § 1071 *et seq.*, a scheme for the provision of fringe benefits to members of the uniformed services on a competitive basis with business and industry. Thus, under 37 U.S.C. § 403, a member of the uniformed services with dependents is entitled to an increased "basic allowance for quarters" and, under 10 U.S.C. § 1076, a member's dependents are provided comprehensive medical and dental care.

Appellant Sharron Frontiero, a lieutenant in the United States Air Force, sought increased quarters allowances, and housing and medical benefits for her husband, appellant Joseph Frontiero, on the ground that he was her "dependent." Although such benefits would automatically have been granted with respect to the wife of a male member of the uniformed services, appellant's application was de-

* 411 U.S. 677, 93 S. Ct. 1764, 36 L.Ed.2d 583 (1973).

nied because she failed to demonstrate that her husband was dependent on her for more than one-half of his support. Appellants then commenced this suit, contending that, by making this distinction, the statutes unreasonably discriminate on the basis of sex in violation of the Due Process Clause of the Fifth Amendment. In essence, appellants asserted that the discriminatory impact of the statutes is twofold: first, as a procedural matter, a female member is required to demonstrate her spouse's dependency, while no such burden is imposed upon male members; and, second, as a substantive matter, a male member who does not provide more than one-half of his wife's support receives benefits, while a similarly situated female member is denied such benefits.

II

At the outset, appellants contend that classifications based upon sex, like classifications based upon race, alienage, and national origin, are inherently suspect and must therefore be subjected to close judicial scrutiny. We agree and, indeed, find at least implicit support for such an approach in our unanimous decision only last Term in *Reed v. Reed*, 404 U.S. 71 (1971).

There can be no doubt that our Nation has had a long and unfortunate history of sex discrimination. Traditionally, such discrimination was rationalized by an attitude of "romantic paternalism" which, in practical effect, put women, not on a pedestal, but in a cage. Indeed, this paternalistic attitude became so firmly rooted in our national consciousness that, 100 years ago, a distinguished Member of this Court was able to proclaim:

"Man is, or should be, woman's protector and defender. The natural and proper timidity and delicacy which belongs to the female sex evidently unfits it for many of the occupations of civil life. The constitution of the family organization, which is founded in the divine ordinance, as well as in the nature of things, indicates the domestic sphere as that which properly belongs to the domain and functions of womanhood. The harmony, not to say identity, of interests and views which belong, or should belong, to the family institution is repugnant to the idea of a woman adopting a distinct and independent career from that of her husband. . . .

". . . The paramount destiny and mission of woman are to fulfil the noble and benign offices of wife and mother. This is the law of the

Creator." *Bradwell v. State*, 16 Wall. 130, 141 (1873) (Bradley, J., concurring).

As a result of notions such as these, our statute books gradually became laden with gross, stereotyped distinctions between the sexes and, indeed, throughout much of the 19th century the position of women in our society was, in many respects, comparable to that of blacks under the pre–Civil War slave codes. Neither slaves nor women could hold office, serve on juries, or bring suit in their own names, and married women traditionally were denied the legal capacity to hold or convey property or to serve as legal guardians of their own children. . . . And although blacks were guaranteed the right to vote in 1870, women were denied even that right—which is itself "preservative of other basic civil and political rights"—until adoption of the Nineteenth Amendment half a century later.

It is true, of course, that the position of women in America has improved markedly in recent decades. Nevertheless, it can hardly be doubted that, in part because of the high visibility of the sex characteristic, women still face pervasive, although at times more subtle, discrimination in our educational institutions, in the job market and, perhaps most conspicuously, in the political arena. . . .

Moreover, since sex, like race and national origin, is an immutable characteristic determined solely by the accident of birth, the imposition of special disabilities upon the members of a particular sex because of their sex would seem to violate "the basic concept of our system that legal burdens should bear some relationship to individual responsibility. . . ." . . . And what differentiates sex from such nonsuspect statuses as intelligence or physical disability, and aligns it with the recognized suspect criteria, is that the sex characteristic frequently bears no relation to ability to perform or contribute to society. . . .

. . . [O]ur prior decisions make clear that although efficacious administration of governmental programs is not without some importance, "the Constitution recognizes higher values than speed and efficiency." . . . And when we enter the realm of "strict judicial scrutiny," there can be no doubt that "administrative convenience" is not a shibboleth, the mere recitation of which dictates constitutionality. . . . On the contrary, any statutory scheme which draws a sharp line between the sexes, *solely* for the purpose of achieving administrative convenience, necessarily commands "dissimilar treatment for men and women who are . . . similarly situated," and therefore involves the "very kind of arbitrary legislative choice forbidden by the Constitution. . . ." *Reed v. Reed*, 404 U.S., at 77, 76. We therefore conclude that, by according differential treatment to male and female members of the uniformed services for the sole purpose of achieving administrative convenience, the challenged statutes violate the Due Process Clause of the Fifth Amendment insofar as they require a female member to prove the dependency of her husband.

MR. JUSTICE POWELL, with whom THE CHIEF JUSTICE and MR. JUSTICE BLACKMUN join, concurring in the judgment.

I agree that the challenged statutes constitute an unconstitutional discrimination against servicewomen in violation of the Due Process Clause of the Fifth Amendment, but I cannot join the opinion of MR. JUSTICE BRENNAN, which would hold that all classifications based upon sex, "like classifications based upon race, alienage, and national origin," are "inherently suspect and must therefore be subjected to close judicial scrutiny." *Ante*, at 682. It is unnecessary for the Court in this case to characterize sex as a suspect classification, with all of the far-reaching implications of such a holding. *Reed v. Reed*, 404 U.S. 71 (1971), which abundantly supports our decision today, did not add sex to the narrowly limited group of classifications which are inherently suspect. In my view, we can and should decide this case on the authority of *Reed* and reserve for the future any expansion of its rationale.

There is another, and I find compelling, reason for deferring a general categorizing of sex classifications as invoking the strictest test of judicial scrutiny. The Equal Rights Amendment, which if adopted will resolve the substance of this precise question, has been approved by the Congress and submitted for ratification by the States. If this Amendment is duly adopted, it will represent the will of the people accomplished in the manner prescribed by the Constitution. By acting prematurely and unnecessarily, as I view it, the Court has assumed a decisional responsibility at the very time when state legislatures, functioning within the traditional democratic process, are debating the proposed Amendment. It seems to me that this reaching out to pre-empt by judicial action a major political decision which is currently in process of resolution does not reflect appropriate respect for duly prescribed legislative processes.

There are times when this Court, under our system, cannot avoid a constitutional decision on issues which normally should be resolved by the elected representatives of the people. But democratic institutions are weakened, and confidence in the restraint of the Court is impaired, when we appear unnecessarily to decide sensitive issues of broad social and political importance at the very time they are under consideration within the prescribed constitutional processes.

NOTE

In *Frontiero*, there is no majority opinion. Four justices urge that gender should be treated as a suspect classification; four others agree with the result in the case but do not join Justice Brennan's opinion. Despite the failure of the Court to agree on a standard of review, it was clear after this case, if it was not already evident from *Reed v. Reed*, that the Court was prepared to strike down gender classifications unless they were supported by powerful justifications. In subsequent cases, the Court did invalidate a succession of laws drawing lines between men and women.

The reason why *Frontiero* presents an issue under the due process clause of the Fifth Amendment, rather than under the equal protection clause of the Fourteenth Amendment, is because the latter applies only to state governments, while the Fifth Amendment restricts the federal government. Despite the absence of any explicit equal protection language applicable against the federal government, the Supreme Court has treated it as subject to the same sorts of constraints on classification as the states.

The classification in *Frontiero* is typical of many of those drawn on gender lines. One class of women is disadvantaged while another class of women benefits. The woman wage earner is denied a privilege afforded her male counterpart; the female spouse of the male wage earner is afforded benefits not given to her male counterpart. In this and similar cases, the Supreme Court has not believed it relevant that some other women may benefit from the classification; instead it has focused on the women who are denied privileges that males have.

QUESTION

Should gender, like race, be treated as a "suspect" basis for classification? Is it morally defensible to treat women, as a class, differently from men if most women are different in the relevant respect from most men? In other words, if most female spouses of servicemen are dependent on their husbands for half of their support and most male spouses of women in service are not so dependent, is that a sufficient justification for the statutory distinction challenged in *Frontiero*?

*Craig v. Boren**

MR. JUSTICE BRENNAN delivered the opinion of the Court.

The interaction of two sections of an Oklahoma statute, Tit. 37 Okla. Stat. §§ 241 and 245 (1958 and Supp. 1976), prohibits the sale of "nonintoxicating" 3.2% beer to males under the age of 21 and to females under the age of 18. The question to be decided is whether such a gender-based differential constitutes a denial to males 18–20 years of age of the equal protection of the laws in violation of the Fourteenth Amendment. . . .

II

A

. . . Analysis may appropriately begin with the reminder that *Reed* emphasized that statutory classifications that distinguish between males and females are "subject to scrutiny under the Equal Protection Clause." 404 U.S., at 75. To withstand constitutional challenge, previous cases establish that classifications by gender must serve important governmental objectives and must be substantially related to achievement of those objectives. Thus, in *Reed*, the objectives of "reducing the workload on probate courts," *id.*, at 76, and "avoiding intrafamily controversy," *id.*, at 77, were deemed of insufficient importance to sustain use of an overt gender criterion in the appointment of administrators of intestate decedents' estates. Decisions following *Reed* similarly have rejected administrative ease and convenience as sufficiently important objectives to justify gender-based classifications. . . .

B

The District Court recognized that *Reed v. Reed* was controlling. In applying the teachings of that case, the court found the requisite

* 429 U.S. 190, 97 S. Ct. 451, 50 L.Ed.2d 397 (1976).

important governmental objective in the traffic-safety goal proffered by the Oklahoma Attorney General. It then concluded that the statistics introduced by the appellees established that the gender-based distinction was substantially related to achievement of that goal.

C

We accept for purposes of discussion the District Court's identification of the objective underlying §§ 241 and 245 as the enhancement of traffic safety. Clearly, the protection of public health and safety represents an important function of state and local governments. However, appellees' statistics in our view cannot support the conclusion that the gender-based distinction closely serves to achieve that objective and therefore the distinction cannot under *Reed* withstand equal protection challenge.

The appellees introduced a variety of statistical surveys. First, an analysis of arrest statistics for 1973 demonstrated that 18–20-year-old male arrests for "driving under the influence" and "drunkenness" substantially exceeded female arrests for that same age period. Similarly, youths aged 17–21 were found to be overrepresented among those killed or injured in traffic accidents, with males again numerically exceeding females in this regard. Third, a random roadside survey in Oklahoma City revealed that young males were more inclined to drive and drink beer than were their female counterparts. Fourth, Federal Bureau of Investigation nationwide statistics exhibited a notable increase in arrests for "driving under the influence." . . .

Even were this statistical evidence accepted as accurate, it nevertheless offers only a weak answer to the equal protection question presented here. The most focused and relevant of the statistical surveys, arrests of 18–20-year-olds for alcohol-related driving offenses, exemplifies the ultimate unpersuasiveness of this evidentiary record. Viewed in terms of the correlation between sex and the actual activity that Oklahoma seeks to regulate—driving while under the influence of alcohol—the statistics broadly establish that .18% of females and 2% of males in that age group were arrested for that offense. While such a disparity is not trivial in a statistical sense, it hardly can form the basis for employment of a gender line as a classifying device. Certainly if maleness is to serve as a proxy for drinking and driving, a correlation of 2% must be considered an unduly tenuous "fit." Indeed, prior cases have consistently rejected the use of sex as a decisionmaking factor even though the statutes in question certainly rested on far more predictive empirical relationships than this.

Moreover, the statistics exhibit a variety of other shortcomings that seriously impugn their value to equal protection analysis. Setting aside the obvious methodological problems, the surveys do not adequately justify the salient features of Oklahoma's gender-based traffic-safety law. None purports to measure the use and dangerousness of 3.2% beer as opposed to alcohol generally, a detail that is of particular importance since, in light of its low alcohol level, Oklahoma apparently considers the 3.2% beverage to be "nonintoxicating." . . .

. . . [T]he showing offered by the appellees does not satisfy us that sex represents a legitimate, accurate proxy for the regulation of drinking and driving. In fact, when it is further recognized that Oklahoma's statute prohibits only the selling of 3.2% beer to young males and not their drinking the beverage once acquired (even after purchase by their 18–20-year-old female companions), the relationship between gender and traffic safety becomes far too tenuous to satisfy *Reed's* requirement that the gender-based difference be substantially related to achievement of the statutory objective.

We hold, therefore, that under *Reed*, Oklahoma's 3.2% beer statute invidiously discriminates against males 18–20 years of age.

NOTE

This rather unimportant case marks the emergence in a majority opinion of an intermediate standard of review in gender cases. The Court says that to withstand attack, classifications by gender "must serve important governmental objectives and must be substantially related to achievement of those objectives." Clearly, this implies more exacting examination than the traditional rational basis test. But by not demanding that the classification be *necessary* to the achievement of a *compelling* state interest, the test is more relaxed than the strict scrutiny applicable to racial classifications. The Supreme Court's subsequent approval of draft registration limited to males demonstrates its continuing willingness to accept gender classifications that it finds to be supported by substantial reasons. (For comment on the standard of review, see Essay, p. 77.)

QUESTIONS

1.   Is the statistical foundation for the Oklahoma statute more persuasive than the Court indicates, particularly when one considers the relative insignificance of the right to drink 3.2% beer? Are any distinctions drawn on the basis of age between males and females morally defensible? Is it, for example, proper to treat consensual sexual intercourse between a twenty-year-old male and a sixteen-year-old female as the crime of statutory rape committed by the male, and not to make criminal at all such intercourse between a twenty-year-old female and a sixteen-year-old male?

2.   Is an intermediate standard of review appropriate for gender cases? Does it represent a proper allocation of responsibility between the legislatures and the courts in this area? What is the justification for a stricter standard of review than "rational basis"? The fact that gender is an immutable characteristic? The underrepresentation of females in legislative bodies? Some other reason?

The Equal Rights Amendment, Proposed Amendment XXVII to the Constitution

Section 1. Equality of rights under the law shall not be denied or abridged by the United States or by any State on account of sex.

Section 2. The Congress shall have the power to enforce, by appropriate legislation, the provisions of this article.

NOTE

Had this amendment been ratified by the requisite number of states, it, rather than the equal protection clause of the Fourteenth Amendment, would then have become the point of focus for claims of gender discrimination. Proponents of the amendment indicated that it was not intended to be an absolute ban on all forms of sexual classification, permitting, for example, men's and women's restrooms.

QUESTION

Does the language of the amendment appear to bar all sexual differentiations? What practices do you think might have been forbidden under the amendment that might be allowable under the equal protection clause? A military draft for males only? Would ratification of the amendment have been valuable for symbolic reasons?

VII.

The Modern Law of Discrimination: Statutory and Administrative Protections

Civil Rights Act of 1964, * *Title III*

§ 2000A. PROHIBITION AGAINST DISCRIMINATION OR SEGREGATION IN PLACES OF PUBLIC ACCOMMODATION—EQUAL ACCESS

(a) All persons shall be entititled to the full and equal enjoyment of the goods, services, facilities, privileges, advantages, and accommodations of any place of public accommodation, as defined in this section, without discrimination or segregation on the ground of race, color, religion, or national origin.

ESTABLISHMENTS AFFECTING INTERSTATE COMMERCE OR
SUPPORTED IN THEIR ACTIVITIES BY STATE ACTION AS PLACES OF
PUBLIC ACCOMMODATION; LODGINGS; FACILITIES PRINCIPALLY
ENGAGED IN SELLING FOOD FOR CONSUMPTION ON THE PREMISES;
GASOLINE STATIONS; PLACES OF EXHIBITION OR ENTERTAINMENT:
OTHER COVERED ESTABLISHMENTS

(b) Each of the following establishments which serves the public is a place of public accommodation within the meaning of this subchapter if its operations affect commerce, or if discrimination or segregation by it is supported by State action:

(1) any inn, hotel, motel, or other establishment which provides lodging to transient guests, other than an establishment located within a building which contains not more than five rooms for rent or hire and which is actually occupied by the proprietor of such establishment as his residence;

(2) any restaurant, cafeteria, lunchroom, lunch counter, soda fountain, or other facility principally engaged in selling food for

* 42 U.S.C.

consumption on the premises, including, but not limited to, any such facility located on the premises of any retail establishment; or any gasoline station;

(3) any motion picture house, theater, concert hall, sports arena, stadium or other place of exhibition or entertainment; and

(4) any establishment (A) (i) which is physically located within the premises of any establishment otherwise covered by this subsection, or (ii) within the premises of which is physically located any such covered establishment, and (B) which holds itself out as serving patrons of such covered establishment.

OPERATIONS AFFECTING COMMERCE: CRITERIA; "COMMERCE" DEFINED

(c) The operations of an establishment affect commerce within the meaning of this subchapter if (1) it is one of the establishments described in paragraph (1) of subsection (b) of this section; (2) in the case of an establishment described in paragraph (2) of subsection (b) of this section, it serves or offers to serve interstate travelers or a substantial portion of the food which it serves, or gasoline or other products which it sells, has moved in commerce; (3) in the case of an establishment described in paragraph (3) of subsection (b) of this section, it customarily presents films, performances, athletic teams, exhibitions, or other sources of entertainment which move in commerce; and (4) in the case of an establishment described in paragraph (4) of subsection (b) of this section, it is physically located within the premises of, or there is physically located within its premises, an establishment the operations of which affect commerce within the meaning of this subsection. For purposes of this section, "commerce" means travel, trade, traffic, commerce, transportation, or communication among the several States, or between the District of Columbia and any State, or between any foreign country or any territory or possession and any State or the District of Columbia, or between points in the same State but through any other State or the District of Columbia or a foreign country.

SUPPORT BY STATE ACTION

(d) Discrimination or segregation by an establishment is supported by State action within the meaning of this subchapter if such discrimination or segregation (1) is carried on under color of any law, statute, ordinance, or regulation; or (2) is carried on under color of any custom or usage required or enforced by officials of the State or political subdivision thereof; or (3) is required by action of the State or political subdivision thereof.

PRIVATE ESTABLISHMENTS

(e) The provisions of this subchapter shall not apply to a private club or other establishment not in fact open to the public, except to the extent that the facilities of such establishment are made available to the customers or patrons of an establishment within the scope of subsection (b) of this section.

NOTE

The Civil Rights Act of 1964 was the Congress's first major piece of civil rights legislation in this century. It was passed a little more than half a year after John F. Kennedy's assassination, Lyndon B. Johnson having made an emotional appeal to Congress to guarantee equal rights for blacks. The public accommodations section was in part responsive to sit-in demonstrations, in which blacks had been engaging for some years, refusing to leave lunch counters and other facilities when asked to do so by owners whose policy was to segregate.

At the time the act was passed, the most obvious basis of congressional power seemed to be the commerce clause, and the statute is framed in those terms. Note, however, that it reaches establishments whose connection with interstate commerce is not too powerful. It covers any restaurant or lunchroom that "offers to serve interstate travelers" or serves food a "substantial portion" of which has moved in commerce. Despite its broad reach, the Supreme Court had little difficulty sustaining the public accommodations section as a proper exercise of Congress's power to regulate interstate commerce. (For further comment, see Essay, pp. 12–13.)

QUESTIONS

1.   Does the act go too far in infringing the liberty of owners of establishments selling food? For example, should a local soda fountain that very occasionally serves an interstate traveler and gets some of its food from out-of-state be required to refrain from racial

discrimination? If it is appropriate that even such establishments not be allowed to discriminate, is it appropriate that the rule be laid down by the federal government, or should the matter be left for state or local regulation?

    2.   Does the act create too many exceptions? For example, should a family that rents rooms overnight in its own home be permitted to discriminate as paragraph (1) of subsection (b) provides? Should private clubs that have dining facilities be permitted to discriminate?

Civil Rights Act of 1964,* ═══════════════
Title VII
§ 2000e. DEFINITIONS

For the purposes of this subchapter—

(a) The term "person" includes one or more individuals, governments, governmental agencies, political subdivisions, labor unions, partnerships, associations, corporations, legal representatives, mutual companies, joint-stock companies, trusts, unincorporated organizations, trustees, trustees in bankruptcy, or receivers.

    (b) The term "employer" means a person engaged in an industry affecting commerce who has fifteen or more employees for each working day in each of twenty or more calendar weeks in the current or preceding calendar year. . . .

§ 2000e–2. UNLAWFUL EMPLOYMENT PRACTICES— EMPLOYER PRACTICES

(a) It shall be an unlawful employment practice for an employer—

    (1) to fail or refuse to hire or to discharge any individual, or otherwise to discriminate against any individual with respect to his compensation, terms, conditions, or privileges of employment, because of such individual's race, color, religion, sex, or national origin; or

    (2) to limit, segregate, or classify his employees or applicants for employment in any way which would deprive or tend to deprive any individual of employment opportunities or other-

* 42 U.S.C.

wise adversely affect his status as an employee, because of such individual's race, color, religion, sex, or national origin.

NOTE

The inclusion of sex as an impermissible basis of differentiation was proposed by opponents of a congressional ban on racial discrimination in employment; they hoped that including a prohibition on sexual discrimination would lead to defeat of the entire bill. But Title VII of the 1964 act was nevertheless adopted and, during a period before the full swell of women's liberation, gave women a very important weapon in the fight for job opportunities. Although the federal legislation reaches only employers of fifteen or more persons, state and local legislation often goes further, prohibiting discrimination in employment relationships much more broadly.

In *Griggs v. Duke Power Co.* 401 U.S. 424 (1971), the Supreme Court said that an employer could violate the act even without engaging in intentional discrimination. If it used a test for employment, such as an aptitude test or requirement of a high school diploma, that disproportionately excluded blacks or women, and it could not demonstrate a correlation between successful performance on the test and successful performance of the relevant job, then use of the test had the effect of discriminating and was forbidden by the statute. This reading of the statute to bar use of tests with a "disproportionate impact" that are not required by "business necessity" considerably strengthens the hand of those challenging hiring policies, because it means they need not necessarily prove that an employer consciously discriminated.

The scope of appropriate remedies presents some of the most complex issues in cases arising under the statute and in related cases in which governmental discrimination in employment is determined to be unconstitutional. Generally, trial courts have considerable latitude in determining precisely what remedy will be afforded in a particular situation; and when the parties can agree on a remedy, that is likely to be accepted. Both through agreement and by decision of trial courts, remedies in employment discrimination cases have frequently included an obligation on the employer's part to hire a specified percentage of new employees from the group previously discriminated against. (For further comment, see Essay, pp. 42–47.)

QUESTIONS

1. Are there any employment relationships in which you believe employers should be permitted to discriminate on racial or sexual grounds? In the hiring of a baby-sitter for one's child?

2. Is it unfair to the employer to base a finding of discrimination on its use of employment tests that have a disproportionate impact and are not required by "business necessity"?

3. Are remedies that require an employer to hire a specified percentage of members of a certain group appropriate? In order to prevent covert discrimination against members of that group? In order to give jobs to some persons who were previously the victims of the employer's discrimination but cannot now be individually identified as such? In order to avoid continuing effects of prior discrimination? In order to compensate some members of the group for wrongs done to other members of the group? Should women or blacks now entering the job market be given special treatment because women and blacks entering the job market five years ago were subject to discrimination?

Civil Rights Act of 1968*

§ 3604. DISCRIMINATION IN SALE OR RENTAL OF HOUSING

As made applicable by section 3603 of this title and except as exempted by sections 3603(b) and 3607 of this title, it shall be unlawful—

(a) To refuse to sell or rent after the making of a bona fide offer, or to refuse to negotiate for the sale or rental of, or otherwise make unavailable or deny, a dwelling to any person because of race, color, religion, sex, or national origin.

(b) To discriminate against any person in the terms, conditions, or privileges of sale or rental of a dwelling, or in the provision of services or facilities in connection therewith, because of race, color, religion, sex, or national origin.

* 42 U.S.C.

156 *Discrimination and Reverse Discrimination*

(c) To make, print, or publish, or cause to be made, printed, or published any notice, statement, or advertisement, with respect to the sale or rental of a dwelling that indicates any preference, limitation, or discrimination based on race, color, religion, sex, or national origin, or an intention to make any such preference, limitation, or discrimination.

(d) To represent to any person because of race, color, religion, sex, or national origin that any dwelling is not available for inspection, sale, or rental when such dwelling is in fact so available.

NOTE

Section 3603(b) exempts from the ban on discrimination sales of single-family houses when the owner does not use a real estate broker; and the rental of rooms in an owner's own residence.

Shortly after the passage of this legislation, the Supreme Court interpreted the 1866 Civil Rights Act to bar racial discrimination in the sale of private property. Over a vigorous dissent arguing that the Reconstruction statute meant to afford blacks only equal legal power to hold, buy, and sell property, the majority in *Jones v. Alfred H. Mayer Co.*, 392 U.S. 409 (1968), decided that the right of blacks to purchase property meant a right not to be discriminated against because of race by a private seller. This reading of the 1866 act made the substantive coverage of the 1968 act mostly redundant, although the 1968 act also contains remedial provisions of independent importance. In a later case, the Court said that the right of blacks to make and enforce contracts guaranteed by the 1866 act includes a right not to suffer racial discrimination in the choice of pupils by a private school.

In the *Jones* case, the Court sustained the 1866 act by a broad reading of Congress's power under the Thirteenth Amendment, holding that the enforcement clause of the amendment grants Congress authority to attack private racial discrimination as a means of eliminating the "badges and incidents" of slavery.

QUESTIONS

1. Should a family that rents a room in its own home to a boarder be permitted to discriminate on racial or sexual grounds? Are there other situations involving housing in which such discrimination should be permitted?

THE MODERN LAW OF DISCRIMINATION: PROTECTIONS

2. Do you think the language of the 1866 act supports the reading of the majority in *Jones* or that of the dissenters?

Civil Rights Act of 1964,* Title VI

§ 2000d. PROHIBITION AGAINST EXCLUSION FROM PARTICIPATION IN, DENIAL OF BENEFITS OF, AND DISCRIMINATION UNDER FEDERALLY ASSISTED PROGRAMS ON GROUND OF RACE, COLOR, OR NATIONAL ORIGIN

No person in the United States shall, on the ground of race, color or national origin, be excluded from participation in, be denied the benefits of, or be subjected to discrimination under any program or activity receiving Federal financial assistance.

Executive Order 11246 (1965), Equal Employment Opportunity

Under and by virtue of the authority vested in me as President of the United States by the Constitution and statutes of the United States, it is ordered as follows:

PART I—NONDISCRIMINATION IN GOVERNMENT EMPLOYMENT

SECTION 101. It is the policy of the Government of the United States to provide equal opportunity in Federal employment for all qualified persons, to prohibit discrimination in employment because of race, creed, color, or national origin, and to promote the full realization of equal employment opportunity through a positive, continuing program in each executive department and agency. The policy of equal opportunity applies to every aspect of Federal employment policy and practice.

SEC. 102. The head of each executive department and agency shall establish and maintain a positive program of equal employment opportunity for all civilian employees and applicants for employment within his jurisdiction in accordance with the policy set forth in Section 101.

* 42 U.S.C.

PART II—NONDISCRIMINATION IN EMPLOYMENT BY GOVERNMENT CONTRACTORS AND SUBCONTRACTORS

SUBPART A—DUTIES OF THE SECRETARY OF LABOR

SEC. 201. The Secretary of Labor shall be responsible for the administration of Parts II and III of this Order and shall adopt such rules and regulations and issue such orders as he deems necessary and appropriate to achieve the purposes thereof.

SUBPART B—CONTRACTORS' AGREEMENTS

SEC. 202. . . . Government contracting agencies shall include in every Government contract hereafter entered into the following provisions:

"During the performance of this contract, the contractor agrees as follows:

"(1) The contractor will not discriminate against any employee or applicant for employment because of race, creed, color, or national origin. The contractor will take affirmative action to ensure that applicants are employed, and that employees are treated during employment, without regard to their race, creed, color, or national origin. Such action shall include, but not be limited to the following: employment, upgrading, demotion, or transfer; recruitment or re-cruitment advertising; layoff or termination; rates of pay or other forms of compensation; and selection for training, including appren-ticeship. The contractor agrees to post in conspicuous places, avail-able to employees and applicants for employment, notices to be provided by the contracting officer setting forth the provisions of this nondiscrimination clause.

"(2) The contractor will, in all solicitations or advertisements for employees placed by or on behalf of the contractor, state that all qualified applicants will receive consideration for employment with-out regard to race, creed, color, or national origin.

"(3) The contractor will send to each labor union or representa-tive of workers with which he has a collective bargaining agreement or other contract or understanding, a notice, to be provided by the agency contracting officer, advising the labor union or workers' representative of the contractor's commitments under Section 202 of Executive Order No. 11246 of September 24, 1965, and shall post copies of the notice in conspicuous places available to employees and applicants for employment."

. . .

Executive Order 11375 (1967), Amending Executive Order No 11246, Relating To Equal Employment Opportunity

It is the policy of the United States Government to provide equal opportunity in Federal employment and in employment by Federal contractors on the basis of merit and without discrimination because of race, color, religion, sex or national origin.

The Congress, by enacting Title VII of the Civil Rights Act of 1964, enunciated a national policy of equal employment opportunity in private employment, without discrimination because of race, color, religion, sex or national origin.

. Executive Order No. 11246 of September 24, 1965, carried forward a program of equal employment opportunity in Government employment, employment by Federal contractors and subcontractors and employment under Federally assisted construction contracts regardless of race, creed, color or national origin.

It is desirable that the equal employment opportunity programs provided for in Executive order No. 11246 expressly embrace discrimination on account of sex.

NOW, THEREFORE, by virtue of the authority vested in me as President of the United States by the Constitution and statutes of the United States, it is ordered that Executive Order No. 11246 of September 24, 1965, be amended as follows:

(1) Section 101 of Part I, concerning nondiscrimination in Government employment, is revised to read as follows:

"Sec. 101. It is the policy of the Government of the United States to provide equal opportunity in Federal employment for all qualified persons, to prohibit discrimination in employment because of race, color, religion, sex or national origin, and to promote the full realization of equal employment opportunity through a positive, continuing program in each executive department and agency. The policy of equal opportunity applies to every aspect of Federal employment policy and practice." . . .

(3) Paragraph (1) . . . of the quoted required contract provisions in section 202 of Part II, concerning nondiscrimination in

employment by Government contractors and subcontractors, is revised to read as follows:

"(1) The contractor will not discriminate against any employee or applicant for employment because of race, color, religion, sex, or national origin. The contractor will take affirmative action to ensure that applicants are employed, and that employees are treated during employment, without regard to their race, color, religion, sex or national origin. Such action shall include, but not be limited to the following: employment, upgrading, demotion, or transfer; recruitment or recruitment advertising; layoff or termination; rates of pay or other forms of compensation; and selection for training, including apprenticeship. The contractor agrees to post in conspicuous places, available to employees and applicants for employment, notices to be provided by the contracting officer setting forth the provisions of this nondiscrimination clause.

*Regulations of Department of Health, Education, and Welfare**

PART 80—NONDISCRIMINATION UNDER PROGRAMS RECEIVING FEDERAL ASSISTANCE THROUGH THE DEPARTMENT OF HEALTH, EDUCATION, AND WELFARE EFFECTUATION OF TITLE VI OF THE CIVIL RIGHTS ACT OF 1964

§ 80.1 PURPOSE

The purpose of this part is to effectuate the provisions of title VI of the Civil Rights Act of 1964 (hereafter referred to as the "Act") to the end that no person in the United States shall: on the ground of race, color, or national origin, be excluded from participation in, be denied the benefits of, or be otherwise subjected to discrimination under any program or activity receiving Federal financial assistance from the Department of Health, Education, and Welfare.

* * *

§ 80.3 DISCRIMINATION PROHIBITED

(a) *General.* No person in the United States shall, on the ground

* 45 CFR 80 (1977).

of race, color, or national origin be excluded from participation in, be denied the benefits of, or be otherwise subjected to discrimination under any program to which this part applies.

(b) *Specific discriminatory actions prohibited.* . . .

(6)(i) In administering a program regarding which the recipient has previously discriminated against persons on the ground of race, color, or national origin, the recipient must take affirmative action to overcome the effects of prior discrimination.

(ii) Even in the absence of such prior discrimination, a recipient in administering a program may take affirmative action to overcome the effects of conditions which resulted in limiting participation by persons of a particular race, color, or national origin.

* * *

§ 80.5 ILLUSTRATIVE APPLICATION

(i) . . . In some situations, even though past discriminatory practices attributable to a recipient or applicant have been abandoned, the consequences of such practices continue to impede the full availability of a benefit. If the efforts required of the applicant or recipient to provide information as to the availability of the program or activity and the rights of beneficiaries under this regulation, have failed to overcome these consequences, it will become necessary under the requirement stated in (i) of § 80.3(b) (6) for such applicant or recipient to take additional steps to make the benefits fully available to racial and nationality groups previously subject to discrimination. This action might take the form, for example, of special arrangements for obtaining referrals or making selections which will insure that groups previously subjected to discrimination are adequately served.

(j) Even though an applicant or recipient has never used discriminatory policies, the services and benefits of the program or activity it administers may not in fact be equally available to some racial or nationality groups. In such circumstances, an applicant or recipient may properly give special consideration to race, color, or national origin to make the benefits of its program more widely available to such groups, not then being adequately served. For example, where a university is not adequately serving members of a particular racial or nationality group, it may establish special recruitment policies to make its program better known and more readily available to such group, and take other steps to provide that group with more adequate service.

Title VI of the 1964 Civil Rights Act forbade racial discrimination by recipients of federal funds. Executive Order 11246 implements this prohibition in regard to employment, and Executive Order 11375 extends the prohibition in employment to gender discrimination. These are both orders issued by the President in his role as chief administrator for the executive branch. The Department of Health, Education, and Welfare was for a number of years responsible for administering these rules as they applied to universities, and developed regulations for that task. The Labor Department, which was responsible for administering the nondiscrimination requirement for most private firms that contract to do work financed by the government, and now is responsible for universities as well, has had similar regulations. Both the Labor Department and HEW required fund recipients who underutilized women or members of minorities to set goals for hiring women or minority group members. Underutilization was, and is, determined by comparing the percentage of a group hired with the percentage of qualified potential applicants from that group. Although the goals do not constitute fixed quotas that must necessarily be met, success in meeting the goals is likely to be taken as strong evidence of nondiscrimination, and failure will call for explanation. Thus recipients may consciously seek out a sufficient number of minority groups members and women to meet their goals. Recent comprehensive regulations on this subject issued by the Office of Federal Contract Compliance Programs are found in 41 Code of Federal Regulations, Chapter 60 (1980). (For further comments, see Essay, pp. 47–49.)

Is it proper for the government to demand goals for hiring women and minority group members when there has been no demonstration of prior discrimination? Is it morally defensible for employers receiving government money to hire a minority group member or woman in order to meet a goal, even if they believe some white male is actually better qualified for the position?

VIII.
The Problem of Reverse Discrimination: Gender

Kahn v. Shevin*

MR. JUSTICE DOUGLAS delivered the opinion of the Court.

Since at least 1885, Florida has provided for some form of property tax exemption for widows. The current law granting all widows an annual $500 exemption, Fla. Stat. § 196.202 (Supp. 1974–1975), has been essentially unchanged since 1941. Appellant Kahn is a widower who lives in Florida and applied for the exemption to the Dade County Tax Assessor's Office. It was denied because the statute offers no analogous benefit for widowers. Kahn then sought a declaratory judgment in the Circuit Court for Dade County, Florida, and that court held the statute violative of the Equal Protection Clause of the Fourteenth Amendment because the classification "widow" was based upon gender. The Florida Supreme Court reversed, finding the classification valid because it has a "'fair and substantial relation to the object of the legislation,'" that object being the reduction of "the disparity between the economic capabilities of a man and a woman." . . .

There can be no dispute that the financial difficulties confronting the lone woman in Florida or in any other State exceed those facing the man. Whether from overt discrimination or from the socialization process of a male-dominated culture, the job market is inhospitable to the woman seeking any but the lowest paid jobs. There are, of course, efforts under way to remedy this situation. On the federal level, Title VII of the Civil Rights Act of 1964 prohibits covered employers and labor unions from discrimination on the basis of sex, 78 Stat. 253, 42 U.S.C. §§ 2000c 2 (a), (c), as does the Equal Pay Act of 1963. 77 Stat. 56.29 U.S.C. §§ 206 (d). But firmly entrenched practices are resistant to such pressures, and, indeed, data compiled by the Women's Bureau of the United States Department of Labor show that in 1972 a woman working full time had a median income which was only 57.9% of the median for males—a figure actually six points lower than had been achieved in 1955. Other data point in the same direction. The disparity is likely to be exacerbated for the widow. While the widower can usually continue in the occupation which preceded his spouse's death, in many cases the widow will

---

* 416 U.S. 351, 94 S. Ct. 1734, 40 L.Ed.2d 189 (1974).

find herself suddenly forced into a job market with which she is unfamiliar, and in which, because of her former economic dependency, she will have fewer skills to offer.

There can be no doubt, therefore, that Florida's differing treatment of widows and widowers "'rest[s] upon some ground of difference having a fair and substantial relation to the object of the legislation.' " *Reed* v. *Reed*, 404 U.S. 71, 76, quoting *Royster Guano Co.* v. *Virginia*, 253 U.S. 412, 415.

. . .

MR. JUSTICE BRENNAN, with whom MR. JUSTICE MARSHALL joins, dissenting.

. . . In my view, . . . a legislative classification that distinguishes potential beneficiaries solely by reference to their gender-based status as widows or widowers, like classifications based upon race, alienage, and national origin, must be subjected to close judicial scrutiny, because it focuses upon generally immutable characteristics over which individuals have little or no control, and also because gender-based classifications too often have been inexcusably utilized to stereotype and stigmatize politically powerless segments of society. See *Frontiero* v. *Richardson*, 411 U.S. 677 (1973). The Court is not, therefore, free to sustain the statute on the ground that it rationally promotes legitimate governmental interests; rather, such suspect classifications can be sustained only when the State bears the burden of demonstrating that the challenged legislation serves overriding or compelling interests that cannot be achieved either by a more carefully tailored legislative classification or by the use of feasible, less drastic means. While, in my view, the statute serves a compelling governmental interest by "cushioning the financial impact of spousal loss upon the sex for which that loss imposes a disproportionately heavy burden," I think that the statute is invalid because the State's interest can be served equally well by a more narrowly drafted statute.

. . . Section 196.191 (7) is plainly overinclusive, for the $500 property tax exemption may be obtained by a financially independent heiress as well as by an unemployed widow with dependent children. The State has offered nothing to explain why inclusion of widows of substantial economic means was necessary to advance the State's interest in ameliorating the effects of past economic discrimination against women.

NOTE

Kahn v. *Shevin* involved a classification that unambiguously prefers women in comparison with men. Justice Douglas, who had joined Justice Brennan in *Frontiero v. Richardson* in concluding that gender is a suspect classification, nevertheless wrote the opinion for the majority in this case, which applies a more "relaxed" standard of review. Justice Brennan's dissenting opinion uses the compelling interest test generally employed for "suspect" classifications: although he asserts that aiding needy female widows to counter economic injustice to women would be a sufficiently powerful justification, he rejects Florida's property tax exemption because the class benefited is too broad for that purpose.

In *Califano v. Webster*, 430 U.S. 313, 97 S. Ct. 1192, 51 L.Ed.2d. 360 (1977), the Supreme Court sustained another classification that unambiguously favored women. Under the Social Security Act, women were permitted to compute their "average monthly wage" for old age insurance benefits in a manner that produced a slightly higher figure than the figure for men with equivalent earnings over a period of years. In a *per curiam* opinion, that is, an unsigned majority opinion, five members of the Court employed the intermediate standard of review developed in *Craig v. Boren* and held the distinction between women and men valid as a means of reducing disparities caused by discrimination against women.

QUESTION

Should the Court use the same standard of review for classifications that favor women as it uses for classifications that disfavor them? Should the Court uphold any classification that unambiguously favors women? What should the courts do about classifications that favor women but are not designed to reduce disparities caused by discrimination, such as a rule that women are to be favored in child custody contests? Are such rules, whether announced or simply followed as a matter of practice by courts, justified?

The Problem of Reverse Discrimination: Race*

*DeFunis v. Odegaard***

PER CURIAM.

In 1971 the petitioner Marco DeFunis, Jr., applied for admission as a first-year student at the University of Washington Law School, a

---

* For general comment on the ethical dimensions, see Essay, pp. 49–69.
** 416 U.S. 321, 94 S. Ct. 1704, 40 L.Ed.2d 164 (1974).

state-operated institution. The size of the incoming first-year class was to be limited to 150 persons, and the Law School received some 1,600 applications for these 150 places. DeFunis was eventually notified that he had been denied admission. He thereupon commenced this suit in a Washington trial court, contending that the procedures and criteria employed by the Law School Admissions Committee invidiously discriminated against him on account of his race in violation of the Equal Protection Clause of the Fourteenth Amendment to the United States Constitution.

DeFunis brought the suit on behalf of himself alone, and not as the representative of any class, against the various respondents, who are officers, faculty members, and members of the Board of Regents of the University of Washington. He asked the trial court to issue a mandatory injunction commanding the respondents to admit him as a member of the first-year class entering in September 1971, on the ground that the Law School admissions policy had resulted in the unconstitutional denial of his application for admission. The trial court agreed with his claim and granted the requested relief. DeFunis was, accordingly, admitted to the Law School and began his legal studies there in the fall of 1971. On appeal, the Washington Supreme Court reversed the judgment of the trial court and held that the Law School admissions policy did not violate the Constitution. By this time DeFunis was in his second year at the Law School.

He then petitioned this Court for a writ of certiorari, and MR. JUSTICE DOUGLAS, as Circuit Justice, stayed the judgment of the Washington Supreme Court pending the "final disposition of the case by this Court." By virtue of this stay, DeFunis has remained in law school, and was in the first term of his third and final year when this Court first considered his certiorari petition in the fall of 1973. Because of our concern that DeFunis' third-year standing in the Law School might have rendered this case moot, we requested the parties to brief the question of mootness before we acted on the petition. . . .

The respondents have represented that, without regard to the ultimate resolution of the issues in this case, DeFunis will remain a student in the Law School for the duration of any term in which he has already enrolled. Since he has now registered for his final term, it is evident that he will be given an opportunity to complete all academic and other requirements for graduation, and, if he does so, will receive his diploma regardless of any decision this Court might reach on the merits of this case.

Because the petitioner will complete his law school studies at the end of the term for which he has now registered regardless of any decision this Court might reach on the merits of this litigation, we conclude that the Court cannot, consistently with the limitations of Art. III of the Constitution, consider the substantive constitutional issues tendered by the parties.

MR. JUSTICE DOUGLAS, dissenting.
I agree with MR. JUSTICE BRENNAN that this case is not moot, and because of the significance of the issues raised I think it is important to reach the merits.

I

The University of Washington Law School received 1,601 applications for admission to its first-year class beginning in September 1971. There were spaces available for only about 150 students, but in order to enroll this number the school eventually offered admission to 275 applicants. All applicants were put into two groups, one of which was considered under the minority admissions program. Thirty-seven of those offered admission had indicated on an optional question on their application that their "dominant" ethnic origin was either black, Chicano, American Indian, or Filipino, the four groups included in the minority admissions program. Answers to this optional question were apparently the sole basis upon which eligibility for the program was determined. Eighteen of these 37 actually enrolled in the Law School.

In general, the admissions process proceeded as follows: An index called the Predicted First Year Average (Average) was calculated for each applicant on the basis of a formula combining the applicant's score on the Law School Admission Test (LSAT) and his grades in his last two years in college. On the basis of its experience with previous years' applications, the Admissions Committee, consisting of faculty, administration, and students, concluded that the most outstanding applicants were those with averages above 77; the highest average of any applicant was 81. Applicants with averages above 77 were considered as their applications arrived by random distribution of their files to the members of the Committee who would read them and report their recommendations back to the Committee. As a result of the first three Committee meetings in February, March, and April 1971, 78 applicants from this group were admitted, although virtually no other applicants were offered admission this early. By the final conclusion of the admissions process in August 1971, 147 applicants with averages above 77 had been admitted, including all applicants with averages above 78, and 93 of 105 applicants with averages between 77 and 78.

Also beginning early in the admissions process was the culling out of applicants with averages below 74.5. These were reviewed by the Chairman of the Admissions Committee, who had the authority to reject them summarily without further consideration by the rest of the Committee. A small number of these applications were saved by the Chairman for Committee consideration on the basis of information in the file indicating greater promise than suggested by the Average. Finally during the early months the Committee accumulated the applications of those with averages between 74.5 and 77 to be considered at a later time when most of the applications had been received and thus could be compared with one another. Since DeFunis' average was 76.23, he was in this middle group.

Beginning in their May meeting the Committee considered this middle group of applicants, whose folders had been randomly distributed to Committee members for their recommendations to the Committee. Also considered at this time were remaining applicants with averages below 74.5 who had not been summarily rejected, and some of those with averages above 77 who had not been summarily admitted but instead held for further consideration. Each Committee member would consider the applications competitively, following rough guidelines as to the proportion who could be offered admission. After the Committee had extended offers of admission to somewhat over 200 applicants, a waiting list was constructed in the same fashion, and was divided into four groups ranked by the Committee's assessment of their applications. DeFunis was on this waiting list, but was ranked in the lowest quarter. He was ultimately told in August 1971 that there would be no room for him.

Applicants who had indicated on their application forms that they were either black, Chicano, American Indian, or Filipino were treated differently in several respects. Whatever their Averages, none were given to the Committee Chairman for consideration of summary rejection, nor were they distributed randomly among Committee members for consideration along with the other applications. Instead, all applications of black students were assigned separately to two particular Committee members: a first-year black law student on the Committee, and a professor on the Committee who had worked the previous summer in a special program for disadvantaged college students considering application to the Law School. Applications from among the other three minority groups were assigned to an assistant dean who was on the Committee. The minority applications, while considered competitively with one another, were never directly compared to the remaining applications, either by the subcommittee or by the full Committee. As in the admissions process generally, the Committee sought to find "within the minority category those persons who we thought had the highest probability of succeeding in Law School." In reviewing the minority applications, the Committee attached less weight to the Average "in making a total judgmental evaluation as to the relative ability of the particular applicant to succeed in law school." 82 Wash. 2d 11, 21, 507 P. 2d 1169, 1175. In its publicly distributed Guide to Applicants, the Committee explained that "[a]n applicant's racial or ethnic background was considered as one factor in our general attempt to convert formal credentials into realistic predictions."

Thirty-seven minority applicants were admitted under this procedure. Of these, 36 had Averages below DeFunis' 76.23, and 30 had Averages below 74.5, and thus would ordinarily have been summarily rejected by the Chairman. There were also 48 nonminority applicants admitted who had Averages below DeFunis. Twenty-three of these were returning veterans . . . and 25 were others who presumably were admitted because of other factors in their applications that made them attractive candidates despite their relatively low Averages.

It is reasonable to conclude from the above facts that while other factors were considered by the Committee, and were on occasion crucial, the Average was for most applicants a heavily weighted factor, and was at the extremes virtually dispositive. A different balance was apparently struck, however, with regard to the minority applicants. Indeed, at oral argument, the respondents' counsel advised us that were the minority applicants considered under the same procedure as was generally used, none of those who eventually enrolled at the Law School would have been admitted.

The educational policy choices confronting a university admissions committee are not ordinarily a subject for judicial oversight; clearly it is not for us but for the law school to decide which tests to employ, how heavily to weigh recommendations from professors or undergraduate grades, and what level of achievement on the chosen criteria are sufficient to demonstrate that the candidate is qualified for admission. What places this case in a special category is the fact that the school did not choose one set of criteria but two, and then determined which to apply to a given applicant on the basis of his race. The Committee adopted this policy in order to achieve "a reasonable representation" of minority groups in the Law School. 82 Wash. 2d. at 20, 507 P. 2d. at 1175. Although it may be speculated that the Committee sought to rectify what it perceived to be cultural or racial biases in the LSAT or in the candidates' undergraduate records, the record in this case is devoid of any evidence of such bias, and the school has not sought to justify its procedures on this basis. . . .

It . . . appears that by the Committee's own assessment, it admitted minority students who, by the tests given, seemed less qualified than some white students who were not accepted, in order to achieve a "reasonable representation." In this regard it may be pointed out that for the year 1969–1970—two years before the class to which DeFunis was seeking admission—the Law School reported an enrollment of eight black students out of a total of 356. Defendants' Ex. 7. That percentage, approximately 2.2%, compares to a percentage of blacks in the population of Washington of approximately 2.1%.

II

. . .

The [LSAT] test purports to predict how successful the applicant will be in his first year of law school, and consists of a few hours' worth of multiple-choice questions. But the answers the student can give to a multiple-choice question are limited by the creativity and intelligence of the test-maker; the student with a better or more original understanding of the problem than the test-maker may realize that none of the alternative answers are any good, but there is no way for him to demonstrate his understanding. "It is obvious from the nature of the tests that they do not give the candidate a significant opportunity to express himself. If he is subtle in his choice of answers it will go against him; and yet there is no other way for him to show any individuality. If he is strong-minded, nonconformist, unusual, original, or creative—as so many of the truly important people are—he must stifle his impulses and conform as best he can to the norms that the multiple-choice testers set up in their unimaginative, scientific way. The more profoundly gifted the candidate is, the more his resentment will rise against the mental strait jacket into which the testers would force his mind." B. Hoffmann. The Tyranny of Testing 91–92 (1962).

Those who make the tests and the law schools which use them point, of course, to the high correlations between the test scores and the grades at law school the first year. . . .Certainly the tests do seem to do better than chance. But they do not have the value that their deceptively precise scoring system suggests. The proponents' own data show that, for example, most of those scoring in the bottom 20% on the test do better than that in law school—indeed six of every 100 of them will be in the *top* 20% of their law school class. . . .

Of course, the tests are not the only thing considered; here they were combined with the prelaw grades to produce a new number called the Average. The grades have their own problems; one school's A is another school's C. And even to the extent that this formula predicts law school grades, its value is limited.

III

The Equal Protection Clause did not enact a requirement that law schools employ as the sole criterion for admissions a formula based upon the LSAT and undergraduate grades, nor does it prohibit law schools from evaluating an applicant's prior achievements in light of the barriers that he had to overcome. A black applicant who pulled himself out of the ghetto into a junior college may thereby demonstrate a level of motivation, perseverance, and ability that would lead a fairminded admissions committee to conclude that he shows more promise for law study than the son of a rich alumnus who achieved better grades at Harvard. That applicant would be offered admission not because he is black, but because as an individual he has shown he has the potential, while the Harvard man may have taken less advantage of the vastly superior opportunities offered him. Because of the weight of the prior handicaps, that black applicant may not realize his full potential in the first year of law school, or even in the full three years, but in the long pull of a legal career his achievements may far outstrip those of his classmates whose earlier records appeared superior by conventional criteria. There is currently no test available to the Admissions Committee that can predict such possibilities with assurance, but the Committee may nevertheless seek to gauge it as best it can, and weigh this factor in its decisions. Such a policy would not be limited to blacks, or Chicanos or Filipinos, or American Indians, although undoubtedly groups such as these may in practice be the principal beneficiaries of it. But a poor Appalachian white, or a second generation Chinese in San Francisco, or some other American whose lineage is so diverse as to defy ethnic labels, may demonstrate similar potential and thus be accorded favorable consideration by the Committee.

The difference between such a policy and the one presented by this case is that the Committee would be making decisions on the basis of individual attributes, rather than according a preference solely on the basis of race.

There is no constitutional right for any race to be preferred. The years of slavery did more than retard the progress of blacks. Even a greater wrong was done the whites by creating arrogance instead of humility and by encouraging the growth of the fiction of a superior race. There is no superior person by constitutional standards. A DeFunis who is white is entitled to no advantage by reason of that fact; nor is he subject to any disability, no matter what his race or color. Whatever his race, he had a constitutional right to have his application considered on its individual merits in a racially neutral manner.

. . . The key to the problem is consideration of . . . applications *in a racially neutral way*. Abolition of the LSAT would be a start. . . .

The argument is that a "compelling" state interest can easily justify the racial discrimination that is practiced here. To many, "compelling" would give members of one race even more than *pro rata* representation. The public payrolls might then be deluged say with Chicanos because they are as a group the poorest of the poor and need work more than others, leaving desperately poor individual blacks and whites without employment. By the same token large quotas of blacks or browns could be added to the Bar, waiving examinations required of other groups, so that it would be better racially balanced. The State, however, may not proceed by racial classification to force strict population equivalencies for every group in every occupation, overriding individual preferences. The Equal Protection Clause commands the elimination of racial barriers, not their creation in order to satisfy our theory as to how society ought to be organized. The purpose of the University of Washington cannot be to produce black lawyers for blacks, Polish lawyers for Poles, Jewish lawyers for Jews, Irish lawyers for Irish. . . .A segregated admissions process creates suggestions of stigma and caste no less than a segregated classroom, and in the end it may produce that result despite its contrary intentions. One other assumption must be clearly disapproved: that blacks or browns cannot make it on their individual merit. That is a stamp of inferiority that a State is not permitted to place on any lawyer.

If discrimination based on race is constitutionally permissible when those who hold the reins can come up with "compelling" reasons to justify it, then constitutional guarantees acquire an accordionlike quality.

NOTE

The *DeFunis* case was the Supreme Court's first involvement with programs of preferential treatment for blacks. Only Justice Douglas wrote about the merits of the substantive issue, concluding that racial preferences are unconstitutional. The majority decided that the case was moot, which means that the issue originally presented was no longer a live one. Since DeFunis was going to graduate from the law school in any event, it ceased to matter whether his original denial of admission had been improper. The traditional rule is that courts will not decide cases when the issue becomes moot.

Justice Douglas is highly critical of heavy reliance for admissions on aptitude tests and college grades. He is right that the Law School Aptitude Tests are uncertain predictors of law school performance, but studies indicate that the tests predict about as accurately for minority group members as for whites. This, of course, does not necessarily prove that the tests are free of "cultural bias" in some sense; but if they are biased, it is plausible to suppose that legal education and the practice of law may be "culturally biased" in similar respects.

QUESTION

Do you agree with Justice Douglas that admissions policies should be neutral among races? That the attempt to train "black lawyers for blacks" is an unacceptable policy for the state to pursue?

*University of California Regents v. Bakke**

To make it easier to understand the statutory and constitutional issues, the materials separate the parts of the various opinions that address those issues. After Justice Powell's initial statement about the Supreme Court's disposition of the case, his presentation of the relevant facts, and his treatment of the statutory question, the discussion of that question in other opinions is presented. Then comes the consideration of the constitutional issues by the California Supreme Court, followed by excerpts from the Supreme Court opinions dealing with those issues. An an aid, the following schematic list is provided:

MR. JUSTICE POWELL announced the judgment of the Court.

This case presents a challenge to the special admissions program of the petitioner, the Medical School of the University of California at Davis, which is designed to assure the admission of a specified number of students from certain minority groups. The Superior Court of California sustained respondent's challenge, holding that petitioner's program violated the California Constitution, Title VI of the Civil Rights Act of 1964, 42 USC §2000d [42 USCS §2000d], and the Equal Protection Clause of the Fourteenth Amendment. The court enjoined petitioner from considering respondent's race or the race of any other applicant in making admissions decisions. It refused, however, to order respondent's admission to the Medical School,

* 438 U.S. 265, 98 S. Ct. 2733, 57 L.Ed.2d 750 (1978).

holding that he had not carried his burden of proving that he would have been admitted but for the constitutional and statutory violations. The Supreme Court of California affirmed those portions of the trial court's judgment declaring the special admissions program unlawful and enjoining petitioner from considering the race of any applicant. It modified that portion of the judgment denying respondent's requested injunction and directed the trial court to order his admission.

For the reasons stated in the following opinion, I believe that so much of the judgment of the California court as holds petitioner's special admissions program unlawful and directs that respondent be admitted to the Medical School must be affirmed. For the reasons expressed in a separate opinion, my Brothers THE CHIEF JUSTICE, MR. JUSTICE STEWART, MR. JUSTICE REHNQUIST, and MR. JUSTICE STEVENS concur in this judgment.

I also conclude for the reasons stated in the following opinion that the portion of the court's judgment enjoining petitioner from according any consideration to race in its admissions process must be reversed. For reasons expressed in separate opinions, my Brothers MR. JUSTICE BRENNAN, MR. JUSTICE WHITE, MR. JUSTICE MARSHALL, and MR. JUSTICE BLACKMUN concur in this judgment.

Affirmed in part and reversed in part.

I

The Medical School of the University of California at Davis opened in 1968 with an entering class of 50 students. In 1971, the size of the entering class was increased to 100 students, a level at which it remains. No admissions program for disadvantaged or minority students existed when the school opened, and the first class contained three Asians but no blacks, no Mexican-Americans, and no American Indians. Over the next two years, the faculty devised a special admissions program to increase the representation of "disadvantaged" students in each medical school class. The special program consisted of a separate admissions system operating in coordination with the regular admissions process.

Under the regular admissions procedure, a candidate could submit his application to the medical school beginning in July of the year preceding the academic year for which admission was sought. Record 149. Because of the large number of applications, the admissions committee screened each one to select candidates for further consideration. Candidates whose overall undergraduate grade point averages fell below 2.5 on a scale of 4.0 were summarily rejected. Id., at 63. About one out of six applicants was invited for a personal interview. Ibid. Following the interviews, each candidate was rated on a scale of 1 to 100 by his interviewers and four other members of the admissions committee. The rating embraced the interviewers' summaries, the candidate's overall grade point average, grade point average in science courses, and scores on the Medical College Admissions Test (MCAT), letters of recommendation, extracurricular activities, and other biographical data. Id., at 62. The ratings were added together to arrive at each candidate's "benchmark" score. Since five committee members rated each candidate in 1973, a perfect score was 500; in 1974, six members rated each candidate, so that a perfect score was 600. The full committee then reviewed the file and scores of each applicant and made offers of admission on a "rolling" basis. The chairman was responsible for placing names on the waiting list. They were not placed in strict numerical order; instead, the chairman had discretion to include persons with "special skills." Ibid.

The special admissions program operated with a separate committee, a majority of whom were members of minority groups. Id., at 163. On the 1973 application form, candidates were asked to indicate whether they wished to be considered as "economically and/or educationally disadvantaged" applicants; on the 1974 form the question was whether they wished to be considered as members of a "minority group," which the medical school apparently viewed as "Blacks," "Chicanos," "Asians," and "American Indians." Id., at 65-66, 146, 197, 203–205, 216–218. If these questions were answered affirmatively, the application was forwarded to the special admissions committee. No formal definition of "disadvantage" was ever produced, id., at 163–164, but the chairman of the special committee screened each application to see whether it reflected economic or educational deprivation. Having passed this initial hurdle, the applications then were rated by the special committee in a fashion similar to that used by the general admissions committee, except that special candidates did not have to meet the 2.5 grade point average cut-off applied to regular applicants. About one-fifth of the total number of special applicants were invited for interviews in 1973 and 1974. Following each interview, the special committee assigned each special applicant a benchmark score. The special committee then presented its top choices to the general admissions committee. The latter did not rate or compare the special candidates against the general applicants, id., at 388, but could reject recommended special candidates for failure to meet course requirements or other specific deficiencies. Id., at 171–172. The special committee continued to recommend special applicants until a number prescribed by faculty vote were admitted. While the overall class size was still 50, the prescribed number was eight; in 1973 and 1974, when the class size had doubled to 100, the prescribed number of special admissions also doubled, to 16. Id., at 164, 166.

From the year of the increase in class size—1971—through 1974, the special program resulted in the admission of 21 black students, 30 Mexican-Americans, and 12 Asians, for a total of 63 minority students. Over the same period, the regular admissions program produced one black, six Mexican-Americans, and 12 Asians, for a total of 44 minority students. Although disadvantaged whites applied to the special program in large numbers, see n. 5, supra, none received an offer of admission through that process. Indeed, in 1974, at least, the special committee explicitly considered only "disadvantaged" special applicants who were members of one of the designated minority groups. Record 171.

Allan Bakke is a white male who applied to the Davis Medical School in both 1973 and 1974. In both years Bakke's application was considered by the general admissions program, and he received an interview. His 1973 interview was with Dr. Theodore H. West, who considered Bakke "a very desirable applicant to [the] medical school." Id., at 225. Despite a strong benchmark score of 468 out of 500, Bakke was rejected. His application had come late in the year, and no applicants in the general admissions process with scores below 470 were accepted after Bakke's application was completed. Id., at 69. There were four special admissions slots unfilled at that time, however, for which Bakke was not considered. Id., at 70. After his 1973 rejection, Bakke wrote to Dr. George H. Lowrey, Associate Dean and Chairman of the Admissions Committee, protesting that the special admissions program operated as a racial and ethnic quota. Id., at 259.

Bakke's 1974 application was completed early in the year. Id., at 70. His student interviewer gave him an overall rating of 94, finding him "friendly, well tempered, conscientious and delightful to speak with." Id., at 229. His faculty interviewer was, by coincidence, the same Dr. Lowrey to whom he had written in protest of the special admissions program. Dr. Lowrey found Bakke "rather limited in his approach" to the problems of the medical profession and found disturbing Bakke's "very definite opinions which were based more on his personal viewpoints than upon a study of the total problem." Id., at 226. Dr. Lowrey gave Bakke the lowest of his six ratings, an 86; his total was 549 out of 600. Id., at 230. Again, Bakke's application was rejected. In neither year did the chairman of the admissions committee, Dr. Lowrey, exercise his discretion to place Bakke on the waiting list. Id., at 64. In both years, applicants were admitted under the special program with grade point averages, MCAT scores, and benchmark scores significantly lower than Bakke's.

After the second rejection, Bakke filed the instant suit in the Superior Court of California. He sought mandatory, injunctive, and declaratory relief compelling his admission to the Medical School. . . .

B

The language of § 601, like that of the Equal Protection Clause, is majestic in its sweep:

"No person in the United States shall, on the ground of race, color, or national origin, be excluded from participation in, be denied the benefits of, or be subjected to discrimination under any program or activity receiving Federal financial assistance."

The concept of "discrimination," like the phrase "equal protection of the laws," is susceptible to varying interpretations, for as Mr. Justice Holmes declared, "[a] word is not a crystal, transparent and unchanged, it is the skin of a living thought and may vary greatly in color and content according to the circumstances and the time in which it is used." . . . Examination of the voluminous legislative history of Title VI reveals a congressional intent to halt federal funding of entities that violate a prohibition of racial discrimination similar to that of the Constitution. Although isolated statements of various legislators, taken out of context, can be marshalled in support of the proposition that § 601 enacted a purely colorblind scheme, without regard to the reach of the Equal Protection Clause, these comments must be read against the background of both the problem that Congress was addressing and the broader view of the statute that emerges from a full examinaton of the legislative debates.

The problem confronting Congress was discrimination against Negro citizens at the hands of recipients of federal moneys. Indeed, the colorblindness pronouncements . . . generally occur in the midst of extended remarks dealing with the evils of segregation in federally funded programs. Over and over again, proponents of the bill detailed the plight of Negroes seeking equal treatment in such programs. There simply was no reason for Congress to consider the validity of hypothetical preferences that might be accorded minority citizens; the legislators were dealing with the real and pressing problem of how to guarantee those citizens equal treatment.

In addressing that problem, supporters of Title VI repeatedly declared that the bill enacted constitutional principles. For example, Representative Celler, the Chairman of the House Judiciary Committee and floor manager of the legislation in the House, emphasized this in introducing the bill:

> "The bill would offer assurance that hospitals financed by Federal money would not deny adequate care to Negroes. It would prevent abuse of food distribution programs whereby Negroes have been known to be denied food surplus supplies when white persons were given such food. It would assure Negroes the benefits now accorded only white students in programs of higher education financed by Federal funds. It would, in short, *assure the existing right to equal treatment* in the enjoyment of Federal funds. It would not destroy any rights of private property or freedom of association." 110 Cong Rec 1519 (1964) (emphasis added).

Other sponsors shared Representative Celler's view that Title VI embodied constitutional principles.

In the Senate, Senator Humphrey declared that the purpose of Title VI was "to insure that Federal funds are spent in accordance with the Constitution and the moral sense of the Nation." Id., at 6544. Senator Ribicoff agreed that Title VI embraced the constitutional standard: "Basically, there is a constitutional restriction against discrimination in the use of federal funds; and title VI simply spells out the procedure to be used in enforcing that restriction." Id., at 13333. Other Senators expressed similar views. . . .

In view of the clear legislative intent, Title VI must be held to proscribe only those racial classifications that would violate the Equal Protection Clause or the Fifth Amendment.

Opinion of MR. JUSTICE BRENNAN, MR. JUSTICE WHITE, MR. JUSTICE MARSHALL, and MR. JUSTICE BLACKMUN, concurring in the judgment in part and dissenting in part.

II

The threshold question we must decide is whether Title VI of the Civil Rights Act of 1964 bars recipients of federal funds from giving preferential consideration to disadvantaged members of racial minorities as part of a program designed to enable such individuals to surmount the obstacles imposed by racial discrimination. . . .

In our view, Title VI prohibits only those uses of racial criteria that would violate the Fourteenth Amendment if employed by a State or its agencies; it does not bar the preferential treatment of racial minorities as a means of remedying past societal discrimination to the extent that such action is consistent with the Fourteenth Amendment. The legislative history of Title VI, administrative regulations interpreting the statute, subsequent congressional and executive action, and the prior decisions of this Court compel this conclusion. None of these sources lends support to the proposition that Congress intended to bar all race conscious efforts to extend the benefits of federally financed programs to minorities who have been historically excluded from the full benefits of American life.

MR. JUSTICE STEVENS, with whom THE CHIEF JUSTICE, MR. JUSTICE STEWART, and MR. JUSTICE REHNQUIST join, concurring in the judgment in part and dissenting in part. . . .

The University, through its special admissions policy, excluded Bakke from participation in its program of medical education because of his race. The University also acknowledges that it was, and still is, receiving federal financial assistance. The plain language of the statute therefore requires affirmance of the judgment below. A different result cannot be justified unless that language misstates the actual intent of the Congress that enacted the statute or the statute is not enforceable in a private action. Neither conclusion is warranted.

Title VI is an integral part of the far-reaching Civil Rights Act of 1964. No doubt, when this legislation was being debated, Congress was not directly concerned with the legality of "reverse discrimination" or "affirmative action" programs. Its attention was focused on the problem at hand, "the glaring . . . discrimination against Negroes which exists throughout our Nation," and, with respect to Title VI, the federal funding of segregated facilities. The genesis of the legislation, however, did not limit the breadth of the solution adopted. Just as Congress responded to the problem of employment discrimination by enacting a provision that protects all races, . . . so too its answer to the problem of federal funding of segregated facilities stands as a broad prohibition against the exclusion of *any* individual from a federally funded program "on the ground of race." In the words of the House Report, Title VI stands for "the general principle that *no person* . . . be excluded from participation . . . on the ground of race, color, or national origin under any program or activity receiving Federal financial assistance." . . . This same broad view of Title VI and § 601 was echoed throughout the congressional debate and was stressed by every one of the major spokesmen for the Act.

*University of California Regents v. Bakke**

The general rule is that classifications made by government regulations are valid "if any state of facts reasonably may be conceived" in their justification. . . . This yardstick generally called the "rational basis" test, is employed in a variety of contexts to determine the validity of government action, . . . and its use signifies that a reviewing court will strain to find any legitimate purpose in order to uphold the propriety of the state's conduct.

But in some circumstances a more stringent standard is imposed. Classification by race is subject to strict scrutiny, at least where the classification results in detriment to a person because of his race. In the case of such a racial classification, not only must the purpose of the classification serve a "compelling state interest," but it must be demonstrated by rigid scrutiny that there are no reasonable ways to achieve the state's goals by means which impose a lesser limitation on the rights of the group disadvantaged by the classification. The burden in both respects is upon the government. . . . It has been more than three decades since any decision of the United States

* 18 Cal. 3d 34, 553 P.2d 1152 (1976).

Supreme Court upheld a classification which resulted in detriment solely on the basis of race: *Korematsu v. United States* (1944) . . . and *Hirabayashi v. United States* (1943) 320 U.S. 81 . . . both of which were war-inspired cases that have been severely criticized subsequently.

The University asserts that the appropriate standard to be applied in determining the validity of the special admission program is the more lenient "rational basis" test. It contends that the "compelling interest" measure is applicable only to a classification which discriminates against a minority, reasoning that racial classifications are suspect only if they result in invidious discrimination . . . and that invidious discrimination occurs only if the classification excludes, disadvantages, isolates, or stigmatizes a minority or is designed to segregate the races. The argument is that white applicants denied admission are not stigmatized in the sense of having cast about them an aura of inferiority; therefore, it is sufficient if the special admission program has a rational relation to the University's goals.

We cannot agree with the proposition that deprivation based upon race is subject to a less demanding standard of review under the Fourteenth Amendment if the race discriminated against is the majority rather than a minority. We have found no case so holding, and we do not hesitate to reject the notion that racial discrimination may be more easily justified against one race than another, nor can we permit the validity of such discrimination to be determined by a mere census count of the races.

That whites suffer a grievous disadvantage by reason of their exclusion from the University on racial grounds is abundantly clear. The fact that they are not also invidiously discriminated against in the sense that a stigma is cast upon them because of their race, as is often the circumstance when the discriminatory conduct is directed against a minority, does not justify the conclusion that race is a suspect classification only if the consequences of the classification are detrimental to minorities.

Regardless of its historical origin, the equal protection clause by its literal terms applies to "any person," and its lofty purpose, to secure equality of treatment to all, is incompatible with the premise that some races may be afforded a higher degree of protection against unequal treatment than others. . . .

We come, then, to the question whether the University has demonstrated that the special admission program is necessary to serve a compelling governmental interest and that the objectives of the program cannot reasonably be achieved by some means which would impose a lesser burden on the rights of the majority.

The University seeks to justify the program on the ground that the admission of minority students is necessary in order to integrate the medical school and the profession. The presence of a substantial number of minority students will not only provide diversity in the student body, it is said, but will influence the students and the remainder of the profession so that they will become aware of the medical needs of the minority community and be encouraged to assist in meeting those demands. Minority doctors will, moreover, provide role models for younger persons in the minority community, demonstrating to them that they can overcome the residual handicaps inherent from past discrimination.

Furthermore, the special admission program will assertedly increase the number of doctors willing to serve the minority community, which is desperately short of physicians. While the University concedes it cannot guarantee that all the applicants admitted under the special program will ultimately practice as doctors in disadvantaged communities, they have expressed an interest in serving those communities and there is a likelihood that many of them will thus fashion their careers.

Finally, it is urged, black physicians would have a greater rapport with patients of their own race and a greater interest in treating diseases which are especially prevalent among blacks, such as sickle cell anemia, hypertension, and certain skin ailments.

We reject the University's assertion that the special admission program may be justified as compelling on the ground that minorities would have more rapport with doctors of their own race and that black doctors would have a greater interest in treating diseases prevalent among blacks. The record contains no evidence to justify the parochialism implicit in the latter assertion; and as to the former, we cite as eloquent refutation to racial exclusivity the comment of Justice Douglas in his dissenting opinion in *DeFunis:* "The Equal Protection Clause commands the elimination of racial barriers, not their creation in order to satisfy our theory as to how society ought to be organized. The purpose of the University of Washington cannot be to produce black lawyers for blacks, Polish lawyers for Poles, Jewish lawyers for Jews, Irish lawyers for Irish. It should be to produce good lawyers for Americans. . . ." (416 U.S. at p. 342. . . .)

We may assume arguendo that the remaining objectives which the University seeks to achieve by the special admission program meet the exacting standards required to uphold the validity of a racial classification insofar as they establish a compelling governmental interest. Nevertheless, we are not convinced that the University has met its burden of demonstrating that the basic goals of the program cannot be substantially achieved by means less detrimental to the rights of the majority.

The two major aims of the University are to integrate the student body and to improve medical care for minorities. In our view, the University has not established that a program which discriminates against white applicants because of their race is necessary to achieve either of these goals.

It is the University's claim that if special consideration is not afforded to disadvantaged minority applicants, almost none of them would gain admission because, no matter how large the pool of applicants, the grades and test scores of most minority applicants are lower than those of white applicants. . . .

We observe and emphasize in this connection that the University is not required to choose between a racially neutral admission standard applied strictly according to grade point averages and test scores, and a standard which accords preference to minorities because of their race.

While minority applicants may have lower grade point averages and test scores than others, we are aware of no rule of law which requires the University to afford determinative weight in admissions to these quantitative factors. . . . The University is entitled to consider, as it does with respect to applicants in the special program, that low grades and test scores may not accurately reflect the abilities of some disadvantaged students; and it may reasonably conclude that although their academic scores are lower, their potential for success in the school and the profession is equal to or greater than that of an applicant with higher grades who has not been similarly handicapped. . . .

. . . Disadvantaged applicants of all races must be eligible for sympathetic consideration, and no applicant may be rejected because of his race, in favor of another who is less qualified, as measured by standards applied without regard to race. . . .

University of California Regents v. Bakke*

Opinion of MR. JUSTICE POWELL.

III

A

. . . Racial and ethnic distinctions of any sort are inherently suspect and thus call for the most exacting judicial examination.

B

Although many of the Framers of the Fourteenth Amendment conceived of its primary function as bridging the vast distance between members of the Negro race and the white "majority," *Slaughter-House Cases*, supra, the Amendment itself was framed in universal terms, without reference to color, ethnic origin, or condition of prior servitude. . . .

Over the past 30 years, this Court has embarked upon the crucial mission of interpreting the Equal Protection Clause with the view of assuring to all persons "the protection of equal laws." . . .

Petitioner urges us to adopt for the first time a more restrictive view of the Equal Protection Clause and hold that discrimination against members of the white "majority" cannot be suspect if its purpose can be characterized as "benign." The clock of our liberties, however, cannot be turned back to 1868. . . .

Once the artificial line of a "two-class theory" of the Fourteenth Amendment is put aside, the difficulties entailed in varying the level of judicial review according to a perceived "preferred" status of a particular racial or ethnic minority are intractable. The concepts of "majority" and "minority" necessarily reflect temporary arrangements and political judgments. . . . [T]he white "majority" itself is composed of various minority groups, most of which can lay claim to a history of prior discrimination at the hands of the state and private individuals. Not all of these groups can receive preferential treatment

* 438 U.S. 265, 98 S. Ct. 2733, 57 L.Ed.2d 570 (1978).

and corresponding judicial tolerance of distinctions drawn in terms of race and nationality, for then the only "majority" left would be a new minority of White Anglo-Saxon Protestants. There is no principled basis for deciding which groups would merit "heightened judicial solicitude" and which would not. Courts would be asked to evaluate the extent of the prejudice and consequent harm suffered by various minority groups. Those whose societal injury is thought to exceed some arbitrary level of tolerability then would be entitled to preferential classifications at the expense of individuals belonging to other groups. Those classifications would be free from exacting judicial scrutiny. As these preferences began to have their desired effect, and the consequences of past discrimination were undone, new judicial rankings would be necessary. The kind of variable sociological and political analysis necessary to produce such rankings simply does not lie within the judicial competence—even if they otherwise were politically feasible and socially desirable. . . .

Nor is petitioner's view as to the applicable standard supported by the fact that gender-based classifications are not subjected to this level of scrutiny. . . . Gender-based distinctions are less likely to create the analytical and practical problems present in preferential programs premised on racial or ethnic criteria. With respect to gender there are only two possible classifications. The incidence of the burdens imposed by preferential classifications is clear. There are no rival groups who can claim that they, too, are entitled to preferential treatment. Classwide questions as to the group suffering previous injury and groups which fairly can be burdened are relatively manageable for reviewing courts. . . . The resolution of these same questions in the context of racial and ethnic preferences presents far more complex and intractable problems than gender-based classifications. More importantly, the perception of racial classifications as inherently odious stems from a lengthy and tragic history that gender-based classifications do not share. In sum, the Court has never viewed such classification as inherently suspect or as comparable to racial or ethnic classifications for the purpose of equal-protection analysis.

IV

We have held that in "order to justify the use of a suspect classification, a State must show that its purpose or interest is both constitutionally permissible and substantial, and that its use of the classification is 'necessary . . . to the accomplishment' of its purpose or the safeguarding of its interest." . . . The special admissions program purports to serve the purposes of: (i) "reducing the historic deficit of traditionally disfavored minorities in medical schools and the medical profession," Brief for Petitioner 32; (ii) countering the effects of societal discrimination; (iii) increasing the number of physicians who will practice in communities currently underserved; and (iv) obtaining the educational benefits that flow from an ethnically diverse student body. It is necessary to decide which, if any, of these purposes is substantial enough to support the use of a suspect classification.

A

If petitioner's purpose is to assure within its student body some specified percentage of a particular group merely because of its race or ethnic origin, such a preferential purpose must be rejected not as insubstantial but as facially invalid. Preferring members of any one group for no reason other than race or ethnic origin is discrimination for its own sake. This the Constitution forbids.

B

The State certainly has a legitimate and substantial interest in ameliorating, or eliminating where feasible, the disabling effects of identified discrimination. The line of school desegregation cases, commencing with Brown, attests to the importance of this state goal and the commitment of the judiciary to affirm all lawful means towards its attainment. In the school cases, the States were required by court order to redress the wrongs worked by specific instances of racial discrimination. That goal was far more focused than the remedying of the effects of "societal discrimination," an amorphous concept of injury that may be ageless in its reach into the past.

We have never approved a classification that aids persons perceived as members of relatively victimized groups at the expense of other innocent individuals in the absence of judicial, legislative, or administrative findings of constitutional or statutory violations. . . . After such findings have been made, the governmental interest in preferring members of the injured groups at the expense of others is substantial, since the legal rights of the victims must be vindicated. In such a case, the extent of the injury and the consequent remedy will have been judicially, legislatively, or administratively defined. Also, the remedial action usually remains subject to continuing oversight to assure that it will work the least harm possible to other innocent persons competing for the benefit. Without such findings of constitutional or statutory violations, it cannot be said that the government has any greater interest in helping one individual than in refraining from harming another. Thus, the government has no compelling justification for inflicting such harm.

Petitioner does not purport to have made, and is in no position to make, such findings. Its broad mission is education, not the formulation of any legislative policy or the adjudication of particular claims of illegality. For reasons similar to those stated in Part III of this opinion, isolated segments of our vast governmental structures are not competent to make those decisions, at least in the absence of legislative mandates and legislatively determined criteria.

C

Petitioner identifies, as another purpose of its program, improving the delivery of health care services to communities currently underserved. It may be assumed that in some situations a State's interest in facilitating the health care of its citizens is sufficiently compelling to support the use of a suspect classification. But there is virtually no evidence in the record indicating that petitioner's special admissions program is either needed or geared to promote that goal.

Petitioner simply has not carried its burden of demonstrating that it must prefer members of particular ethnic groups over all other individuals in order to promote better health care delivery to deprived citizens. Indeed, petitioner has not shown that its preferential classification is likely to have any significant effect on the problem.

D

The fourth goal asserted by petitioner is the attainment of a diverse student body. This clearly is a constitutionally permissible goal for an institution of higher education. Academic freedom, though not a specifically enumerated constitutional right, long has been viewed as a special concern of the First Amendment. The freedom of a university to make its own judgments as to education includes the selection of its student body. The atmosphere of "speculation, experiment and creation"—so essential to the quality of

higher education—is widely believed to be promoted by a diverse
student body. . . .

It may be argued that there is greater force to these views at the
undergraduate level than in a medical school where the training is
centered primarily on professional competency. But even at the
graduate level, our tradition and experience lend support to the view
that the contribution of diversity is substantial. In *Sweatt v Painter*,
339 US 629, . . . (1950), the Court made a similar point with specific
reference to legal education:

> "The law school, the proving ground for legal learning and practice,
> cannot be effective in isolation from the individuals and institutions with
> which the law interacts. Few students and no one who has practiced law
> would choose to study in an academic vacuum, removed from the inter-
> play of ideas and the exchange of views with which the law is concerned."

Physicians serve a heterogeneous population. An otherwise qualified
medical student with a particular background—whether it be ethnic,
geographic, culturally advantaged or disadvantaged—may bring to a
professional school of medicine experiences, outlooks and ideas that
enrich the training of its student body and better equip its graduates
to render with understanding their vital service to humanity.

V

A

 . . The diversity that furthers a compelling state interest encompasses a far broader array of qualifications and characteristics of
which racial or ethnic origin is but a single though important
element. Petitioner's special admissions program, focused *solely* on
ethnic diversity, would hinder rather than further attainment of
genuine diversity.

The experience of other university admissions programs, which
take race into account in achieving the educational diversity valued
by the First Amendment, demonstrates that the assignment of a fixed
number of places to a minority group is not a necessary means toward
that end. An illuminating example is found in the Harvard College
program:

> "In recent years Harvard College has expanded the concept of diversity
> to include students from disadvantaged economic, racial and ethnic

groups. Harvard College now recruits not only Californians or Louisianans but also blacks and Chicanos and other minority students.

. . .

"In practice, this new definition of diversity has meant that race has been a factor in some admission decisions. When the Committee on Admissions reviews the large middle group of applicants who are 'admissible' and deemed capable of doing good work in their courses, the race of an applicant may tip the balance in his favor just as geographic origin or a life spent on a farm may tip the balance in other candidates' cases. A farm boy from Idaho can bring something to Harvard College that a Bostonian cannot offer. Similarly, a black student can usually bring something that a white person cannot offer." . . .

This kind of program treats each applicant as an individual in the admissions process. The applicant who loses out on the last available seat to another candidate receiving a "plus" on the basis of ethnic background will not have been foreclosed from all consideration for that seat simply because he was not the right color or had the wrong surname. It would mean only that his combined qualifications, which may have included similar nonobjective factors, did not outweigh those of the other applicant. His qualifications would have been weighed fairly and competitively, and he would have no basis to complain of unequal treatment under the Fourteenth Amendment.

It has been suggested that an admissions program which considers race only as one factor is simply a subtle and more sophisticated—but no less effective—means of according racial preference than the Davis program. A facial intent to discriminate, however, is evident in petitioner's preference program and not denied in this case. No such facial infirmity exists in an admissions program where race or ethnic background is simply one element—to be weighed fairly against other elements—in the selection process. . . . And a Court would not assume that a university, professing to employ a facially nondiscriminatory admissions policy, would operate it as a cover for the functional equivalent of a quota system. In short, good faith would be presumed in the absence of a showing to the contrary in the manner permitted by our cases.

. . .

Opinion of MR. JUSTICE BRENNAN, MR. JUSTICE WHITE, MR. JUSTICE MARSHALL, and MR. JUSTICE BLACKMUN.

III

A

The assertion of human equality is closely associated with the proposition that differences in color or creed, birth or status, are neither significant nor relevant to the way in which persons should be treated. Nonetheless, the position that such factors must be "[c]onstitutionally an irrelevance," . . . has never been adopted by this Court as the proper meaning of the Equal Protection Clause. Indeed, we have expressly rejected this proposition on a number of occasions.

Our cases have always implied that an "overriding statutory purpose," . . . could be found that would justify racial classifications. . . .

We conclude, therefore, that racial classifications are not per se invalid under the Fourteenth Amendment. Accordingly, we turn to the problem of articulating what our role should be in reviewing state action that expressly classifies by race.

B

. . .

Unquestionably we have held that a government practice or statute which restricts "fundamental rights" or which contains "suspect classifications" is to be subjected to "strict scrutiny" and can be justified only if it furthers a compelling government purpose and, even then, only if no less restrictive alternative is available. But no fundamental right is involved here. Nor do whites as a class have any of the "traditional indicia of suspectness: the class is not saddled with such disabilities, or subjected to such a history of purposeful unequal treatment, or relegated to such a position of political powerlessness as to command extraordinary protection from the majoritarian political process."

Moreover, if the University's representations are credited, this is not a case where racial classifications are "irrelevant and therefore prohibited." *Hirabayashi*, . . . Nor has anyone suggested that the

University's purposes contravene the cardinal principle that racial classifications that stigmatize—because they are drawn on the presumption that one race is inferior to another or because they put the weight of government behind racial hatred and separatism—are invalid without more. . . .

On the other hand, the fact that this case does not fit neatly into our prior analytic framework for race cases does not mean that it should be analyzed by applying the very loose rational-basis standard of review that is the very least that is always applied in equal protection cases. " '[T]he mere recitation of a benign, compensatory purpose is not an automatic shield which protects against any inquiry into the actual purposes underlying a statutory scheme.' " Instead, a number of considerations—developed in gender discrimination cases but which carry even more force when applied to racial classifications—lead us to conclude that racial classifications designed to further remedial purposes " 'must serve important governmental objectives and must be substantially related to achievement of those objectives.' "

First, race, like "gender-based classifications too often [has] been inexcusably utilized to stereotype and stigmatize politically powerless segments of society." . . .While a carefully tailored statute designed to remedy past discrimination could avoid these vices, we nonetheless have recognized that the line between honest and thoughtful appraisal of the effects of past discrimination and paternalistic stereotyping is not so clear and that a statute based on the latter is patently capable of stigmatizing all women with a badge of inferiority. State programs designed ostensibly to ameliorate the effects of past racial discrimination obviously create the same hazard of stigma, since they may promote racial separatism and reinforce the views of those who believe that members of racial minorities are inherently incapable of succeeding on their own.

Second, race, like gender and illegitimacy, . . . is an immutable characteristic which its possessors are powerless to escape or set aside. While a classification is not per se invalid because it divides classes on the basis of an immutable characteristic, it is nevertheless true that such divisions are contrary to our deep belief that "legal burdens should bear some relationship to individual responsibility or wrongdoing," and that advancement sanctioned, sponsored, or approved by the State should ideally be based on individual merit or achievement, or at the least on factors within the control of an individual.

Because this principle is so deeply rooted it might be supposed that it would be considered in the legislative process and weighed against the benefits of programs preferring individuals because of their race. But this is not necessarily so: The "natural consequence of our governing processes [may well be] that the most 'discrete and insular' of whites . . . will be called upon to bear the immediate, direct costs of benign discrimination." Moreover, it is clear from our cases that there are limits beyond which majorities may not go when they classify on the basis of immutable characteristics. Thus, even if the concern for individualism is weighed by the political process, that weighing cannot waive the personal rights of individuals under the Fourteenth Amendment. . . .

IV

Davis' articulated purpose of remedying the effects of past societal discrimination is, under our cases, sufficiently important to justify the use of race-conscious admissions programs where there is a sound basis for concluding that minority underrepresentation is substantial and chronic, and that the handicap of past discrimination is impeding access of minorities to the medical school.

A

At least since *Green v County School Board*, it has been clear that a public body which has itself been adjudged to have engaged in racial discrimination cannot bring itself into compliance with the Equal Protection Clause simply by ending its unlawful acts and adopting a neutral stance. Three years later, *Swann v Charlotte-Mecklenburg Board of Ed.,* . . . and its companion cases, reiterated that racially neutral remedies for past discrimination were inadequate where consequences of past discriminatory acts influence or control present decisions. And the Court further held both that courts could enter desegregation orders which assigned students and faculty by reference to race, and that local school boards could *voluntarily* adopt desegregation plans which made express reference to race if this was necessary to remedy the effects of past discrimination. Moreover, we stated that school boards, even in the absence of a judicial finding of past discrimination, could voluntarily adopt plans which assigned students with the end of creating racial pluralism by establishing fixed ratios of black and white students in each school. In each instance, the creation of unitary school systems, in which the effects of past discrimination had been "eliminated root and branch," was recognized as a compelling social goal justifying the overt use of race.

Finally, the conclusion that state educational institutions may constitutionally adopt admissions programs designed to avoid exclusion of historically disadvantaged minorities, even when such programs explicitly take race into account, finds direct support in our cases construing congressional legislation designed to overcome the present effects of past discrimination. Congress can and has outlawed actions which have a disproportionately adverse and unjustified impact upon members of racial minorities and has required or authorized race-conscious action to put individuals disadvantaged by such impact in the position they otherwise might have enjoyed. Such relief does not require as a predicate proof that recipients of preferential advancement have been individually discriminated against; it is enough that each recipient is within a general class of persons likely to have been the victims of discrimination. Nor is it an objection to such relief that preference for minorities will upset the settled expectations of nonminorities. . . .

These cases cannot be distinguished simply by the presence of judicial findings of discrimination, for race-conscious remedies have been approved where such findings have not been made. Indeed, the requirement of a judicial determination of a constitutional or statutory violation as a predicate for race-conscious remedial actions would be self-defeating. Such a requirement would severely undermine efforts to achieve voluntary compliance with the requirements of law. And, our society and jurisprudence have always stressed the value of voluntary efforts to further the objectives of the law. Judicial intervention is a last resort to achieve cessation of illegal conduct or the remedying of its effects rather than a prerequisite to action.

. . . Moreover, the presence or absence of past discrimination by universities or employers is largely irrelevant to resolving respondent's constitutional claims. The claims of those burdened by the race-conscious actions of a university or employer who has never been adjudged in violation of an antidiscrimination law are not any more or less entitled to deference than the claims of the burdened nonminority workers in *Franks v Bowman*, 424 U.S. 747, . . . in which the employer had violated Title VII, for in each case the employees are innocent of past discrimination. And, although it might be argued that, where an employer has violated an anti-discrimination law, the expectations of nonminority workers are themselves products of discrimination and hence "tainted," . . . and therefore more easily upset, the same argument can be made with respect to respondent. If it was reasonable to conclude—as we hold that it was—that the failure of minorities to qualify for admission at Davis under regular procedures was due principally to the effects of past discrimination, then there is a reasonable likelihood that, but for pervasive racial discrimination, respondent would have failed to qualify for admission even in the absence of Davis' special admissions program.

B

Properly construed, therefore, our prior cases unequivocally show that a state government may adopt race-conscious programs if the purpose of such programs is to remove the disparate racial impact its actions might otherwise have and if there is reason to believe that the disparate impact is itself the product of past discrimination, whether its own or that of society at large. There is no question that Davis' program is valid under this test.

Certainly, on the basis of the undisputed factual submissions before this Court, Davis had a sound basis for believing that the problem of underrepresentation of minorities was substantial and chronic and that the problem was attributable to handicaps imposed on minority applicants by past and present racial discrimination. Until at least 1973, the practice of medicine in this country was, in fact, if not in law, largely the prerogative of whites. In 1950, for example, while Negroes comprised 10% of the total population, Negro physicians constituted only 2.2% of the total number of physicians. The overwhelming majority of these, moreover, were educated in two predominantly Negro medical schools, Howard and Meharry. By 1970, the gap between the proportion of Negroes in medicine and their proportion in the population had widened: The number of Negroes employed in medicine remained frozen at 2.2% while the Negro population had increased to 11.1%. The number of Negro admittees to predominantly white medical schools, moreover, had declined in absolute numbers during the years 1955 to 1964. . . .

Moreover, Davis had very good reason to believe that the national pattern of underrepresentation of minorities in medicine would be perpetuated if it retained a single admissions standard. For example, the entering classes in 1968 and 1969, the years in which such a standard was used, included only one Chicano and two Negroes out of 100 admittees. Nor is there any relief from this pattern of underrepresentation in the statistics for the regular admissions program in later years.

Davis clearly could conclude that the serious and persistent underrepresentation of minorities in medicine depicted by these statistics is the result of handicaps under which minority applicants labor as a consequence of a background of deliberate, purposeful discrimination against minorities in education and in society generally, as well as in the medical profession. . . .

. . . The generation of minority students applying to Davis Medical School since it opened in 1968—most of whom were born before or about the time Brown I was decided—clearly have been victims of this discrimination. Judicial decrees recognizing discrimination in public education in California testify to the fact of widespread discrimination suffered by California-born minority applicants; many minority group members living in California, moreover, were born and reared in school districts in southern States segregated by law. Since separation of school children by race "generates a feeling of inferiority as to their status in the community that may affect their hearts and minds in a way unlikely ever to be undone," . . . the conclusion is inescapable that applicants to medical school must be few indeed who endured the effects of de jure segregation, the resistance to Brown I, or the equally debilitating pervasive private discrimination fostered by our long history of official discrimination. . . . and yet come to the starting line with an education equal to whites.

C

The second prong of our test—whether the Davis program stigmatizes any discrete group or individual and whether race is reasonably used in light of the program's objectives—is clearly satisfied by the Davis program.

It is not even claimed that Davis' program in any way operates to stigmatize or single out any discrete and insular, or even any identifiable, nonminority group. Nor will harm comparable to that imposed upon racial minorities by exclusion or separation on grounds of race be the likely result of the program. It does not, for example, establish an exclusive preserve for minority students apart from and exclusive of whites. Rather, its purpose is to overcome the effects of segregation by bringing the races together. True, whites are excluded from participation in the special admissions program, but this fact only operates to reduce the number of whites to be admitted in the regular admissions program in order to permit admission of a reasonable percentage—less than their proportion of the California population—of otherwise underrepresented qualified minority applicants.

Nor was Bakke in any sense stamped as inferior by the Medical School's rejection of him. Indeed, it is conceded by all that he satisfied those criteria regarded by the School as generally relevant to academic performance better than most of the minority members who were admitted. Moreover, there is absolutely no basis for concluding that Bakke's rejection as a result of Davis' use of racial preference will affect him throughout his life in the same way as the segregation of the Negro school children in Brown I would have affected them. Unlike discrimination against racial minorities, the use of racial preferences for remedial purposes does not inflict a pervasive injury upon individual whites in the sense that wherever they go or whatever they do there is a significant likelihood that they will be treated as second-class citizens because of their color. This distinction does not mean that the exclusion of a white resulting from the preferential use of race is not sufficiently serious to require justification; but it does mean that the injury inflicted by such a policy is not distinguishable from disadvantages caused by a wide range of government actions, none of which has ever been thought impermissible for that reason alone.

In addition, there is simply no evidence that the Davis program discriminates intentionally or unintentionally against any minority group which it purports to benefit. The program does not establish a quota in the invidious sense of a ceiling on the number of minority applicants to be admitted. Nor can the program reasonably be regarded as stigmatizing the program's beneficiaries or their race as inferior. The Davis program does not simply advance less qualified applicants; rather, it compensates applicants, whom it is uncontested are fully qualified to study medicine, for educational disadvantage which it was reasonable to conclude was a product of state-fostered discrimination. Once admitted, these students must satisfy the same degree requirements as regularly admitted students; they are taught by the same faculty in the same classes; and their performance is evaluated by the same standards by which regularly admitted students are judged. Under these circumstances, their performance and degrees must be regarded equally with the regularly admitted students with whom they compete for standing. Since minority graduates cannot justifiably be regarded as less well qualified than nonminority graduates by virtue of the special admissions program, there is no reasonable basis to conclude that minority graduates at schools using such programs would be stigmatized as inferior by the existence of such programs.

D

We disagree with the lower courts' conclusion that the Davis program's use of race was unreasonable in light of its objectives. First, as petitioner argues, there are no practical means by which it could achieve its ends in the foreseeable future without the use of race-conscious measures. With respect to any factor (such as poverty or family educational background) that may be used as a substitute for race as an indicator of past discrimination, whites greatly outnumber racial minorities simply because whites make up a far larger percentage of the total population and therefore far outnumber minorities in absolute terms at every socioeconomic level. For example, of a class of recent medical school applicants from families with less than $10,000 income, at least 71% were white. Of all 1970 families headed by a person *not* a high school graduate which included related children under 18, 80% were white and 20% were racial minorities. Moreover, while race is positively correlated with differences in GPA and MCAT scores, economic disadvantage is not. Thus, it appears that economically disadvantaged whites do not score less well than economically advantaged whites, while economically advantaged blacks score less well than do disadvantaged whites. These statistics graphically illustrate that the University's purpose to integrate its classes by compensating for past discrimination could not be achieved by a general preference for the economically disadvantaged or the children of parents of limited education unless such groups were to make up the entire class.

Second, the Davis admissions program does not simply equate minority status with disadvantage. Rather, Davis considers on an individual basis each applicant's personal history to determine

whether he or she has likely been disadvantaged by racial discrimination. . . .

E

Finally, Davis' special admissions program cannot be said to
violate the Constitution simply because it has set aside a predeter-
mined number of places for qualified minority applicants rather than
using minority status as a positive factor to be considered in evaluating the applications of disadvantaged minority applicants. For purposes of constitutional adjudication, there is no difference between
the two approaches. In any admissions program which accords special
consideration to disadvantaged racial minorities, a determination of
the degree of preference to be given is unavoidable, and any given
preference that results in the exclusion of a white candidate is no
more or less constitutionally acceptable than a program such as that
at Davis. Furthermore, the extent of the preference inevitably
depends on how many minority applicants the particular school is
seeking to admit in any particular year so long as the number of
qualified minority applicants exceeds that number. There is no
sensible, and certainly no constitutional, distinction between, for
example, adding a set number of points to the admissions rating of
disadvantaged minority applicants as an expression of the preference
with the expectation that this will result in the admission of an
approximately determined number of qualified minority applicants
and setting a fixed number of places for such applicants as was done
here. . . .

Opinion of MR. JUSTICE MARSHALL.

I

A

Three hundred and fifty years ago, the Negro was dragged to this
country in chains to be sold into slavery. Uprooted from his home-
land and thrust into bondage for forced labor, the slave was deprived
of all legal rights. It was unlawful to teach him to read; he could be
sold away from his family and friends at the whim of his master; and
killing or maiming him was not a crime. The system of slavery
brutalized and dehumanized both master and slave.

The denial of human rights was etched into the American
colonies' first attempts at establishing self-government. When the

colonists determined to seek their independence from England, they drafted a unique document cataloguing their grievances against the King and proclaiming as "self-evident" that "all men are created equal" and are endowed "with certain unalienable Rights," including those to "Life, Liberty and the pursuit of Happiness." The self-evident truths and the unalienable rights were intended, however, to apply only to white men. An earlier draft of the Declaration of Independence, submitted by Thomas Jefferson to the Continental Congress, had included among the charges against the King that

> "[h]e has waged cruel war against human nature itself, violating its most sacred rights of life and liberty in the persons of a distant people who never offended him, captivating and carrying them into slavery in another hemisphere, or to incur miserable death in their transportation thither." Franklin 88.

The Southern delegation insisted that the charge be deleted; the colonists themselves were implicated in the slave trade, and inclusion of this claim might have made it more difficult to justify the continuation of slavery once the ties to England were severed. Thus, even as the colonists embarked on a course to secure their own freedom and equality, they ensured perpetuation of the system that deprived a whole race of those rights.

The implicit protection of slavery embodied in the Declaration of Independence was made explicit in the Constitution, which treated a slave as being equivalent to three-fifths of a person for purposes of apportioning representatives and taxes among the States. Art I, § 2. The Constitution also contained a clause ensuring that the "migration or importation" of slaves into the existing States would be legal until at least 1808, Art I, § 9, and a fugitive slave clause requiring that when a slave escaped to another State, he must be returned on the claim of the master, Art IV, § 2. In their declaration of the principles that were to provide the cornerstone of the new Nation, therefore, the Framers made it plain that "we the people," for whose protection the Constitution was designed, did not include those whose skins were the wrong color. As Professor John Hope Franklin has observed, Americans "proudly accepted the challenge and responsibility of their new political freedom by establishing the machinery and safeguards that insured the continued enslavement of blacks." Franklin 100.

The individual States likewise established the machinery to protect the system of slavery through the promulgation of the Slave Codes, which were designed primarily to defend the property interest of the owner in his slave. The position of the Negro slave as mere property was confirmed by this Court in *Dred Scott v. Sandford*, 19 How. 393 (1857), holding that the Missouri Compromise—which prohibited slavery in the portion of the Louisiana Purchase Territory north of Missouri—was unconstitutional because it deprived slave owners of their property without due process. The Court declared that under the Constitution a slave was property, and "[t]he right to traffic in it, like an ordinary article of merchandise and property, was guarantied to the citizens of the United States. . . ." Id., at 451. The Court further concluded that Negroes were not intended to be included as citizens under the Constitution but were "regarded as beings of an inferior order . . . altogether unfit to associate with the white race, either in social or political relations; and so far inferior, that they had no rights which the white man was bound to respect . . . ." Id., at 407.

B

The status of the Negro as property was officially erased by his emancipation at the end of the Civil War. But the long awaited emancipation, while freeing the Negro from slavery, did not bring him citizenship or equality in any meaningful way. Slavery was replaced by a system of "laws which imposed upon the colored race onerous disabilities and burdens, and curtailed their rights in the pursuit of life, liberty, and property to such an extent that their freedom was of little value." *Slaughter House Cases*, 16 Wall. 36, 70, . . . (1873). Despite the passage of the Thirteenth, Fourteenth, and Fifteenth Amendments, the Negro was systematically denied the rights those amendments were supposed to secure. The combined actions and inactions of the State and Federal Government maintained Negroes in a position of legal inferiority for another century after the Civil War.

II

The position of the Negro today in America is the tragic but inevitable consequence of centuries of unequal treatment. Measured by any benchmark of comfort or achievement, meaningful equality remains a distant dream for the Negro.

A Negro child today has a life expectancy which is shorter by more than five years than that of a white child. The Negro child's mother is over three times more likely to die of complications in childbirth, and the infant mortality rate for Negroes is nearly twice that for whites. The median income of the Negro family is only 60% that of the median of a white family, and the percentage of Negroes who live in families with incomes below the poverty line is nearly four times greater than that of whites.

When the Negro child reaches working age, he finds that America offers him significantly less than it offers his white counterpart. For Negro adults, the unemployment rate is twice that of whites, and the unemployment rate for Negro teenagers is nearly three times that of white teenagers. A Negro male who completes four years of college can expect a median annual income of merely $110 more than a white male who has only a high school diploma. Although Negroes represent 11.5% of the population, they are only 1.2% of the lawyers and judges, 2% of the physicians, 2.3% of the dentists, 1.1% of the engineers and 2.6% of the college and university professors.

The relationship between those figures and the history of unequal treatment afforded to the Negro cannot be denied. At every point from birth to death the impact of the past is reflected in the still disfavored position of the Negro.

In light of the sorry history of discrimination and its devastating impact on the lives of Negroes, bringing the Negro into the mainstream of American life should be a state interest of the highest order. To fail to do so is to ensure that America will forever remain a divided society.

III

I do not believe that the Fourteenth Amendment requires us to accept that fate. Neither its history nor our past cases lend any support to the conclusion that a University may not remedy the cumulative effects of society's discrimination by giving consideration to race in an effort to increase the number and percentage of Negro doctors.

IV

. . . The experience of Negroes in America has been different in kind, not just in degree, from that of other ethnic groups. It is not merely the history of slavery alone but also that a whole people were marked as inferior by the law. And that mark has endured. The dream of America as the great melting pot has not been realized for the Negro; because of his skin color he never even made it into the pot.

These differences in the experience of the Negro make it difficult for me to accept that Negroes cannot be afforded greater protection under the Fourteenth Amendment where it is necessary to remedy the effects of past discrimination. . . .

Opinion of MR. JUSTICE BLACKMUN.

. . . Governmental preference has not been a stranger to our legal life. We see it in veterans' preferences. We see it in the aid-to-the-handicapped programs. We see it in the progressive income tax. We see it in the Indian programs. We may excuse some of these on the ground that they have specific constitutional protection or, as with Indians, that those benefited are wards of the Government. Nevertheless, these preferences exist and may not be ignored. And in the admissions field, as I have indicated, educational institutions have always used geography, athletic ability, anticipated financial largess, alumni pressure, and other factors of that kind.

I add these only as additional components on the edges of the central question as to which I join my Brothers BRENNAN, WHITE, and MARSHALL in our more general approach. It is gratifying to know that the Court at least finds it constitutional for an academic institution to take race and ethnic background into consideration as one factor, among many, in the administration of its admissions program. I presume that that factor always has been there, though perhaps not conceded or even admitted. It is a fact of life, however, and a part of the real world of which we are all a part. The sooner we get down the road toward accepting and being a part of the real world, and not shutting it out and away from us, the sooner will these difficulties vanish from the scene.

I suspect that it would be impossible to arrange an affirmative action program in a racially neutral way and have it successful. To ask that this be so is to demand the impossible. In order to get beyond racism, we must first take account of race. There is no other way. And in order to treat some persons equally, we must treat them differently. We cannot—we dare not—let the Equal Protection Clause perpetuate racial supremacy.

As Justice Powell explains at the beginning of his opinion in *Bakke*, four justices believe that Title VI of the 1964 Civil Rights Act bars racial preferences altogether, so they join him to make a majority opposed to a fixed number of places being set aside for minority group members. Four justices think a program like Davis's is permissible under both the statute and the Constitution, so they join Justice Powell in asserting that some consideration of race is allowable in admissions decisions. In *Bakke* Justice Powell is the middle man, and he determines the disposition. But even apart from changes in the Court's membership, it is not clear from *Bakke* that he will occupy that status in future Title VI cases. The traditional principle has been that once a majority of the Court has interpreted a federal statute, that interpretation should be accepted for subsequent cases, the theory being that Congress can change the statute if it does not like the interpretation. If Justice Stevens and other justices joining his opinion do in future cases accept the majority view that Title VI bars only unconstitutional discrimination, then their constitutional views would become important. If even one justice thinks the Constitution allows preferences for members of disadvantaged groups more broadly than does Justice Powell, Justice Powell will no longer be in the middle. The post-*Bakke* cases are important partly because they shed light on these constitutional views. (For further comment on the opinions in *Bakke*, see Essay, pp. 70–83 and, especially, the table on p. 72.)

1.   Whose position on the question of statutory interpretation is most persuasive?

2.   For purposes of constitutional law, how carefully should courts review decisions to give preferences to members of minority groups? Is it proper, given the origins of the Fourteenth Amendment, to interpret the amendment, as Justice Powell does, to make it easier to adopt preferences for women than to adopt preferences for blacks.

3.   Are whites who are excluded because of preferences for blacks "innocent victims"? Does their status make such preferences morally wrong? Should it affect the standard of review used

by a court or the ultimate acceptability of a preferential program?

4.   Justices Brennan, White, Marshall, and Blackmun indicate that racial classifications that stigmatize are unconstitutional. What exactly do they mean? Is the crucial consideration whether most legislators mean to stigmatize a group or whether some do? How are courts to determine the motives that lead legislators to pass statutes? Is the test whether the classification has the effect of stigmatizing a group in the eyes of the public? If so, how are courts to make that evaluation, and what percentage of the public must take that view? Is stigmatization a workable concept in constitutional law?

5.   Are the arguments for preferential programs sufficient to justify them? Even if a fixed number of places is set aside for minority group members? Which arguments are most significant in your view? If you were on a faculty of law, would you vote for a preferential program, and if so, how would you want it constructed?

6.   Is the problem of deciding on the groups that will receive a preference manageable, or is it too difficult to say whether American Indians, Puerto Ricans, Chicanos, Asian-Americans, etc. will be included in a preferential policy that encompasses blacks? Does the opinion of Justices Brennan, White, Marshall, and Blackmun adequately face this problem in *Bakke*?

7.   In deciding on statutory interpretation and constitutionality, how far should a justice be consciously influenced by his own judgment as to whether preferential admissions policies are socially desirable or socially undesirable?

8.   Is segregation requested by blacks morally justified? For example, should blacks be able to have dormitories or student organizations from which whites are excluded? Should such practices at a state university be held constitutionally permissible? If white administrators accede to a request for a black dormitory, is it relevant what their motive is? How is a court to determine their motive?

9.   Is it morally justifiable to exclude a black applicant from an apartment in order to maintain an integrated housing project? Should courts accept that form of racial classification?

United Steelworkers of America v. Weber*

MR. JUSTICE BRENNAN delivered the opinion of the Court. Challenged here is the legality of an affirmative action plan—collectively bargained by an employer and a union—that reserves for black employees 50% of the openings in an in-plant craft-training program until the percentage of black craftworkers in the plant is commensurate with the percentage of blacks in the local labor force. The question for decision is whether Congress, in Title VII of the Civil Rights Act of 1964, 78 Stat. 253, as amended, 42 U.S.C § 2000e *et seq.,* left employers and unions in the private sector free to take such race-conscious steps to eliminate manifest racial imbalances in traditionally segregated job categories. We hold that Title VII does not prohibit such race-conscious affirmative action plans. . . .

We emphasize at the outset the narrowness of our inquiry. Since the Kaiser-USWA plan does not involve state action, this case does not present an alleged violation of the Equal Protection Clause of the Fourteenth Amendment. Further, since the Kaiser-USWA plan was adopted voluntarily, we are not concerned with what Title VII requires or with what a court might order to remedy a past proved violation of the Act. The only question before us is the narrow statutory issue of whether Title VII *forbids* private employers and unions from voluntarily agreeing upon bona fide affirmative action plans that accord racial preferences in the manner and for the purpose provided in the Kaiser-USWA plan. . . .

Respondent argues that Congress intended in Title VII to prohibit all race-conscious affirmative action plans. Respondent's argument rests upon a literal interpretation of §§ 703 (a) and (d) of the Act. Those sections make it unlawful to "discriminate . . . because of . . . race" in hiring and in the selection of apprentices for training programs. Since, the argument runs, *McDonald v. Santa Fe Trail Transp. Co., supra,* settled that Title VII forbids discrimination against whites as well as blacks, and since the Kaiser-USWA affirmative action plan operates to discriminate against white employees solely because they are white, it follows that the Kaiser-USWA plan violates Title VII.

*443, U.S. 193, 99 S. Ct. 2721, 61 L.Ed.2d 480 (1979).

Respondent's argument is not without force. But it overlooks the significance of the fact that the Kaiser-USWA plan is an affirmative action plan voluntarily adopted by private parties to eliminate traditional patterns of racial segregation. . . .

Given the legislative history, we cannot agree with respondent that Congress intended to prohibit the private sector from taking effective steps to accomplish the goal that Congress designed Title VII to achieve. The very statutory words intended as a spur or catalyst to cause "employers and unions to self-examine and to self-evaluate their employment practices and to endeavor to eliminate, so far as possible, the last vestiges of an unfortunate and ignominious page in this country's history," . . . cannot be interpreted as an absolute prohibition against all private, voluntary, race-conscious affirmative action efforts to hasten the elimination of such vestiges. It would be ironic indeed if a law triggered by a Nation's concern over centuries of racial injustice and intended to improve the lot of those who had "been excluded from the American dream for so long," 110 Cong. Rec. 6552 (1964) (remarks of Sen. Humphrey), constituted the first legislative prohibition of all voluntary, private, race-conscious efforts to abolish traditional patterns of racial segregation and hierarchy. . . .

We need not today define in detail the line of demarcation between permissible and impermissible affirmative action plans. It suffices to hold that the challenged Kaiser-USWA affirmative action plan falls on the permissible side of the line. The purposes of the plan mirror those of the statute. Both were designed to break down old patterns of racial segregation and hierarchy. Both were structured to "open employment opportunities for Negroes in occupations which have been traditionally closed to them." 110 Cong. Rec. 6548 (1964) (remarks of Sen. Humphrey).

At the same time, the plan does not unnecessarily trammel the interests of the white employees. The plan does not require the discharge of white workers and their replacement with new black hirees. . . . Nor does the plan create an absolute bar to the advancement of white employees; half of those trained in the program will be white. Moreover, the plan is a temporary measure; it is not intended to maintain racial balance, but simply to eliminate a manifest racial imbalance. Preferential selection of craft trainees at the Gramercy plant will end as soon as the percentage of black skilled craftworkers in the Gramercy plant approximates the percentage of blacks in the local labor force.

NOTE

Neither Justice Stevens nor Justice Powell took part in the case. Chief Justice Burger and Justice Rehnquist dissented, the latter writing a lengthy opinion to demonstrate that Congress had intended to bar all racial preferences. Thus of the four justices who took a colorblind view of Title VI in *Bakke*, only Justice Stewart was persuaded that Title VII permitted private employers to use preferences in favor of minorities. One possibility that does not emerge from the majority opinion is that Kaiser Aluminum may well have accepted the idea of preferences because it feared that if it did not do so, it would be sued for past discrimination. The color-blind view of Title VII would make matters difficult for a firm unsure whether it had discriminated. A firm could not adopt a preferential program without admitting discrimination or laying itself open to suits by white applicants or both; if the firm declined to adopt such a program, it would risk a court's declaring it to have discriminated and imposing a similar preferential program as a remedy for the violation.

QUESTIONS

1.   Given the language of Title VII, is the majority's position defensible? Should it have been influenced by the justice or social desirability of preferential programs in private employment?

2.   From the ethical point of view, should private employers institute programs like the one involved in *Weber*?

*Fullilove v. Klutznick** ══════════════

MR. CHIEF JUSTICE BURGER announced the judgment of the Court and delivered an opinion in which MR. JUSTICE WHITE and MR. JUSTICE POWELL joined.

We granted certiorari to consider a facial constitutional challenge to a requirement in a congressional spending program that, absent an

* U.S. 448 100 S.Ct. 2758, 65 L.Ed.2d 902 (1980).

administrative waiver, 10% of the federal funds granted for local public works projects must be used by the state or local grantee to procure services or supplies from businesses owned and controlled by members of statutorily identified minority groups. . . .

I

In May 1977, Congress enacted the Public Works Employment Act of 1977, Pub. L. 95–28, 91 Stat. 116, which amended the Local Public Works Capital Development and Investment Act of 1976, Pub. L. 94–369, 90 Stat. 999. The 1977 amendments authorized an additional $4 billion appropriation for federal grants to be made by the Secretary of Commerce, acting through the Economic Development Administration (EDA), to state and local governmental entities for use in local public works projects. Among the changes made was the addition of the provision that has become the focus of this litigation. Section 103(f)(2) of the 1977 Act, referred to as the "minority business enterprise" or "MBE" provision, requires that:

> "Except to the extent that the Secretary determines otherwise, no grant shall be made under this Act for any local public works project unless the applicant gives satisfactory assurance to the Secretary that at least 10 per centum of the amount of each grant shall be expended for minority business enterprises. For purposes of this paragraph, the term "minority business enterprise" means a business at least 50 per centum of which is owned by minority group members or, in case of a publicly owned business, at least 51 per centum of the stock of which is owned by minority group members. For the purposes of the preceding sentence minority group members are citizens of the United States who are Negroes, Spanish-speaking, Orientals, Indians, Eskimos, and Aleuts."

Here we pass, not on a choice made by a single judge or a school board but on a considered decision of the Congress and the President. However, in no sense does that render it immune from judicial scrutiny and it "is not to say we 'defer' to the judgment of the Congress . . . on a constitutional question," or that we would hesitate to invoke the Constitution should we determine that Congress has overstepped the bounds of its constitutional power. . . .

. . . The MBE provision . . . was designed to ensure that, to the extent federal funds were granted under the Public Works Employment Act of 1977, grantees who elect to participate would not employ procurement practices that Congress had decided might result in perpetuation of the effects of prior discrimination which had impaired or foreclosed access by minority businesses to public contracting opportunities. The MBE program does not mandate the allocation of federal funds according to inflexible percentages solely based on race or ethnicity.

Our analysis proceeds in two steps. At the outset, we must inquire whether the *objectives* of this legislation are within the power of Congress. If so, we must go on to decide whether the limited use of racial and ethnic criteria, in the context presented, is a constitutionally permissible *means* for achieving the congressional objectives and does not violate the equal protection component of the Due Process Clause of the Fifth Amendment. . . .

With respect to the MBE provision, Congress had abundant evidence from which it could conclude that minority businesses have been denied effective participation in public contracting opportunities by procurement practices that perpetuated the effects of prior discrimination. Congress, of course, may legislate without compiling the kind of "record" appropriate with respect to judicial or administrative proceedings. Congress had before it, among other data, evidence of a long history of marked disparity in the percentage of public contracts awarded to minority business enterprises. This disparity was considered to result not from any lack of capable and qualified minority businesses, but from the existence and maintenance of barriers to competitive access which had their roots in racial and ethnic discrimination, and which continue today, even absent any intentional discrimination or other unlawful conduct. Although much of this history related to the experience of minority businesses in the area of federal procurement, there was direct evidence before the Congress that this pattern of disadvantage and discrimination existed with respect to state and local construction contracting as well. In relation to the MBE provision, Congress acted within its competence to determine that the problem was national in scope.

Although the Act recites no preambulary "findings" on the subject, we are satisfied that Congress had abundant historical basis from which it could conclude that traditional procurement practices, when applied to minority businesses, could perpetuate the effects of prior discrimination. Accordingly, Congress reasonably determined that the prospective elimination of these barriers to minority firm access to public contracting opportunities generated by the 1977 Act was appropriate to ensure that those businesses were not denied equal opportunity to participate in federal grants to state and local governments, which is one aspect of the equal protection of the laws. . . .

We now turn to the question whether, as a *means* to accomplish these plainly constitutional objectives, Congress may use racial and ethnic criteria, in this limited way, as a condition attached to a federal grant. We are mindful that "[i]n no matter should we pay more deference to the opinion of Congress than in its choice of instrumentalities to perform a function that is within its power." . . .

As a threshold matter we reject the contention that in the remedial context the . . . Congress must act in a wholly "color-blind" fashion. In *Swann v. Charlotte-Mecklenburg Board of Education,* 402 U.S. 1, 18–21, . . . (1971), we rejected this argument in considering a court-formulated school desegregation remedy on the basis that examination of the racial composition of student bodies was an unavoidable starting point and that racially based attendance assignments were permissible so long as no absolute racial balance of each school was required. . . .

A more specific challenge to the MBE program is the charge that it impermissibly deprives nonminority businesses of access to at least some portion of the government contracting opportunities generated by the Act. It must be conceded that by its objective of remedying the historical impairment of access, the MBE provision can have the effect of awarding some contracts to MBE's which otherwise might be awarded to other businesses, who may themselves be innocent of any prior discriminatory actions. Failure of nonminority firms to receive certain contracts is, of course, an incidental consequence of the program, not part of its objective; similarly, past impairment of minority-firm access to public contracting opportunities may have been an incidental consequence of "business-as-usual" by public contracting agencies and among prime contractors.

It is not a constitutional defect in this program that it may disappoint the expectations of nonminority firms. When effectuating a limited and properly tailored remedy to cure the effects of prior discrimination, such "a sharing of the burden" by innocent parties is not impermissible. . . . Moreover, although we may assume that the complaining parties are innocent of any discriminatory conduct, it was within congressional power to act on the assumption that in the past some nonminority businesses may have reaped competitive benefit over the years from the virtual exclusion of minority firms from these contracting opportunities. . . .

Any preference based on racial or ethnic criteria must necessarily receive a most searching examination to make sure that it does not conflict with constitutional guarantees. This case is one which requires, and which has received, that kind of examination. This opinion does not adopt, either expressly or implicity, the formulas of analysis articulated in such cases as *University of California Regents v. Bakke,* 438 U.S. 265, . . . (1978). However, our analysis demonstrates that the MBE provision would survive judicial review under either "test" articulated in the several *Bakke* opinions. The MBE provision of the Public Works Employment Act of 1977 does not violate the Constitution.

MR. JUSTICE POWELL, concurring.

Although I would place greater emphasis than THE CHIEF JUSTICE on the need to articulate judicial standards of review in conventional terms, I view his opinion announcing the judgment as substantially in accord with my own views. Accordingly, I join that opinion and write separately to apply the analysis set forth by my opinion in *University of California Regents v. Bakke.* . . .

Because the distinction between permissible remedial action and impermissible racial preference rests on the existence of a constitutional or statutory violation, the legitimate interest in creating a race-conscious remedy is not compelling unless an appropriate governmental authority has found that such a violation has occurred. In other words, two requirements must be met. First, the governmental body that attempts to impose a race-conscious remedy must have the authority to act in response to identified discrimination. . . . Second, the governmental body must make findings that demonstrate the existence of illegal discrimination. In *Bakke,* the Regents failed both requirements. They were entrusted only with educational functions, and they made no findings of past discrimination. Thus, no compelling governmental interest was present to justify the use of a racial quota in medical school admissions. . . .

In reviewing the constitutionality of § 103(f)(2), we must decide: (i) whether Congress is competent to make findings of unlawful discrimination; (ii) if so, whether sufficient findings have been made to establish that unlawful discrimination has affected adversely minority business enterprises, and (iii) whether the 10% set-aside is a permissible means for redressing identifiable past discrimination. None of these questions may be answered without explicit recognition that we are reviewing an Act of Congress.

The history of this Court's review of congressional action demonstrates beyond question that the National Legislature is competent to find constitutional and statutory violations. Unlike the Regents of the University of California, Congress properly may—and indeed must—address directly the problems of discrimination in our society. . . .

In my view, the legislative history of § 103(f)(2) demonstrates that Congress reasonably concluded that private and governmental discrimination had contributed to the negligible percentage of public contracts awarded minority contractors. . . .

Consideration . . . persuades me that the set-aside is a reasonably necessary means of furthering the compelling governmental interest in redressing the discrimination that affects minority contractors. Any marginal unfairness to innocent nonminority contractors is not sufficiently significant—or sufficiently identifiable—to outweigh the governmental interest served by § 103(f)(2). When Congress acts to remedy identified discrimination, it may exercise discretion in choosing a remedy that is reasonably necessary to accomplish its purpose. Whatever the exact breadth of that discretion, I believe that it encompasses the selection of the set-aside in this case.

MR. JUSTICE MARSHALL, with whom MR. JUSTICE BRENNAN and MR. JUSTICE BLACKMUN join, concurring in the judgment.

My resolution of the constitutional issue in this case is governed by the separate opinion I coauthored in *University of California Regents v. Bakke.* . . . In my view, the 10% minority set-aside provision of the Public Works Employment Act of 1977 passes constitutional muster under the standard announced in that opinion.

As MR. CHIEF JUSTICE BURGER demonstrates, . . . it is indisputable that Congress' articulated purpose for enacting the set-aside provision was to remedy the present effects of past racial discrimination. See also the concurring opinion of my BROTHER POWELL, . . . Congress had a sound basis for concluding that minority-owned construction enterprises, though capable, qualified, and ready and willing to work, have received a disproportionately small amount of public contracting business because of the continuing effects of past discrimination. Here, as in *Bakke*, . . . (joint separate opinion), "minority underrepresentation is substantial and chronic, and . . . the handicap of past discrimination is impeding access of minorities to" the benefits of the governmental program. In these circumstances remedying these present effects of past racial discrimination is a sufficiently important governmental interest to justify the use of racial classifications. . . .

Because the means chosen by Congress to implement the set-aside provision are substantially related to the achievement of its remedial purpose, the provision also meets the second prong of our *Bakke* test. Congress reasonably determined that race-conscious means were necessary to break down the barriers confronting participation by minority enterprises in federally funded public works projects. That the set-aside creates a quota in favor of qualified and available minority business enterprises does not necessarily indicate that it stigmatizes. . . . Since under the set-aside provision a contract may be awarded to a minority enterprise only if it is qualified to do the work, the provison stigmatizes as inferior neither a minority firm that benefits from it nor a nonminority firm that is burdened by it. Nor does the set-aside "establish a quota in the invidious sense of a ceiling," *Bakke* . . . (joint separate opinion), on the number of minority firms that can be awarded public works contracts. In addition, the set-aside affects only a miniscule amount of the funds annually expended in the United States for construction work. . . .

MR. JUSTICE STEWART, with whom MR. JUSTICE REHNQUIST joins, dissenting.

"Our Constitution is color-blind, and neither knows nor tolerates classes among citizens. . . . The law regards man as man, and takes no account of his surroundings or of his color. . . ." Those words were written by a Member of this Court 84 years ago. *Plessy v. Ferguson,* 163 U.S. 537, 559, . . . (Harlan, J., dissenting). His colleagues disagreed with him, and held that a statute that required the separation of people on the basis of their race was constitutionally valid because it was a "reasonable" exercise of legislative power and had been "enacted in good faith for the promotion [of] the public good. . . . " Today, the Court upholds a statute that accords a preference to citizens who are "Negroes, Spanish-speaking, Orientals, Indians, Eskimos, and Aleuts," for much the same reasons. I think today's decision is wrong for the same reason that *Plessy v. Ferguson* was wrong, and I respectfully dissent. . . .

The Fourteenth Amendment was adopted to ensure that every person must be treated equally by each State regardless of the color of his skin. The Amendment promised to carry to its necessary conclusion a fundamental principle upon which this Nation had been founded—that the law would honor no preference based on lineage. Tragically, the promise of 1868 was not immediately fulfilled, and decades passed before the States and the Federal Government were finally directed to eliminate detrimental classifications based on race. Today, the Court derails this achievement and places its imprimatur on the creation once again by government of privileges based on birth.

The Court, moreover, takes this drastic step without, in my opinion, seriously considering the ramifications of its decision. Laws that operate on the basis of race require definitions of race. Because of the Court's decision today, our statute books will once again have to contain laws that reflect the odious practice of delineating the qualities that make one person a Negro and make another white. Moreover, racial discrimination, even "good faith" racial discrimination, is inevitably a two-edged sword. "[P]referential programs may only reinforce common stereotypes holding that certain groups are unable to achieve success without special protection based on a factor having no relationship to individual worth." *University of California Regents v. Bakke,* . . . .(opinion of POWELL, J.) Most importantly, by making race a relevant criterion once again in its own affairs, the Government implicitly teaches the public that the apportionment of rewards and penalties can legitimately be made according to race— rather than according to merit or ability—and that people can, and perhaps should, view themselves and others in terms of their racial characteristics. Notions of "racial entitlement" will be fostered, and private discrimination will necessarily be encouraged. . . .

There are those who think that we need a new Constitution, and their views may someday prevail. But under the Constitution we have, one practice in which government may never engage is the practice of racism—not even "temporarily" and not even as an "experiment."

For these reasons, I would reverse the judgment of the Court of Appeals.

MR. JUSTICE STEVENS, dissenting.

The 10% set-aside contained in the Public Works Employment Act of 1977, 91 Stat. 116 ("the Act") creates monopoly privileges in a $400,000,000 market for a class of investors defined solely by racial characteristics. The direct beneficiaries of these monopoly privileges are the relatively small number of persons within the racial classification who represent the entrepreneurial subclass—those who have, or can borrow, working capital. . . .

The Act may also be viewed as a much narrower remedial measure—one designed to grant relief to the specific minority business enterprises that have been denied access to public contracts by discriminatory practices. . . .

Assuming, however, that some firms have been denied public business for racial reasons, the instant statutory remedy is nevertheless demonstrably much broader than is necessary to right any such past wrong. For the statute grants the special preference to a class that includes (1) those minority owned firms that have successfully obtained business in the past on a free competitive basis and undoubtedly are capable of doing so in the future as well; (2) firms that have never attempted to obtain any public business in the past; (3) firms that were initially formed after the Act was passed, including those that may have been organized simply to take advantage of its provisions; (4) firms that have tried to obtain public business but were unsuccessful for reasons that are unrelated to the racial characteristics of their stockholders; and (5) those firms that have been victimized by racial discrimination.

Since there is no reason to believe that any of the firms in the first four categories had been wrongfully excluded from the market for public contracts, the statutory preference for those firms cannot be justified as a remedial measure. And since a judicial remedy was already available for the firms in the fifth category, it seems inappropriate to regard the preference as a remedy designed to redress any specific wrongs. In any event, since it is highly unlikely that the composition of the fifth category is at all representative of the entire class of firms to which the statute grants a valuable preference, it is ill-fitting to characterize this as a "narrowly tailored" remedial measure. . . .

Although it is traditional for judges to accord the same presumption of regularity to the legislative process no matter how obvious it may be that a busy Congress has acted precipitately, I see no reason why the character of their procedures may not be considered relevant to the decision whether the legislative product has caused a deprivation of liberty or property without due process of law. Whenever Congress creates a classification that would be subject to strict scrutiny under the Equal Protection Clause of the Fourteenth Amendment if it had been fashioned by a state legislature, it seems to me that judicial review should include a consideration of the procedural character of the decisionmaking process. A holding that the classification was not adequately preceded by a consideration of less drastic alternatives or adequately explained by a statement of legislative purpose would be far less intrusive than a final determination that the substance of the decision is not "narrowly tailored to the achievement of that goal." If the general language of the Due Process Clause of the Fifth Amendment authorizes this Court to review acts of Congress under the standards of the Equal Protection Clause of the Fourteenth Amendment—a clause that cannot be found in the Fifth Amendment—there can be no separation of powers objection to a more tentative holding of unconstitutionality based on a failure to follow procedures that guarantee the kind of deliberation that a fundamental constitutional issue of this kind obviously merits.

In all events, rather than take the substantive position expressed in MR. JUSTICE STEWART's dissenting opinion, I would hold this statute unconstitutional on a narrower ground. It cannot fairly be characterized as a "narrowly tailored" racial classification because it simply raises too many serious questions that Congress failed to answer or even to address in a responsible way. The risk that habitual attitudes toward classes of persons, rather than analysis of the relevant characteristics of the class, will serve as a basis for a legislative classification is present when benefits are distributed as well as when burdens are imposed. In the past, traditional attitudes too often provided the only explanation for discrimination against women, aliens, illegitimates, and black citizens. Today there is a danger that awareness of past injustice will lead to automatic acceptance of new classifications that are not in fact justified by attributes characteristic of the class as a whole.

When Congress creates a special preference, or a special disability, for a class of persons, it should identify the characteristic that justifies the special treatment.

When the classification is defined in racial terms, I believe that such particular identification is imperative.

In this case, only two conceivable bases for differentiating the preferred classes from society as a whole have occurred to me: (1) that they were the victims of unfair treatment in the past and (2) that they are less able to compete in the future. Although the first of these factors would justify an appropriate remedy for past wrongs, for reasons that I have already stated, this statute is not such a remedial measure. The second factor is simply not true. Nothing in the record of this case, the legislative history of the Act, or experience that we may notice judicially provides any support for such a proposition. It is up to Congress to demonstrate that its unique statutory preference is justified by a relevant characteristic that is shared by the members of the preferred class. In my opinion, because it has failed to make that demonstration, it has also failed to discharge its duty to govern impartially embodied in the Fifth Amendment to the United States Constitution.

I respectfully dissent.

NOTE

The set-aside provision involved in *Fullilove v. Klutznick* represents an explicit racial preference adopted by Congress. Six of the nine justices accepted it. Of the four justices who, in *Bakke*, had interpreted Title VI to require colorblind action, two justices, Stewart and Rehnquist, urged that the equal protection clause forbids the government to classify persons by race. Justice Stevens objected to the broad coverage of the set-aside benefit and to Congress's lack of care in deciding on that breadth; although unsympathetic to the idea of racial preferences, he did not take the position that the Constitution forecloses them. Chief Justice Burger approved the set-aside provision and wrote an opinion in which Justices White and Powell joined. That opinion emphasized the remedial nature of the set-aside, and evidenced substantial deference to congressional determinations about how to correct past discrimination and its effects. Justice Powell's emphasis on the authority of Congress demonstrated just how critical it had been for him that the admissions preferences in *Bakke* were created not by Congress or a state legislature, but by an educational institution. Justices Marshall, Brennan, and Blackmun relied on their approach in *Bakke* to sustain the set-aside. (For further comment, see Essay, pp. 83–84.)

QUESTIONS

1. Given the obvious truth of Justice Stevens's conclusion that many of the minority businesses that benefit from the set-aside will not themselves have suffered from prior discrimination, can the set-aside be justified as a remedial measure? Is Justice Powell right in suggesting that Congress can remedy only *illegal* discrimination, or can Congress properly try to remedy the effects of discrimination that was immoral but not illegal at the time it occurred?

2. What would be the benefits and drawbacks of the Court's adopting a color-blind view of the Constitution? Would not identification of people by race still be necessary for courts providing remedies for specific violations of law? Would an important distinction remain between when race could and when it could not be taken into account?

3. Given its legal power to do so, should Congress initiate, or continue, programs that set aside specified portions of federal grants for minorities?

Bibliographic Essay

Relevant background material on constitutional law includes M. Perry, *Modern Equal Protection: A Conceptualization and Appraisal*, 79 Colum. L. Rev. 1023 (1979), which outlines and criticizes the present dimensions of the equal protection clause. General problems of equal and unequal treatment, and their relation to the purposes of laws, are analyzed in J. Tussman & J. Tenbroek, *The Equal Protection of the Laws*, 37 Calif. L. Rev. 341 (1949). Sources of historical background on racial discrimination are C. Vann Woodward, *The Strange Career of Jim Crow*, 3rd rev. ed. (New York: Oxford University Press, 1974), which recounts the history of the development of segregation, and R. Kluger, *Simple Justice* (New York: Vintage, 1975), a history of the legal attacks on racial discrimination up through *Brown v. Board of Education*. Jo Freeman identifies the historical areas of sex discrimination in the laws, in *The Legal Basis of the Sexual Caste System*, 5 Valparaiso L. Rev. 203 (1971); a more detailed study, covering state and federal law through the 1960s, is L. Kanowitz, *Women and the Law: The Unfinished Revolution* (Albuquerque: University of New Mexico Press, 1969).

A readable nonlegal treatment of reverse discrimination, arguing that racial classification is both morally unjustifiable and unwise, is T. Eastland & W. J. Bennett, *Counting by Race* (New York: Basic Books, 1979). J. Dreyfuss & C. Lawrence III offer a similarly accessible narrative of the *Bakke* litigation, coming out strongly in favor of affirmative action, in *The Bakke Case: The Politics of Inequality* (New York: Harcourt Brace Jovanovich, 1979). A more analytical approach is taken in R. K. Fullinwider, *The Reverse Discrimination Controversy* (Totowa, N.J.: Rowman & Littlefield,

1980), giving measured support to racial preferences, and A. H. Goldman, *Justice and Preferential Treatment* (Princeton, N.J.: Princeton University Press, 1979), a philosophical account generally unsympathetic to reverse discrimination. J. Nickel discusses various arguments for preferential treatment, then examines special claims for and against such treatment for members of racial and ethnic minorities that have been subject to discrimination in the past, in *Preferential Policies in Hiring and Admissions: A Jurisprudential Approach*, 75 Colum. L. Rev. 534 (1975).

M. K. Vetterling, in *Some Common Sense Notes on Preferential Hiring,* Phil. Forum (Boston) Vol. 5, nos. 1–2, 320 (1973–1974), says that the general ethical problem raised by reverse discrimination is whether social justice may be gained at the expense of the welfare of some individuals. R. Wasserstrom, in *Racism, Sexism, and Preferential Treatment: An Approach to the Topic*, U.C.L.A. L. Rev. 24 (1977), maintains that preferential treatment is an acceptable program for trying to achieve a society in which race and sex do not affect life prospects of individuals, even if the program involves inexactness in classification. J. Thompson adopts a compensatory justice rationale, in *Preferential Hiring*, Phil. & Pub. Affs., Vol. 2, no. 4, 364 (1973), in which she says that past injustices to blacks and women justify the use of racial and sexual criteria to choose between equally qualified candidates. Still another perspective on the ethical issues is found in T. Nagel, *Equal Treatment and Compensatory Discrimination*, Phil. & Pub. Affs., Vol. 2, no. 4, 349 (1973), in which it is suggested that the victim of reverse discrimination has no claim of justice at all, on the ground that choice by ability is essentially not a matter of justice but one of efficiency. Contradicting the positions of these writers is B. Gross, *Discrimination in Reverse: Is Turnabout Fair Play?* (New York: New York University Press, 1978), arguing that programs of compensation and preference are morally unjustifiable if extended generally to members of racial and ethnic groups; such programs, he says, must be based on individual characteristics.

Federal requirements of affirmative action in university faculty hiring have prompted some of the writing on preferential treatment, including much that addresses the claims of specific preferred groups. T. Sowell opposes preferential hiring of blacks for faculty positions, contending that blacks are not underrepresented on university faculties and that preferential hiring policies will undermine the credibility of black professionals, in *"Affirmative Action" Reconsidered,* (Washington, D.C.: American Enterprise Institute for Public Policy Research, 1975); for a shorter version of this pamphlet, see No. 42 Public Interest, 47 (Winter 1976). G. Ezorsky attacks the suggestion that preferential hiring policies would compromise standards of merit, in *The Fight over University Women*, New York Review of Books, May 16, 1974, in which she argues that standards of merit do not generally govern academic hiring decisions. M. A. Warren says that numerical quotas for female faculty are necessary to counteract the discriminatory effect of irrelevant sex-correlated selection criteria, in *Secondary Sexism and Quota Hiring*, Phil. & Pub. Affs., Vol. 6, no. 3, 240 (1977); while M. Martin offers reasons why a program for hiring more female professors would be good educational policy, in *Pedagogical Arguments for Preferential Hiring and Tenuring of Women Teachers in the University*, Phil. Forum (Boston), Vol. 5, nos. 1–2, 325 (1973–1974). More general discussions of affirmative action have also distinguished the claims of blacks and the claims of women to preferential treatment. G. Sher suggests that blacks have a stronger claim because of the role discrimination has played in denying them the educational and economic opportunities that, he says, women have had, in *Reverse Discrimination in Employment,* Phil. & Pub. Affs., Vol. 4, no. 2, 159 (1975). R. Ginsburg notes differences in the nature and effects of racial discrimination and sex discrimination, in *Realizing the Equality Principle*, 44 U. Cin. L. Rev. 1 (1975), reprinted in W. T. Blackstone & R. D. Helsep (eds.), *Social Justice and Preferential Treatment* (Athens: University of Georgia Press, 1977); she concludes that in the case of gender discrimination, "a clear posting of the welcome sign" could be sufficient remedial action in many settings. The position that reverse gender discrimination is illegitimate is taken by L. Kanowitz, based on the assertion that males as a class have been victims of sexism whereas whites as a class have not been victims of racism, in *Equal Rights: The Male Stake* (Albuquerque: University of New Mexico Press, 1981), Chapter 3.

In addition to the Ginsburg and Kanowitz pieces, legal commentary on reverse discrimination includes R. Posner, *The DeFunis Case and the Constitutionality of Preferential Treatment of Racial Minorities,* Sup. Ct. Rev. 1 (1974). Posner contends that racial preferences are unnecessary and unjust, and that the antidiscrimination principle of the Fourteenth Amendment should not be subject to empirical conjectures about the effects of various kinds of discrimination. R. O'Neil, by contrast, argues that racial preferences serve strong social interests and are therefore constitutional, in *Racial Preference and Higher Education: The Larger Context*, 60 Va. L. Rev. 925 (1974); while T. Sandalow, after examining arguments for and against such preferences, concludes that they are constitutional if enacted by the legislature, in *Racial Preferences in Higher Education: Political Responsibility and the Judicial Role*, 42 U. Chi. L. Rev. 653 (1975). In *The DeFunis Case: The Right to Go to Law School*, New York Review of Books, Feb. 5, 1976, reprinted as Chapter 9 of R. Dworkin, *Taking Rights Seriously* (Cambridge, Mass.: Harvard University Press, 1977), Dworkin says that a member of the white majority has a right to be treated as an equal but does not have a right not to be disadvantaged by preferential treatment of minorities.

Many of the points suggested in the introductory essay of this book are developed in more detail in K. Greenawalt, *Judicial Scrutiny of "Benign" Racial Preference in Law School Admissions*, 75 Colum. L. Rev. 559 (1975), and *The Unresolved Problems of Reverse Discrimination*, 67 Cal. L. Rev. 87 (1979).

Collections of essays on reverse discrimination include B. Gross (ed.), *Reverse Discrimination* (Buffalo, N. Y.: Prometheus, 1977); R. Wasserstrom, *Today's Moral Problems*, 2nd ed. (New York: Macmillan, 1979); *DeFunis Symposium*, 75 Colum. L. Rev., Apr. 1975; and *Symposium on Regents v. Bakke*, 67 Calif. L. Rev., Jan. 1979.

Index

Italicized page numbers indicate document entries.

abortion, 5, 12
act-utilitarianism, 18–19
administrative agencies, 13
affirmative action, 17
American Indians, 50, 59
amicus curiae, 15

Bakke, *see University of California Regents v. Bakke*
Beccaria, 18
Bentham, 18
Bill of Rights, 14
Brown v. Board of Education, 12, 28–29, 38, 40, *121*, 125–126
Brown v. Board of Education (II), 126
Bureau of Indian Affairs, 50
busing, 40–41

Califano v. Webster, 165
capital punishment, 9
certiorari, 15
Civil Rights Act of 1886, 27, *92,* 93–94, 156–157
Civil Rights Act of 1875, 28, *93,* 94, 102–105
Civil Rights Act of 1964, 31–32, *150,* 152–153
   Title VI, 72, 73–75, *157,* 162, 204
   Title VII, 75, 83, *153,* 154, 155, 208
Civil Rights Act of 1968, *155,* 156
Civil Rights Cases, 102, 104–105
commerce power, 13, 152
compensatory justice, *see* justice
Constitution, United States, 12–14
Craig v. Boren, 77, *146,* 165

Declaration of Independence, 26, *89*

About the Author

KENT GREENAWALT is Cardozo Professor of Jurisprudence at Columbia University. A graduate of Swarthmore College, he received a B.Phil. degree at Oxford University, where, as a Keasbey Scholar, he concentrated on political philosophy. He earn an L.L.B. at Columbia Law School, where he was editor-in-chief of the law review. He served as a law clerk for Justice John M. Harlan of the United States Supereme Court and then as a special assistant in the Agency for International Development. After summer work for the Lawyers' Committee for Civil Rights, he returned to Columbia Law School in 1965 to teach. During years of leave, he has been Deputy Solicitor General of the United States (1971–1972), a Fellow of the American Council of Learned Societies (1972–1973), and a Visiting Fellow at All Souls College, Oxford (1979). He has written on diverse areas of legal philosophy and constitutional law, including three articles on preferential treatment for members of minorities.

A Note on the Type

The text of this book was set in a computer version of Times Roman, designed by Stanley Morison for *The Times* (London) and first introduced by that newspaper in 1932.

Among typographers and designers of the twentieth century, Stanley Morison has been a strong forming influence as typographical adviser to the English Monotype Corporation, as a director of two distinguished English publishing houses, and as a writer of sensibility, erudition, and keen practical sense.

Typography by Barbara Sturman. Cover design by Maria Epes. Composition by The Saybrook Press, Inc., Old Saybrook, Connecticut. Printed and bound by Banta Company, Menasha, Wisconsin.

BORZOI BOOKS
IN LAW AND AMERICAN SOCIETY

Law and American History

EARLY AMERICAN LAW AND SOCIETY
Stephen Botein, *Michigan State University*

This volume consists of an essay dealing with the nature of law and early American socioeconomic development from the first settlements to 1776. The author shows how many legal traditions sprang both from English experience and from the influence of the New World. He explores the development of transatlantic legal structures in order to show how they helped rationalize intercolonial affairs. Mr. Botein also emphasizes the relationship between law and religion. The volume includes a pertinent group of documents for classroom discussion, and a bibliographic essay.

LAW IN THE NEW REPUBLIC: *Private Law and the Public Estate*
George Dargo, *Brookline, Massachusetts*

Though the American Revolution had an immediate and abiding impact on American public law (e.g., the formation of the federal and state constitutions), its effect on private law (e.g., the law of contracts, tort law) was less direct but of equal importance. Through essay and documents, Mr. Dargo examines post-Revolutionary public and private reform impulses and finds a shifting emphasis from public to private law which he terms "privatization." To further illustrate the tension between public and private law, the author develops a case study (the Batture land controversy in New Orleans) in early nineteenth century legal, economic, and political history. The volume includes a wide selection of documents and a bibliographic essay.

LAW IN ANTEBELLUM SOCIETY: *Legal Change and Economic Expansion*
Jamil Zainaldin, *Washington, D.C.*

This book examines legal change and economic expansion in the first half of the nineteenth century, integrating major themes in the development of law with key historical themes. Through a series of topical essays and the use of primary source materials, it describes how political, social, and economic interests and values influence law making. The book's focus is on legislation and the common law.

LAW AND THE NATION, 1865–1912
Jonathan Lurie, *Rutgers University*

Using the Fourteenth Amendment as the starting point for his essay, Mr. Lurie examines the ramifications of this landmark constitutional provision on the economic and social development of America in the years following the Civil War. He also explores important late nineteenth-century developments in legal education, and concludes his narrative with some insights on law and social change in the first decade of the twentieth century. The volume is highlighted by a documents section containing statutes, judicial opinions, and legal briefs, with appropriate questions for classroom discussion. Mr. Lurie's bibliographic essay provides information to stimulate further investigation of this period.

ORDERED LIBERTY: *Legal Reform in the Twentieth Century*
Gerald L. Fetner, *University of Chicago*

In an interpretive essay, the author examines the relationship between several major twentieth-century reform movements (e.g., Progressivism, New Deal, and the Great Society) and the law. He shows how policy makers turned increasingly to the legal community for assistance in accommodating economic and social conflict, and how the legal profession responded by formulating statutes, administrative agencies, and private arrangements. Mr. Fetner also discusses how the organization and character of the legal profession were affected by these social changes. Excerpts from relevant documents illustrate issues discussed in the essay. A bibliographic essay is included.

Law and Philosophy

DISCRIMINATION AND REVERSE DISCRIMINATION
Kent Greenawalt, *Columbia Law School*

Using discrimination and reverse discrimination as a model, Mr. Greenawalt examines the relationship between law and ethics. He finds that the proper role of law cannot be limited to grand theory concerning individual liberty and social restraint, but must address what law can effectively discover and accomplish. Such concepts as distributive and compensatory justice and utility are examined in the context of preferential treatment for blacks and other minorities. The analysis draws heavily on the Supreme Court's Bakke decision. The essay is followed by related documents, primarily judicial opinions, with notes and questions, and a bibliography.

THE LEGAL ENFORCEMENT OF MORALITY
Thomas Grey, *Stanford Law School*

This book deals with the traditional issue of whether morality can be legislated and enforced. It consists of an introductory essay and legal texts on three issues: the enforcement of sexual morality, the treatment of human remains, and the duties of potential rescuers. The author shows how philosophical problems differ from classroom hypotheticals when they are confronted in a legal setting. He illustrates this point using material from statutes, regulations, judicial opinions, and law review commentaries. Mr. Grey reviews the celebrated Hart-Devlin debate over the legitimacy of prohibiting homosexual acts. He places the challenging problem of how to treat dead bodies, arising out of developments in the technology of organ transplantation, in the context of the debate over morals enforcement, and discusses the Good Samaritan as an issue concerning the propriety of the legal enforcement of moral duties.

LEGAL REASONING
Martin Golding, *Duke University*

This volume is a blend of text and readings. The author explores the many sides to legal reasoning—as a study in judicial psychology and, in a more narrow sense, as an inquiry into the "logic" of judicial decision making. He shows how judges justify their rulings, and gives examples of the kinds of arguments they use. He challenges the notion that judicial reasoning is rationalization; instead, he argues that judges are guided by a deep concern for consistency and by a strong need to have their decisions stand as a measure for the future conduct of individuals. *(Forthcoming in 1984)*

Law and American Literature

LAW AND AMERICAN LITERATURE
A one-volume collection of the following three essays:

Law as Form and Theme in American Letters
Carl S. Smith, *Northwestern University*

The author explores the interrelationships between law aned literature generally and between American law and American literature in particular. He explores first the literary qualities of legal writing and then the attitudes of major American writers toward the law. Throughout, he studies the links between the legal and literary imaginations. He finds that legal writing has many literary qualities that are essential to its function, and he points out that American writers have long been wary of the power of the law and its special language, speaking out as a compensating voice for the ideal of justice.

Innocent Criminal or Criminal Innocence: The Trial in American Fiction
John McWilliams, *Middlebury College*

Mr. McWilliams explores how law functions as a standard for conduct in a number of major works of American literature, including Cooper's *The Pioneers,* Melville's *Billy Budd,* Dreiser's *An American Tragedy,* and Wright's *Native Son.* Each of these books ends in a criminal trial, in which the reader is asked to choose between his emotional sympathy for the victim and his rational understanding of society's need for criminal sanctions. The author compares these books with James Gould Cozzens' *The Just and the Unjust,* a study of a small town legal system, in which the people's sense of justice contravenes traditional authority.

Law and Lawyers in American Popular Culture
Maxwell Bloomfield, *Catholic University of America*

Melding law, literature, and the American historical experience into a single essay, Mr. Bloomfield discusses popular images of the lawyer. The author shows how contemporary values and attitudes toward the law are reflected in fiction. He concentrates on two historical periods: antebellum America and the Progressive era. He examines fictional works which were not always literary classics, but which exposed particular legal mores. An example of such a book is Winston Churchill's *A Far Country* (1915), a story of a successful corporation lawyer who abandons his practice to dedicate his life to what he believes are more socially desirable objectives.